# BEST NEWSPAPER WRITING
# 1994

## WINNERS: THE AMERICAN SOCIETY OF NEWSPAPER EDITORS COMPETITION

### EDITED BY CHRISTOPHER SCANLAN

98   97   96   95   94                    5   4   3   2   1

International Standard Book Number: 1–56625–014–5
International Standard Serial Number: 0195–895X

**The Poynter Institute for Media Studies**
801 Third Street South
St. Petersburg, Florida 33701

**Bonus Books, Inc.**
160 East Illinois Street
Chicago, Illinois 60611

*Printed in the United States of America*

Book design by Billie M. Keirstead
Cover illustration by Ken Weightman
Photography by Ricardo Ferro

**For Don Murray**

Inspiring coach, generous mentor, valued friend.
You teach journalists that good writing may be magical,
but it's not magic, and teachers that the more you give,
the more you get.

# About this series

The Poynter Institute for Media Studies proudly publishes the 16th volume of its series *Best Newspaper Writing,* valued since 1979 by students, teachers, and professionals as an indispensable text on clear, effective, and graceful newswriting.

As in past years, *Best Newspaper Writing* is a joint venture of the Institute and the American Society of Newspaper Editors. In 1978, ASNE made the improvement of newspaper writing one of its primary goals. The Society inaugurated a contest to select the best writing from newspapers in the United States and Canada, and to reward the winning writers with $2,500 prizes. The Institute volunteered to spread the gospel of good writing by publishing the winning entries along with notes, commentaries, and interviews. That first volume, *Best Newspaper Writing 1979,* sold out long ago and has become a collector's item.

This year's *Best Newspaper Writing* is edited by Christopher Scanlan, an experienced newspaper reporter and writing coach on leave from his job as a national correspondent in the Washington, D.C., bureau of Knight-Ridder Newspapers. Scanlan, a 1994 Visiting Professional at The Poynter Institute, has since joined the Institute faculty as the director of its writing program. He follows in the editing footpaths of former editors Roy Peter Clark, Don Fry, and Karen F. Brown.

The 1994 award categories are non-deadline writing, deadline writing (no award given), commentary, editorial writing, and headline writing. A committee of 15 editors, chaired by Jane Healy, managing editor of *The Orlando Sentinel,* judged this year's entries:

Judith Brown, *New Britain* (Conn.) *Herald*
Michael Fancher, *The Seattle Times*
Robert Giles, *The Detroit News*
James P. Herman, *Rockford* (Ill.) *Register Star*

Deborah Howell, Newhouse News Service, Washington, D.C.
Michael J. Jacobs, *Grand Forks* (N.D.) *Herald*
Pamela Johnson, *Phoenix Gazette*
Beverly Kees, Freedom Forum First Amendment Center
David Lawrence, *The Miami Herald*
Tony Marro, *Newsday,* Long Island, N.Y.
Susan Miller, Scripps Howard, Cincinnati
Acel Moore, *The Philadelphia Inquirer*
Ted Natt, *The Daily News,* Longview, Wash.
Burl Osborne, *Dallas Morning News*

The Institute congratulates the winners and finalists of the ASNE Distinguished Writing Awards, and thanks the judges for their fine work and dedication to good writing.

* * *

Founded in 1975 by the late Nelson Poynter, chairman of the *St. Petersburg Times* and its Washington affiliate, *Congressional Quarterly,* the Institute was bequeathed Poynter's controlling stock in the Times Publishing Company in 1978. It invests its dividends in educational activities in four areas of print and broadcast journalism: writing, graphics, management, and ethics. The faculty teaches beginning and midcareer professionals as well as news executives, publishes teaching tools such as this book, and conducts educational and research projects, all of which seek the same goal: to raise levels of excellence in newspapers and the communications media generally, so that journalists can fulfill their responsibility to empower citizens by informing them.

Robert J. Haiman, President
The Poynter Institute

# Acknowledgments

Like any publication, this book represents a collaboration. The faculty and staff of The Poynter Institute for Media Studies graciously provided the support, expertise, and friendship this enterprise is famous for in newsrooms around the world.

I owe a special debt to:

Billie Keirstead for patience, stewardship, and a creative partnership; Bobbi Alsina for unparalleled support; David Shedden for a historian's reach and a rich bibliography; Sandra Allen and Carla Field for the library's riches; Ken Weightman for an exceptional cover; Ricardo Ferro for superb photojournalism; Joyce Olson for an eagle eye; Jill Gunn for computer support; Vicki Krueger for creative copy editing; Roy Peter Clark, Karen F. Brown, Donald Fry, and Robert Haiman for setting the standards of excellence and helping me reach for them.

Outside the Institute, Don Murray was never too busy to read a draft. Clark Hoyt, vice president/news, and Rich Oppel, chief of the Washington bureau of Knight-Ridder Newspapers, generously approved a leave so a reporter could try to give back something to the profession that has taught him so much. Kathy Fair, my best editor, and our daughters Caitlin, Lianna, and Michaela, furnished steady doses of patience, hugs, and a daily reality check.

Finally, my thanks and congratulations to the newspapers and writers whose work makes this collection possible: the finalists, for their illuminating essays on the writing lessons they learned, and the winners of this year's Distinguished Writing Awards, for their hospitality and willingness to explore the way they write.

This is their book.

# Contents

# A defense against extinction

Shortly before *Jurassic Park* began breaking box-office records, the story's creator came to the National Press Club in Washington, D.C., to discuss what he called "another dinosaur...the American media."

"To my mind," novelist Michael Crichton told his audience, "it is likely that what we now understand as the mass media will be gone within ten years. Vanished, without a trace."

Crichton's doomsday thesis is hardly new. Neither was the familiar evidence he cited in support: declines in newspaper readership and broadcast viewers, negative public attitudes towards the news media, and an information product with serious quality defects. In Crichton's words, "Its information is not reliable, it has too much chrome and glitz, its doors rattle, it breaks down almost immediately, and it is sold without warranty. It's flashy, but it's basically junk. So people have begun to stop buying it."

There is plenty to argue with in Crichton's speech. But if he and others who share his pessimistic view about the media's future are right, the contents of *Best Newspaper Writing 1994* may represent its last, best hope for survival. For if there is a single antidote to extinction for America's newspapers, it is writing that demands to be read.

For the last 16 years, the American Society of Newspaper Editors has spotlighted the best newspaper writing in America with its annual Distinguished Writing Awards competition. Their selections are reprinted in *Best Newspaper Writing,* the collection that since 1979 has influenced and inspired thousands of reporters, editors, teachers, and students.

When the ASNE editors choose the winning entries from hundreds submitted by newspapers around the country, they send a crucial message about what constitutes the best writing. This year's winners are no different. Their stories and headlines and the lessons of craft that lie behind them exemplify the qualities that represent the best writing.

■ **The best writing solves mysteries.**
When a teenager in a public housing project puts a gun to a policewoman's head, feature writer Anne Hull of the *St. Petersburg Times* is a literary detective on the trail of the causes and effects. Hull employs the writer's special talent of empathy to illuminate with unflinching honesty and enormous dignity two often-misunderstood cultures: the insular worlds of the project dweller and the police. Her series, "Metal to Bone," is a stylish spellbinder. Here she recreates Halloween Night in the Ponce de Leon housing project, a scene that strips away stereotypes that breed prejudice endemic in American society today:

For one night of the year, blue police uniforms were traded for a Freddy Krueger mask or an Elvira wig.

Officer Gil Mercado stood at the entrance of the haunted house, acting as doorman and daddy as nearly a thousand kids lined up, waiting their turn to enter the dark, humid corridors, where chain saws buzzed and cobwebs hung.

Gil's partner had her 9mm Glock slipped down into the waistband of her Levi's as a 3-year-old boy named Pooh clung to her neck. Pooh's older sister and a friend screamed with delight as they stepped inside the faded green haunted house.

"Feel my heart," the little girl said, placing her friend's small hand over her chest.

From the doorway of the haunted house, Gil looked out across Rivera Court at the sea of children. Cockroaches crawled on them as they slept at night. The free lunch they ate at school was their only hot meal of the day.

But on Halloween, with their faces painted like witches and tigers, the burdens of their childhood were invisible.

Suddenly, *pop-pop-pop.*

The sound of gunshots rang out in a distant corner of Ponce. The officers outside the haunted house tensed and held perfectly still. The children, though, were oblivious to the familiar sounds of guns. What made them shriek were the cardboard bats that flew in the trees and the plastic fangs worn by middle-aged cops.

A boy ran up to Gil, scared by a goblin in the haunted house.

Gil lifted the child up in his arms. "You all right, my man?"

For hours, Gil chaperoned groups of children inside the haunted house. They clung to his legs and pulled at his shirt. They would not let go.

"Hold on to each other," he shouted, and together, they plunged into the darkness.

## ■ The best writing delivers hard truths.

Columnist Joan Beck of the *Chicago Tribune* is a truth teller whose lucid, informed prose regularly helps readers of her syndicated column make sense of "junk science," AIDS, health care reform, and the space station boondoggle. The best writing touches readers' hearts as well, as Beck does with a poignant summing up of a marriage that spanned five decades. In the complex, confusing age we live in, the best writing cuts through the clutter of jargon and rhetoric that dominates political discourse. In this column about AIDS prevention, Beck displays the muscular style that leaves little doubt about her opinions:

The government isn't going to guard you from AIDS. It can't. President Bush couldn't. President Clinton can't. The White House's new AIDS coordinator, Kristine Gebbie, can't either, no matter how urgently AIDS groups pushed for that post to be created.

Protecting yourself from getting AIDS is something you have to do for yourself.

Doctors can't cure you if you get AIDS.

They can only postpone your death, treat some associated illnesses and keep you feeling a little better as you slowly die. All the politically correct attitudes, all the anti-discrimination laws, all the political activism, all the red AIDS ribbons, all the support groups, all the finger pointing can't change the basic facts about this epidemic.

## ■ The best writing transforms.

*Washington Post* columnist Donna Britt practices the alchemist's art, transforming everyday experiences into extraordinary musings on life and death, love, "gangsta" rap, and violence towards women. With courage and literary grace, her columns explore the personal and yet reveal universal truths. In this column about the destructive nature of gangsta rap, Britt's memory of a teenage girl wearing a rhinestone necklace that spelled "Bitch, Bitch, Bitch" becomes a powerful indictment of the race hatred she sees behind its lyrics:

But maybe, like so much else, it all boils down to money. The fellas who make millions singing their contempt for women—and who at the same time pride themselves for slamming racism in their music—are actually in the business of selling racism's most destructive lies. Singers who wave their Glocks, grab their crotches and dis their women—while thousands of us pay to watch and listen—do more than make themselves and record producers rich.

Too often they tell the world—and the young whites who reportedly are gangsta rap's biggest consumers—what morgues overflowing with the bodies of black men suggest: how deeply some African Americans have internalized the racism they deplore.

The messages many are selling to—and about—blacks:

You don't deserve to live. Your women are sluts and animals. You kill without remorse, and copulate without love or responsibility.

Sure that's all a lie. But slap a beat on it, apply a coat of glamour and someone, somewhere will dance to it.

Or clasp it in rhinestones around her neck.

## ■ The best writing sings.

Michael Gartner, editor of *The Daily Tribune* in Ames, Iowa, is a musician on the editorial page, composing editorials that are lyrical, clear, and meant to be read aloud. One of the nation's staunchest First Amendment defenders, he champions speech and press freedoms with air-tight logic and passion. Here is Gartner's virtuoso style applied to a controversy at the local university:

Let's talk about tattoos.

We haven't seen the arms of Jackson Warren, the food service worker at Iowa State University, but they do sound repulsive. A swastika on one, KKK on the other.

Ugh.

That's obnoxious.

The administrators at the university think so, too, so in response to a student's complaint they've "temporarily reassigned" Warren to a job where he won't be in contact with the general public.

Ugh.

That's outrageous.

What in the world is Iowa State thinking of? Where are those campus champions of liberty and robust debate? Where are the folks who teach about the founding of this country, about freedoms and rights, about the First Amendment? Hasn't anybody there read the Constitution?

In this country, you tolerate speech you despise.

In this country, you tolerate views you abhor.

In this country, you tolerate opinions you loathe.

That's what you're supposed to learn in college. You're supposed to learn that dissent is part of democracy, that the First Amendment is there to protect the outraged and the outrageous, the abhorred and the abhorrent, the despised and the despicable.

## ■ The best writing lures.

Ken Wells of *The Wall Street Journal* is a hoopster of the front page, writing slam-dunk headlines that grab the reader's attention and illuminate a writer's story without giving it away. When the topic is serious, such as molestation by priests, his headlines are sensitive and equally deft. A shameless punster, he adds dazzle and delight to the paper's hallmark Page One features, as in this invitation to read a story about pets on vegetarian diets:

> Ruff! Ruff! Ruffage!
> Here, Rover, Have
> A Nice Bean Sprout
>
> \* \* \*
>
> Turning Pets into Vegetarians
> Is Healthy, Owners Say;
> Veterinarians Are Howling
>
> \* \* \*

Even in the bustle of a lively newsroom, writing is a lonely occupation. With its tradition of reprinting interviews with the winning writers, *Best Newspaper Writing* furnishes uncommon companionship.

I first became aware of *Best Newspaper Writing* in 1980 after Carol McCabe of the *Providence Journal-Bulletin,* where I was a reporter, won the ASNE award that year for newswriting. I admired Carol's work and studied it, hoping to replicate the effects she created through perceptive reporting and graceful prose. Roy Peter Clark's interview with her opened a fascinating window on the work habits of a master writer. Passages jumped off the page, providing advice, comfort, and instruction.

Each succeeding year, I awaited the publication of the latest volume and devoured it, marker pen in hand to highlight the insights, tips, and revelations that spoke to my dreams as a writer. From *Best Newspaper Writing,* I learned how good writers thought.

As I wrestled with a piece on deadline, I remembered the words of Richard Zahler of *The Seattle Times* (*Best Newspaper Writing 1981*): "The mistake that most people make when they are writing on deadline is that they think they can dispense with planning and organizing. I mean taking three or four minutes before you start to think about the material you have, what you want to cover." I tried to follow Zahler's advice to take that brief time "to make a quick list of the high points of the story and to organize my thinking before I write."

As I did my reporting, I tried to remember what Richard Ben Cramer of *The Philadelphia Inquirer* (*BNW 1979*) said: "It's very hard to know what someone would feel in a situation unless you at least feel something of it yourself. It certainly helps to put yourself in the other man's shoes if you are an inch and a half from those shoes. I like to tell the story of the people, to describe the place, to give a sense of how it feels."

From William Blundell of *The Wall Street Journal* (*BNW 1982*), I learned the importance of "building the dimension of time into your story. You look at the past and you also anticipate the future. You don't just deal with the present."

As I sweated over a lead, I was comforted by the way Cynthia Gorney of *The Washington Post* (*BNW 1980*) discovered her stories: "I start to babble, sometimes starting in the middle of the story and usually fairly quickly I see how it's going to start. It just starts shaping itself on the typewriter."

When I heard Rick Bragg of the *St. Petersburg Times* (*BNW 1991*) describe how he talked for 30 minutes to a source before taking out his notebook, or, in the same edition, listened to Jim Dwyer of *Newsday* say, "You've got to be unafraid to look like a complete fool when you're a reporter, because you just have to ask the most obvious questions," they reminded me of lessons I knew I should never forget. And these are just a few of the nuggets that make this series so invaluable as a learning tool and such a well of inspiration for writers, editors, and teachers.

Lillian Ross of *The New Yorker* said it best in the introduction to her classic collection, *Reporting:* "Do not be afraid to acknowledge that you have learned from other writers. Do not spend your time trying to kill off other writers and reporters. The more talented you are, the more you can learn from other writers and the freer you are to admit that you have learned."

That spirit of sharing infects the *Best Newspaper Writing* series. Every year it introduces a new set of talented writers with a variety of valuable lessons about reporting, interviewing, organizing, writing, and revising. They have lessons to teach about how to stay motivated, get along with editors, and other vital areas of job success. These writers share a consuming passion for the written word, unflagging enthusiasm and commitment to their craft, and the unrelenting pursuit of excellence.

By coupling winning entries with penetrating interviews, *Best Newspaper Writing* offers a window into the writing process. Once again, the conversations with this year's winners, as well as stimulating essays written by the eight finalists, demonstrate that good writing is a rational process that can be observed, understood, and, on the best days, repeated.

These writers know that:

## ■ The best writing comes from rewriting.

For Donna Britt, that means drafting her columns quickly, a burst of activity "followed by lots of silence in which I question everything. Can I say this better? Can I be more direct? Can I make this tighter? Can I clarify this point? Is this insensitive? Is this funny? What can I do to make it jump off the page? What's going to make somebody go with me to the end? You know, ride with me the whole way?" The best writers know that "the last act of the writing must be to become one's own reader," as poet John Ciardi says in *Shoptalk: Learning to Write with Writers*, Donald Murray's inspiring collection of quotations from writers on their craft.

■ **The best writing is hard work.**

"I do not know anybody who writes well who writes easily," says Joan Beck. "I think that is important for people to know. After I had been through journalism school and graduate school and was working at the *Tribune,* I was still surprised to see people whose bylines I had admired for a long time still sitting there, head in hand, trying to write. It was a great revelation to me that it did not come easily to anybody that I know."

■ **The best writing seeks the revealing detail.**

In her series "Metal to Bone," Anne Hull consistently populates the page with flesh-and-blood characters, not the stick figures of mediocre writing. She does it with intensive reporting of specific details that are the foundation of good writing. Whatever the story, "you've got to have facts," says Michael Gartner. "In an article, you use them to inform. In an editorial, you use facts to persuade as well as inform." To Hull, "details can help explain the sum of a person."

■ **The best writing has a sense of audience.**

Michael Gartner writes for his 92-year-old father, himself a journalist for 50 years. Ken Wells keeps his mother in Louisiana in mind. Donna Britt aims her columns at an imaginary reader, a young black teenager much like she was, growing up in Gary, Indiana, and trying to find her life reflected in the pages of her daily newspaper.

■ **The best writing comes from editors who listen to writers.**

The best editors "edit people, not copy," in the words of Joel Rawson, deputy executive editor/news of the *Providence Journal-Bulletin. Best Newspaper Writing 1994* includes an instructive conversation with Anne Hull's editor. Chris Lavin sees his role as helping writers find their own voices rather than imposing his own. He says, "When they tell me something, I don't say, 'God, that will make a great lead.' They may have something better in mind, or in their notebook, that they're forgetting to tell me. I don't want to make those judgments for the writer.... We're heading down the road to failure when my words start ending up in your story."

■ **The best writing takes risks.**

Ken Wells credits the risk-taking environment fostered by his boss, *Wall Street Journal* Page One editor, John Brecher, for the flair behind his winning headlines: Brecher "...challenges us to be creative. He says, 'We all recognize that there's a thin line between a really clever, funny headline and one that goes over the line.' Brecher's theory is see what happens, and if it's too clever by half, he will tell you, 'I think this is a little overripe and worth trashing.'"

■ **Most important, the best writing provides models for other writers and editors.**

In an age when the President's health reform plan is available on the Internet at the same moment that reporters are getting their copies in the White House Press Office, readers don't need newspapers the way they used to, certainly not for the stenographic role that reporters too often play.

What readers do need is interpretation, free of bias and gimmicks, that more than meets George Orwell's definition: "Good writing is like a window pane."

The best writing shows readers their world in new, sometimes startling ways.

The best writing takes readers places they cannot go.

And at a time when readers are bombarded by information, the best writing helps them make sense of an increasingly complicated age. Michael Crichton's prediction may come to pass, but don't buy your tickets to *Newsroom Park* yet. As long as writers can be a window onto the world, they won't have to worry about extinction.

# A NOTE ABOUT THIS EDITION

*Best Newspaper Writing 1994* follows in a tradition of learning from excellence set by the previous editors of the series: Roy Peter Clark, Don Fry, and Karen F. Brown. Readers familiar with the series will note several changes in this edition:

**Writers' Workshop:** For many years, each winning story was followed by a list of questions under the heading, "Observations and Questions." In this edition, the section is renamed "Writers' Workshop." As always, it presents a critical evaluation of the stories that can help students, teachers, and working journalists deepen their understanding of the writing craft. In addition to these "Talking Points," a second element called "Assignment Desk" presents a series of writing or reporting exercises. In the spirit of sharing that has infused this series since its inception, these assignments challenge writers to experiment with new shapes, approaches, and voices to discover new ways to write.

These observations, questions, and assignments can be used by individual writers at their desks, by journalism students and their teachers, or by a newsroom staff at a brown-bag writers' lunch. They are an agenda for the best writing.

**Lessons Learned.** To take greater advantage of the expertise recognized by the ASNE judges, each finalist was asked to contribute an essay that answered the question, "What lessons did you learn or re-learn during the writing of this piece that might be of use to someone interested in improving their writing?" Their essays appear after an example of their writing.

**Interviews:** The discussions with the ASNE winners in this book are based on tape-recorded interviews that lasted between four and eight hours. They were conducted in person and supplemented by telephone follow-ups. In editing the voluminous transcripts, I was guided by the standards of the literary, rather than the journalistic, interview. Established by the "Writers at Work" series in the *Paris Review,* the literary interview represents more of a collaboration between interviewer and subject than the journalistic standard. For reasons of clarity or pacing, I reorganized some questions and answers, and in some cases, inserted additional questions. The edited transcripts were reviewed for accuracy and, in some instances, revised slightly by the subjects.

**Deadline Writing.** The ASNE judges did not give an award this year in the deadline writing category. Tony Marro, *Newsday* editor and a member of the ASNE Writing Awards Board, explained their reasons in the ASNE *Bulletin.*

"...It seemed as though many of the entries were being offered up as examples of deadline reporting, rather than writing. There were cleanly-written accounts of traffic accidents, mine cave-ins, train wrecks, legislative actions, and floods. One such offering, representative of many others, had a lead that said, 'The House approved legislation Tuesday that would make it easier for some homeowners to refinance their mortgages...' It was a legitimate story that was likely welcome news to many readers, but nothing approaching the splendid narratives produced by deadline writing winners in the past. And some of the entries seemed not to have been written on deadline at all. So the decision was to not select a winner this year, and to instead send a reminder to ASNE members that the purpose of the contest is to recognize fine writing, not to reward the reporting of spot news."

In that spirit, the final article in this edition, "Storytelling on Deadline," offers advice, tools, and techniques to help writers and editors produce the quality writing that is the hallmark of the ASNE Distinguished Writing Awards.

Christopher Scanlan
July 1994

# Best Newspaper Writing
# 1994

# Anne Hull

## Non-Deadline Writing

A mug shot sits beside Anne Hull's computer in the Newsfeatures department of the *St. Petersburg Times*. The color Polaroid shows a bruised child with the haunted glassy eyes of a crack addict. She is one of the subjects of Hull's latest project, a narrative series exploring the connections between a wealthy, drug-addicted businessman and the street prostitutes he patronized.

"I always get jail mugs. It's one of the first things I do when I start a story," she says. "Thirty cents a pop, the best money the paper can spend."

Hull's feature writing combines the tenacity of the investigative reporter, the novelist's eye for detail, and a passionate curiosity about human behavior; she sees characters where others see sources. Even as a teenage copy clerk answering newsroom phones in the city room of the *St. Petersburg Times,* Hull distinguished herself as

St. Petersburg Times

someone willing to listen to the often sad cases who dial a city desk.

After what she describes as a "brief appearance at Florida State University and a failed attempt as a Revlon sales rep," she was hired as the *Times'* fashion and pop culture writer in 1985, covering the Madonna phenomenon and establishing herself as a writer with a special voice. She traded the fashion beat for newsfeatures general assignment in 1988. A month after she won the ASNE competition, Hull was awarded a Nieman fellowship at Harvard University where she plans to study African-American literature and culture.

# Metal to Bone
## Day 1: Click.

MAY 2, 1993

*It was just the two of them, father and son, living in a tiny apartment where the only luster was a gold picture frame that held the boy's school photo.*

*Their neighborhood stole the young. The father clutched his son fiercely.*

*"I don't want you making the same mistakes I did," he said, the voice of a thousand fathers.*

*On July 4, 1992, at exactly six minutes before midnight, the son stepped from his father's shadow. "I just wanted to be known," he would later say.*

*For his cold-blooded debut, he picked a police officer whose back was turned.*

*The sound she heard from the gun would reverberate for months.*

*Click.*

*It was the same sound the key in the lock makes as the father comes home now to the empty apartment, greeted by the boy in the golden frame.*

*A file at the Hillsborough County Courthouse Annex contains all the information pertinent to the case. But there is no hint of all the things that were lost one Independence Day.*

Officer Lisa Bishop's secret to guarding a sleeping city was pretzels. The crunching kept her awake. She'd pull into a convenience store on Nebraska, say hey to the prostitutes near the pay phone and buy herself a large bag of Rold Gold for the long night ahead. Her shift was from 9 p.m. to 7 a.m.

Four nights a week, Lisa clocked in for duty at the Tampa police station on the frayed outskirts of downtown. In uniform she was petite and muscular, like a beautiful action-figure doll, with piercing green eyes and size 4 steel-toe boots. She kept her hair back in a French braid. Even under a streetlight, her skin seemed carved in pearl.

Her beauty was a curse when she joined the force. She knew what the other officers were thinking: paper doll with a 9mm. Don't break a nail, honey.

After three years of working midnights, her walk got a little tougher and her language a little saltier. Schooled by one too many mean nights, Lisa developed a habit for watching hands. She lost count of all the traffic stops where the driver had a sawed-off shotgun on the floorboard and an outstanding arrest warrant in the computer.

"Take your hands out of your pockets," she'd shout. "Don't get squirrelly on me, and we'll both go home tonight."

Lisa, 30, wasn't unshakable by any stretch. Her biggest fear was rounding a darkened corner. Well, Bishop, she'd tell herself, *somebody's* gotta check behind that building. The hair still rose on the back of her neck.

Funny that she worked nights. As a child, the dark frightened her. Her mother would send her to the corner store at dusk, and she'd run all the way home to beat the falling light. As a cop, she grew to like the night. She drove along the deserted back roads of the Port of Tampa, where the warehouses and giant ships dwarfed her police car. To keep her company, the FM radio was usually turned down low to a country station, her ears perked for a Dwight Yoakam song.

Lisa did not come from a family of cops, never dreamed of being a police officer. She was a varsity cheerleader and star gymnast in high school before entering the University of South Florida. College lasted only a year.

"In my haste, I withdrew to go out and tackle the world," Lisa said. "I ended up working the mall."

She became pregnant when she was 21 and single. Her daughter, Morgan, was born with her mother's same startling green eyes. For years, Lisa bounced from job to job, "bored to tears with my life." She was 27 and struggling to pay the bills when a firefighter friend suggested she put her athletic skills and sense of adventure to use.

Apply to the Tampa Police Academy, he said. Lisa had never handled a weapon before.

She was among 28 cadets who were sworn in with the Tampa Police Department on Oct. 1, 1989. She was issued a badge, a gun and a midnight shift.

Lisa got married the same year she became a cop. Her new career did not always complement her new marriage. "I found something in my life I enjoy," Lisa told Mike, her husband, over his objections. She learned to do what a lot of cops did: She stopped talking about work. All the images of her 10-hour shift—the way a wife's broken jaw hung down, the nightgown worn by a molested child, the beer bottle imbedded in a dashboard of a crumpled car—were filed away in some remote place in Lisa's mind and summed up in one word when her husband asked how the night went:

"Fine."

Her worry revealed itself in other ways. The first thing she did when she arrived home at dawn was strip off her bulletproof vest so she could hold her two young children.

Morgan was 7, and Cody, her new son, was 18 months old.

The Fourth of July was a 93-degree scorcher, with strips of clouds rolled out against blue sky. By early evening, as Lisa buttoned her police uniform, she thought how nice it would be to have a beer and watch the fireworks with the kids. Maybe next year.

As Lisa kissed everyone goodbye, she barely heard her brother-in-law call out to her. The minute he said it, he wished he could take it back.

"Don't get shot."

And she was gone.

Three times a day, a different shift of police officers gathered for roll call in the windowless squad room of District 2. For 20 minutes, a sergeant reviewed the recent tragedies and outstanding warrants before releasing the class of fidgety officers to the streets. On the Fourth of July, the officers were warned to keep their riot helmets ready and be on the alert for flying missiles and gunshots.

Lisa left the station by 9:30 p.m. and drove the short distance into Oscar 8, the zone she patrolled just northeast of I-4 and Ybor City. She and her partner drove in separate cars but answered calls together. One always followed the other for backup. At 10:49, while finishing a domestic dispute complaint, Lisa's radio squawked: Signal 41 —shots fired—at 2003 Cano Court in Ponce de Leon public housing project.

Lisa, who was writing on her clipboard as she stood outside, looked over to Teresa Greiner, her partner. "Wanna go ahead and take it? We're right here," Lisa said, reaching for the radio holstered in her belt to let dispatch know they would respond.

Ponce is usually patrolled by a special squad of Tampa police officers known as the X-ray squad. But if X-ray is busy or off-duty, uniformed officers —such as Lisa—frequently respond to calls there.

Ponce has the highest crime rate of all public housing projects in Tampa. An 8-foot steel fence wraps around the 700 apartments, laid out in flat rows like grimy military barracks. Poverty, drugs and violence have made the neighborhood feel like a bombed-out combat zone. Cigarettes go for a quarter apiece at the corner convenience store, where everything is sold in small quantities that hint of a day-to-day survival.

Some cops in the department avoided taking calls in Ponce. The neighborhood frightened them. Or worse, it didn't seem worth saving. But not Lisa. She jumped at the chance. She always remembered the advice of one of her early mentors: You gotta chill, and the people will respect you. Don't come on all macho or defensive.

As Lisa drove through the streets, the sound of firecrackers and gunshots ricocheted around the treeless, hollow courtyards. Glass flakes glimmered on the sidewalk from a streetlight that had been used for target practice. So many people out tonight, Lisa thought, I bet one of every three is armed.

By 11 p.m., the police had responded to 24 calls to the Ponce area. Among the complaints were car thefts, several domestic disputes, two aggravated

assaults and possession of drugs. Lisa's call was
nearly the last of the day.

"What's goin' on?" she asked, walking up to
the resident who had called the police. The
woman told Lisa that a young man threw ignited
bottle rockets underneath her boyfriend's parked
car, then pumped it full of bullets, just for kicks.
He ran when the police were called, but not before
threatening some of the neighbors with the gun.

As Lisa listened and took notes on her clipboard, someone shouted, "There he goes."

Lisa looked up and glimpsed a figure cutting through a row of buildings. She bolted. Sprinting through the darkness, dodging the wire clotheslines that hung in back of most apartments, she reached for her radio and gave out an alert.

Other officers captured the suspect a block away. Lisa and her partner walked back to finish the investigation.

As they rounded a corner, they used their flashlights to illuminate the sidewalk. Passing a group of teenagers, one of the officers shone the powerful beam in a young man's face. Police flashlights are a familiar form of intimidation to many residents here, especially young men, who often find themselves in a spotlight for no apparent reason.

"I'll kick your ass," the young man yelled. Someone else in the group called one of the officers a whore and a b----.

This is bulls---, Lisa thought. She spun around to face the group.

"Look," she said, walking toward the teenagers, "you can say all you want, but I'll have more units down here than you can shake a stick at. Don't bother with it. Just go on about your business."

Back at Cano Court, Lisa needed to interview a few of the residents who witnessed the suspect shoot at the parked car. Her partner returned to the sector office to finish the report on the captured suspect.

That left Lisa alone on Cano Court.

She could have radioed for backup. Most officers considered it too risky to be alone in Ponce, particularly on a night as unpredictable as the Fourth of July. Lisa didn't.

Though it was nearly midnight, many residents were still on their porches or hanging out on cars, escaping the stultifying heat of the poorly ventilated apartments. Clouds of sulfur from firecrackers drifted through the humid air. Lisa began interviewing William Merrell, one of the people who had had a gun pointed at him. He was still jittery.

Lisa scribbled Merrell's statement, using the hood of her police car to steady her notepad. Merrell stood next to her.

Maybe it was the way Lisa was leaning over. Maybe it was her skin color. Perhaps it was because she was alone, without another officer to cover her. Maybe she had angered a group of boys by shining her flashlight in their eyes earlier in the night.

But there was no way Lisa could have seen it coming.

In an instant, someone forced her down over the hood of the car. A hard object was pressed to the back of her skull, just below her right ear, next to her hair ribbon. Metal to bone: She knew it was a gun. She froze.

"Don't move," the voice behind her ordered.

Maybe it was some other sort of weapon at her head, a lead pipe or something. But a voice in the distance confirmed what she feared.

"He's got a gun."

* * *

The car hood underneath her hand was warm and chalky. It was the only sensation she felt. The rest of the world shut down. Lisa held very still.

If I move he's gonna kill me, Lisa thought.

And then she heard the metallic sound.

Click.

Suddenly, a struggle erupted behind her. The pressure at her skull was gone. She could move. Lift yourself up, she ordered herself. Lift up.

In one sweeping glance, like a movie camera panning a scene, Lisa saw Merrell standing next to her with a terrified look on his face. Just beyond him, someone in a brightly colored outfit was running through a tunnel of screaming neighbors on the sidewalk.

She felt a flash of recognition. She had seen the outfit earlier in the night.

Lisa ran to the back of her car and crouched low for cover. She kept one hand on her holstered weapon and used the other to raise her corporal on the radio. She couldn't see the gunman. Most of the neighbors had fled into their apartments. She was out there alone.

Feeling exposed, she made the 15-yard dash into Merrell's apartment. Inside the small, neat apartment, Lisa was shaking. Merrell was just as panicked. He wondered why Lisa had come into his home. He feared she would draw the gunman inside. Watching her tremble, Merrell could not ask her to leave.

Lisa's corporal screeched up 30 seconds later. Lisa flew out the screen door to meet him.

"Somebody just put a gun to my head," she told him.

"Okay, just hang on," he said, hurrying out to the sidewalk.

Merrell followed Lisa outside. "Did you see a gun?" she asked him.

*"Hell, yeah,"* he said. "I slapped it out of his hand."

Lisa suddenly realized what happened. This stranger had reached out and grabbed the gunman's hand, risking his own life.

"Thank you," she said, stunned. "You saved my life." She hugged him tightly. He could feel her shaking.

Lisa walked over to her corporal. He was bent over a gun on the sidewalk in front of 2005 Cano Court. The gunman must have dropped it as he ran away. Lisa stared at the pistol. Then she looked up at her corporal.

"Oh, my God, Jay, my kids, my kids," she said, beginning to unravel, "What the f--- am I doing out here? My kids."

Her corporal, a burly man with a silver crew cut, put his arm around her tightly and guided her back toward his police car. There was little time for comforting.

"It's okay. It's okay," he said, easing her into the front seat of his car. "Is he still around? Is anybody still around? Tell me what happened, quickly."

Lisa could not give a description of the gunman, only that he wore brightly colored clothes with a bold pattern.

The corporal rushed to the sidewalk to keep an eye on the gun. Police units were everywhere, sirens wailing, lights flashing. The neighbors stood on the sidewalks and their porches. Some disappeared inside their apartments, not wanting to be interviewed as witnesses.

An officer looked at the gun. It was a scrappy, black Colt .25-caliber semiautomatic. He slid the magazine out of the gun. It was empty. Next, he checked the chamber, the small compartment where the bullet rests when ready to fire.

He pulled the slide of the gun back, so he could see inside the slender chamber.

There was a bullet.

Lisa was driven downtown. She could give little detail of the assault. It had all happened behind her. One thing she was positive of was the click she heard from the gun at her head. It had sounded to her like a dry fire, as if the trigger was pulled but the gun did not discharge.

Near dawn, Lisa left the police station and drove home. It was Sunday, and the roads were so eerie and deserted they reminded her of the ending of a Clint Eastwood movie, when he walks out of town alone. The adrenaline of the night had worn off. She felt empty and alone, wanting only to be held.

At home, she looked in on her kids and walked numbly into her bedroom. Michael was in bed, sleeping. He rarely woke up when she came home.

Lisa stood by the dresser and stripped off her gear. Moving in slow motion, she took her radio from her belt and set it in the charger. She unholstered her gun. Michael stirred at the noise and sat up in bed. Something wasn't right. He saw his wife standing at the dresser, gazing blankly at him.

"What's wrong?" he asked.

"Someone tried to kill me tonight," Lisa answered.

Finally, she felt safe enough to cry.

\* \* \*

Officer Gilberto Mercado heard the details at roll call the next afternoon: Someone had crept up behind a police officer last night and placed a loaded gun to her head, execution-style. According to the report, the gunman pulled the trigger but the gun misfired.

Happy Fourth of July.

Gil drove his marked cruiser by the faded pastel buildings of Ponce de Leon. The sun drummed down on the broken sidewalks. Gil wiped sweat from his brow. Bulletproof vests weren't made for Florida summers.

He thought about last night. No mystery how the suspect got a gun. Guns were everywhere. Hell, he'd arrested a 12-year-old with a semiautomatic tucked in the waistband of his Ninja Turtle underwear.

But putting a loaded weapon to a police officer's head? Maybe the walls really were crumbling.

If the suspect was hiding here, Gil and the X-ray squad had the best chance of finding him.

The X-ray squad patrols two neighboring public housing projects—Ponce de Leon and College Hill Homes. The Tampa Police Department created the special unit in 1987 as a last-ditch effort to save the neighborhood from street-level drug dealers and "shootings that were as common as passing transit buses," according to one captain. Residents complained that police officers were rude—at times even physically brutal—and rarely came into the neighborhood unless there was trouble.

The TPD decided to give the two housing projects their own small police force—a handpicked and racially mixed group of 16 officers, called the X squad.

Over the years, the name grew into X-ray. It was a good name. X-ray hinted of a mysterious, special way of seeing things.

To outsiders, even to other police officers in the city, Ponce and College Hill must all look the same: 1,410 residential units stacked side by side like concrete boxes. Best seen through the rolled-up windows of a passing car.

But to Officer Gil Mercado, each apartment has a story, a life behind the screen door that hangs by a loose hinge.

At 31, Gil is a stocky man with thick forearms and the shoulders of a linebacker. He's been on X-ray almost two years. His skin is the color of light coffee, his eyes a shimmering green. Rods of

silver streak through his close-cropped hair. He is
constantly at war with a 5-pound spread around
his middle. Too many plates of *palomilla* and
black beans.

Gil keeps a picture of his son on his key ring.
"That's my heart, right there," Gil likes to say,
tapping the small photo. Before his wife leaves for
work each morning, she takes the baby from the
crib and lays him next to her husband, so the two
Gils can wake up together.

Gil could be brooding or sunny, depending on
his mood, but never volatile. Fair. Patient. Not the
type to go ballistic with a nightstick. He has earned
the respect of many residents in College Hill and
Ponce. A hard thing to do if you are a cop.

Gil knows what it's like to live in poverty. He
grew up in a New Jersey housing project. He was
a 16-year-old street fighter when a high school
teacher saw promise and intelligence behind the
bloody nose and helped him get a football schol-
arship. It was his ticket out.

All it takes is one helping hand, is Gil's theory.
He has reached out to many residents in College
Hill and Ponce.

"You can't be a good officer just taking people
to jail and putting them down," Gil said. He was
a good listener, but he chastised himself for
preaching too much.

One day, walking the beat in Ponce, he saw a
teen mother he knew, pregnant with her third
child. "You need to close those legs and go back
to school," he scolded.

"Tell her, Gil," said the girl's friend, in playful
agreement.

He later brought the woman a sack of diapers.

Gil never fooled himself into thinking he was a
hero here. Old memories run deep. Too many residents remember Melvin Hair, a mentally retarded
man who died in 1987 in a police choke hold outside his home in College Hill.

Some residents feared the police more than
crime itself. A man was pulled over on a minor
traffic violation one night, and as the X-ray officer
approached the car window, the driver raised his

trembling hands in the air and begged, "Don't shoot, don't shoot."

"Man," the officer said, later walking back to his police car, "someone must have f----- with him."

There was no denying the everyday tensions here. Everyone—cops and residents—was on guard.

When riots broke out in Los Angeles in 1992 after the Rodney King verdict, College Hill had its own disturbance. X-ray officers in riot gear were on a sidewalk when bullets whizzed by their heads and into a bus stop sign. For months afterward, the officers stopped to touch the jagged holes left by the slugs.

But no bullets came as close as the one intended for Lisa Bishop on the Fourth of July.

Gil wanted to find who did it. He and Lisa graduated from the police academy together.

On the day after the Fourth of July, the temperature creeped up into the mid-90s, soaking Gil's dark blue polo shirt. The words X-RAY and POLICE were stenciled on the back. A wall of cool air hit him as he walked into the Sector E office, a police substation squarely on the dividing line of Ponce de Leon and College Hill. This is home base for X-ray, complete with lockers, bad coffee, a typewriter, file cabinets and a holding cell.

Inside the sector office, Gil's corporal, Chuck Blount, was flipping through a giant spiral notebook of information on people in the neighborhood who have been arrested or are suspected of criminal activity. A yearbook for offenders. "Courts female rockheads" are the words listed under one man's mug shot, describing his penchant for romancing crack addicts.

The most solid lead Gil and Chuck had to go on was a description read at roll call. Police had canvassed the neighborhood until dawn, interviewing witnesses. This was the composite they came up with:

*Suspect is a B/M, 16–17 years old, 5'9",*
*145 lbs., med bld, dark complexion, nick-*

*name of 'Eugene' who lives with his father in*
*College Hill. He is driving a full-size Bronco,*
*drk blu w/white panels.*

Gil and Chuck tossed names out. Who was bad enough to put a gun to a cop's head? Who had a street name of Eugene? In this neighborhood, lots of young people had nicknames. The two officers came up with a list of possibilities, most of them long shots. They walked outside into the heat and began the hunt.

Riding together, they cruised down each block of Ponce and College Hill. It's a small area, less than a square mile total, but dense with people.

A sleeping bag was rolled out on a second-story roof where someone slept at night to stay cool. Children played makeshift tetherball by stringing a bag of garbage to the top of a pole. Teenage boys with gold teeth and Malcolm X hats pedaled small bikes to nowhere. Because of the holiday weekend, several block parties were humming, with music and cold drinks flowing. When the breeze blew right, like today, it was easy to get a whiff from Caldonia Red Bar-B-Q, a tiny, pink, hot shack where Mr. Caldonia worked his cleaver over a small rack in two seconds flat, good to go.

Gil had the windows in the police car rolled down. He always patrolled that way, to hear things and talk to residents. He drove by 2003 Cano Court, where Lisa Bishop was attacked. He could still see chalk on the sidewalk where the crime scene had been paced off. Everything else looked normal. Almost peaceful, in soft sunlight.

Gil and Chuck passed Cano Court and continued their search. While it was still daylight, they would ride the streets in search of Broncos. After dark, they'd start knocking on doors, making a few surprise visits.

* * *

By Sunday afternoon, William Merrell was tired and agitated. He hadn't slept all night. He didn't even undress for bed. A detective had been by to interview him. One neighbor teased him sourly about being a hero. Merrell knew what the neighbor really meant—he had helped the enemy.

Another neighbor commended his bravery. "You saved that police lady's life," the man said.

Merrell didn't feel courageous. He felt low. And he was afraid. Merrell wanted out of this dangerous place. The event last night only crystallized how life here had disintegrated.

The apartment Merrell and his girlfriend shared was an oasis. Silk flowers were arranged in a vase on a coffee table. Framed paintings of Nelson Mandela and Malcolm X hung over the color TV set. A mesh basket of fresh fruit was in the center of the kitchen table.

But no matter how nice they made the place, Merrell could not escape the gunshots at night or the violence outside his front door. He had to move away from here.

A wiry man with light skin and a close beard, Merrell lived 22 of his 28 years in Ponce de Leon. He moved here with his mother when he was 3. The trim landscape and quiet nights of his childhood vanished long ago.

Under the Housing Act of 1937, Congress directed all states to create low-income housing for urban residents. Ponce de Leon, one of the first properties the Tampa Housing Authority built, opened in 1941. It was occupied by white and Hispanic residents. College Hill was completed in 1945 and occupied by black residents.

Both were beacons of hope. Many older residents remember air that was fragrant with mango and lemon. "We used to suck the nectar out of the hibiscus," said one woman, 42, who spent her childhood in College Hill. "It was like heaven to us."

Public housing originally was conceived as temporary low-income shelter. But over the years, it evolved into a permanent community for the poor. The annual family income of Tampa's public housing residents is less than $5,000 a year. Less than 14 percent of the residents are employed. Nearly 80 percent are black.

Some residents, particularly older ones, will never leave public housing. Despite the crime and physical decay of their neighborhood, it is home.

But others, like William Merrell, are desperate to get out.

Each morning, Merrell waited by the phone to hear if he was needed at work that day. He had a part-time job as a truck driver and was hoping to get on full time. His girlfriend took care of their three small children. They paid $105 a month for their three-bedroom apartment in Ponce. Merrell felt caught in a trap. He could never quite save enough for his family to leave.

Merrell thought about it. People were saying he had saved the life of a police officer. He acted instinctively when he reached out and slapped the gun away. He risked his life for a stranger.

Maybe he could turn his act of valor into a new start for his family.

Maybe the police would give him some sort of reward. He would ask.

\* \* \*

Lisa Bishop's phone was ringing by late afternoon, mostly cops who heard through the grapevine what happened. One of the callers was an officer who used to be on her squad. She considered him a mentor, a "policeman's policeman." He listened as Lisa recounted the sequence of events, the way she held still when the gun was pressed to her head.

"I thought if I moved he would have killed me," she told him.

The officer was supportive, until the end of the conversation. "Lisa," he said, "the next time, think, If you *don't* move, he's gonna kill you."

Another officer told Lisa the same.

"Kick, elbow, do *something*," the officer said.

Others called, offering their support and outrage. "You should have pumped his ass full of lead," a fellow officer told her.

Lisa couldn't shake those words. They ate at her. She sensed the criticism. There was nothing at the academy that had prepared her for that moment in Ponce. What happened last night was all about guts.

She didn't feel guilty for not taking a shot at the suspect. She could have accidentally hit a bystander. For all she knew, the weapon against her head could have been a toy gun. And she wasn't 100 percent sure the man running away from her was the gunman. It had all happened behind her back.

On the hood of that car, she thought, it was just me and him. That was my chance.

She wondered whether the gunman specifically targeted her. Had she angered anyone lately? Were there any outstanding vendettas against her? Hundreds. No one liked getting arrested. She arrested a 12-year-old who shot a man over a $10 rock of cocaine, and the boy was furious at Lisa for interfering with his business deals.

Maybe the gunman didn't care which cop he took down, and Lisa was just the unlucky one.

She didn't tell her kids what happened. What would she say to Morgan? Someone tried to kill Mommy last night? Morgan thought Mommy gave people speeding tickets. Lisa wasn't about to tell her differently. "I'm her Rock of Gibraltar," Lisa said. All those years as a single parent, it was just the two of them.

Lisa's sergeant called to tell her to take the night off, but she needed to work.

In a few hours, she would be back on the street. Where would the gunman be?

* * *

Around 7:30 p.m., Gil and Chuck were cruising through College Hill when they noticed a faded black Bronco with white panels parked on the side of the street. The two officers had pulled over Broncos and Blazers all afternoon, but after running the tags and checking the driver's identification, they kept coming up empty.

They could see a young man sitting on the passenger side. The windows were rolled down. Chuck parked the police cruiser behind the Bronco so that it could not escape. Coolly, the officers walked up to the car. The Bronco had a temporary tag, which made it impossible to check against the computer. Many cars in the projects had paper tags or no tags. License plates and adhesive expiration stickers were always being ripped off from cars and used on uninspected or stolen vehicles.

"This your car?" Chuck asked the passenger.

"No," said the young man, who was about 16 and had his hair styled in a fade.

Gil hoisted himself up on the hood of the car so he could read the vehicle identification number stamped near the dashboard.

"Who's it belong to?" Chuck asked, watching the kid's hands.

"Eugene," he said, unfazed.

Chuck, wearing dark Ray-Bans, flashed his eyes at Gil when he heard the name Eugene. Feeling the rush of a catch, they knew the gunman had to be close by.

Just then, a strapping man in his early 30s walked toward the truck. He had been playing dominoes on a card table with some other men when he saw the officers around the Bronco.

"What's the problem with the truck?" the man asked.

"Is it yours?" Chuck asked.

"It is, but my son is driving it," the man said. "Why?"

"Do you have a son named Eugene?" Gil asked.

"Yeah," he answered. "Why?"

Gil knew this man. He was well known in the neighborhood. His name was Carl Williams.

Years ago, Carl served time in prison. When he got out, he scrubbed floors and earned his money the hard way. Now he was raising a teenage son by himself. He was best known for coaching Little League baseball teams. He coached Dwight Gooden and Gary Sheffield when they were afterschool phenoms. All the young athletes in the projects knew Carl Williams. The X-ray squad even played softball against his teams.

"We need to get to Eugene as soon as possible," Gil told him.

Carl was courteous but asked why they wanted his son.

"I can't explain right now," Gil said. "It's about an incident that occurred last night. We just want to talk to him about it."

Carl sensed the finality in Gil's tone. He said he would find his son.

Carl thought Eugene was at his grandmother's apartment, ⌐ short distance from the truck. With the officers following, Carl walked to the apartment and checked inside. No sign of Eugene.

By foot, he led the officers to his own apartment, in another part of College Hill. Eugene was not there, either. Carl and the officers returned to the Bronco. Several other police units had arrived. Some officers were going through the truck. A crowd had gathered on the sidewalks and under the mossy oak trees.

Gil could see the worry on Carl's face. Raising a child in this neighborhood was not easy. Gil couldn't remember the last time he dealt with a father. This was the land of mothers, grandmothers and aunts. It was the land of tired women.

Again, Carl asked, what did Eugene do?

A sergeant pulled him aside. He told Carl that someone tried to shoot a police officer and his son matched a description of the suspect.

Carl couldn't believe it. He was sure the police had Eugene mixed up with someone else. Trying to shoot a police officer? That wasn't Gene.

"If you want your son alive," Gil told Carl, "you bring me your son. We need to take him in."

Carl didn't take Gil's warning as a threat; he took it as good advice. All he could think about was the police drawing their guns on Eugene in a case of mistaken identity. Carl had to hurry.

"I'll bring him to you," Carl said. "Give me 10 minutes."

# Writers' Workshop

## Talking Points

1) In "Metal to Bone," Hull focuses on the residents of a public housing project, giving detailed and sympathetic media coverage that they rarely receive. "In heart-breaking detail," *St. Petersburg Times* Executive Editor Paul Tash observed, the series gave "a picture of a world we usually try to avoid." She gives the same unusually careful attention to the police. Examine the three parts of this series to see how Hull treats both the police and the residents of the Ponce de Leon public housing project.

2) Solid, painstaking reporting is the foundation of Hull's series. She is especially adept at collecting details that capture the essence of her characters. Consider one such example, her evocative description of police officer Lisa Bishop:

"In uniform she was petite and muscular, like a beautiful action-figure doll, with piercing green eyes and size 4 steel-toe boots. She kept her hair back in a French braid. Even under a streetlight, her skin seemed carved in pearl."

What are the elements that make this passage so descriptive?

3) For her devotion to detail, Hull credits Tom Wolfe who helped school a generation of non-fiction writers with his informative discussion of the techniques of realism in *The New Journalism,* the 1973 anthology he edited with E.W. Johnson.

One key device, Wolfe says, "is the recording of everyday gestures, habits, manners, customs, styles of furniture, clothing, decoration, styles of traveling, eating, keeping house, modes of behaving towards children, servants, superiors, inferiors, peers, plus the various looks, glances, poses, styles of walking, and other symbolic details that might exist within a scene. Symbolic of what? Symbolic, generally, of people's *status life,* using that term in the broad sense of the entire pattern of behavior and possessions through which people express their position in the world or what they think it is or what they hope it to be. The recording of such details is not mere embroidery in prose. It lies as close to the center of the power of realism as any other device in literature."

Examine Hull's series for examples of such revealing status details.

4) The first nine paragraphs of the series are a good example of foreshadowing, a literary device that provides a hint of what is to come later in the story.

Examine how Hull foreshadows the central drama of her entire story and yet doesn't give anything away. Is this an effective lead? What other opening gambits might have worked?

## Assignment Desk

1) Collect a variety of revealing details about a subject in your latest story. Follow Don Murray's advice: "Use all your senses—sight, hearing, smell, taste, touch—to pack your notebook, and your memory, with specifics you may need when writing." To the five senses, add a few more: sense of place, sense of people, sense of drama, sense of time. Discuss what makes them so vivid.

2) Write three new leads for "Metal to Bone." Make sure at least one contains the element of foreshadowing.

# Metal to Bone
# Day 2: Mean streets

MAY 3, 1993

*The day after Officer Lisa Bishop was attacked and held at gunpoint in the Ponce de Leon public housing complex, a special police force that patrols the projects searched the streets for the suspect. The man who would help the police find the gunman was a well-liked and respected figure in the neighborhood. But it was his son the police were looking for. Carl Williams knew how important it was to find his son before the police did.*

Apartment 27 smelled like years of sweat and Lemon Pledge and perfect bacon. The curtains were drawn to keep out the sun. Sports trophies were lined in proud formation on top of the TV. It had looked this way—everything in place, neat and clean—for four decades, though the world outside had completely changed.

Carl Williams first stepped inside this apartment when he was 8. Years later, when his son was born, he would bring a toy or an old baseball for the owl-eyed baby named Eugene.

He had walked across this well-worn carpet so many times.

But no trip had been as painful this one. As the police waited outside, Carl crossed through Mary Robinson's small living room.

His eyes fell on the lanky 16-year-old in swimming trunks with the Red Cross badge sewn on, sitting at his grandmother's kitchen table. Eugene knew the police were looking for him. He had seen the fleet of police cars swarm the Bronco he had been driving. He had watched it all from the screen door of his grandmother's apartment.

"Man, you done messed up," Carl said, moving toward his son.

Eugene panicked. "I didn't do nothin'," he lashed back too quickly.

Carl leveled his cold stare. He knew a lie. "Gene, you didn't do it, did you?"

Eugene just kept shaking his head, his eyes fluttering nervously.

"Man, you know they want you for first-degree attempted murder on a police officer?" Carl asked pleadingly, as if trying to shake his son awake.

*"First-degree attempted murder?"* Eugene said, cocking his head in surprise. "That's not right."

At any minute, Carl feared the police would kick down the door. His neighbors would watch his son being dragged into the back of a police car. He thought he had given everything to this boy.

"You can either go out there now or go out there later," Carl reasoned, "'cause you're eventually gonna have to go. 'Cause if you keep trying to run from the police, these people are gonna try and hurt you."

Eugene kept denying he had done anything wrong.

"You *got* to go out there," Carl ordered.

Eugene shrugged nervously. "I'll go and talk to 'em, but I didn't do nothin'," he said.

They walked out together. Officers Gil Mercado and Chuck Blount of the X-ray squad, the special police force that patrols the projects, looked up.

"Here he is," Carl announced softly. Eugene stood by his side.

Carl was afraid the officers would rush his son and tackle him to the ground. Or worse.

But Gil didn't even handcuff Eugene. They guided him toward a police car and asked him to sit in the back seat.

Out of nowhere, Eugene's mother seemed to appear. Linda Evans had been at a block party nearby when she learned the police were taking her son. It was the day after the Fourth of July, and several block parties were going on throughout the projects. Eugene's mother was quiet and withdrawn, almost nervous. Carl spoke with her quietly and told her to ride with Eugene. She slid in next to her son. Carl followed them in the Bronco.

They drove three blocks to the sector office, a mini-police station that serves the College Hill and Ponce de Leon public housing projects. The officers made small talk with Carl about a recent softball game between the X-ray squad and a team Carl coached.

Carl's skin was black-gold and his eyelashes curled over his eyes, just like Eugene's. His beard needed trimming, and the T-shirt he wore was faded and too small, but there was something proud and impenetrable about him.

Gil liked Carl. It wasn't often he dealt with fathers. They seemed on the verge of extinction in this neighborhood. Of the nearly 1,400 apartments on the tenant rolls for Ponce and College Hill, only 41 belonged to men.

Eugene was soft-spoken and finished his sentences with "Yes, sir." He had a naive, fumbling quality. He was frightened, not defiant. Something didn't fit, the officers thought. Stealing a bag of chips, maybe. But trying to execute a police officer?

And yet he matched the description given to police.

The phone rang in the sector office. It was a detective from downtown. "Bring him in," he said.

Eugene waited in a sergeant's vacant office while someone brought him a soda and a honey bun from a vending machine down the hall. Carl sat on a sofa in the office. Because Eugene was a juvenile, Carl was permitted to be present during the interview. Eugene's mother waited outside the room.

The detective started with the basics.

Eugene was nervous. He glanced at his father before answering each question. He'd say a few words and look over at Carl "like he didn't want to break his dad's heart," the detective would say later.

Eugene denied any knowledge of a police officer being attacked in Ponce.

The detective asked Carl to step outside. Then he turned to Eugene.

"I think you're lying," he said evenly. "Are you embarrassed to tell the truth in front of your father?"

Finally, with Carl out of the room, Eugene began his story.

The Fourth of July had been one of those rare days when he ventured beyond the squalid boundaries of the projects. Eugene, Carl and some other families had driven to Picnic Island, a public park just south of the Gandy Bridge on Tampa Bay. Under one of the shelters that line the small shoreline, barbecue food was spread on the table, and a fresh deck of cards was brought out for later. Eugene saw his first dolphin that day.

By late afternoon, after promising his friends he'd meet up with them later, he rode back to the projects with Carl.

Around 7 p.m., after showering and changing into a new shorts set, Eugene walked the five blocks from his apartment in College Hill over to Ponce. The streets had a Saturday night bustle. People were lined up for blue crab and catfish at the carry-out seafood window on 22nd Street. Rap music thumped through the neighborhood.

Eugene caught up with his friends around Cano Court. They were hanging outside, sitting on the hood of a car listening to Bell Biv DeVoe. They mixed Tanqueray gin with Jack Daniel's wine coolers and drank from paper cups. He couldn't remember exactly how many drinks he had.

"It made my body numb out," Eugene told the detective.

He stayed with the group for a few hours, then left to walk around the projects. The smell of spent fireworks drifted in the air. On his journey around the neighborhood, Eugene stopped to talk with a couple of police officers he knew at the sector office, located between Ponce and College Hill. Some time after 11 p.m., he walked back to Cano Court and hooked up with his buddies.

He learned that one of his friends had shot at a parked car and threatened some neighbors with a gun. The police officer who helped capture their friend was right over there, talking with someone and taking notes near her police car. She was the same officer who shone a flashlight at the group earlier in the night and argued with one of the young men after he called her "bitch."

Eugene's 14-year-old cousin took a gun out of the waistband of his shorts. It was a crummy street pistol, a black Colt .25-caliber not worth more than $30 from a pawnshop. The boy handed it to Eugene in two pieces—the gun and a magazine.

"Stick this gun to the police lady's head," one of his friends dared.

"It was like, ah, all of 'em in that little crowd, just kept yelling at me, 'Go do it' or 'Go ahead,'" Eugene said.

He could see the magazine was empty. But he didn't check the chamber to see whether it contained a bullet.

"I was sat on the car, and when they started telling me, 'Do it,' I went up there and came up from behind. And...stuck it to her head," Eugene told the detective.

"Was your finger on the trigger?" the detective asked.

"Yeah," Eugene said.

"Did you pull the trigger?"

"Unh-uh," Eugene said, shaking his head no.

"When they hit my hand, I was like putting the gun, was like, lowering the gun, and they had hit...hit my hand...and I...I ran. And I threw it some...somewhere between her...her squad car and that first fence."

Eugene kept running. He circled around Ponce, not knowing where to go. For some reason, he came back. Hiding behind the corner of a building, he watched the chaos. Police cars screeched up, their blue and red lights making a pattern on the naked walls of the apartment buildings. He thought the whole police force was out there. He ran home.

The detective closed his notebook.

He stepped outside the office and told Carl of Eugene's confession. Carl walked down the hallway, in shock. His eyes filled with tears. The first person he saw was Gil Mercado, who was stepping off the elevator. They stood there, face to face, in the polished hallway outside the homicide division. Gil could see Carl had been crying.

"He did it," Carl said.

Hours later, Eugene was driven to the Hillsborough Regional Juvenile Detention Center. It was nearly 4 a.m. He changed out of his street clothes into cotton scrubs. He spent the night in a cell by himself.

The next morning, two detectives arrived with an arrest warrant. Eugene was being charged as an adult—first-degree attempted murder of a law enforcement officer, punishable by life in prison. No bail was set.

Eugene was taken to the Hillsborough County Jail. He rode in the back seat, handcuffed. He wasn't sullen or profane or bored, like so many of the juveniles who'd grown used to seeing I-4 through the windows of a police cruiser. He was remorseful.

"I never meant to hurt that police lady," he said.

"It was a stupid thing to do," the detective said, turning his head toward Eugene. "Guns kill people."

The detective added something else. "She had a baby not too long ago."

Eugene was quiet for a moment.

"I never'd want that baby to grow up without a mama."

\* \* \*

Two days after Eugene's arrest, a supporter of the African People's Socialist Party visited Carl's apartment in College Hill. The group, which believes there is an overzealous police presence in black neighborhoods, wanted to help Eugene. The man said Eugene was set up by the Tampa police. This was an example of the "cracker pigs framing up a brother," the man told Carl. His organization was willing to lend its support by publicly raising the issue of racism.

Carl sat in his hot apartment, thinking. Curtains on the front window blocked out the sun, but also any breeze that might find its way to College Hill in July. Two smudged couches jostled for space in

the tiny living room. Outside, a sand pit of litter
and the odd blade of grass.

Options and choices were luxuries that rarely
came into Carl's life. And here was an offer that
might help his son.

Carl refused.

"This isn't a black-and-white issue," he said.

But Carl had tossed and turned all night, trying
to understand how Eugene could have done something so violent, so stupid and so ruinous to his future. Eugene didn't hate the police. He didn't hate
white people. The irony was, Eugene had talked
about being a police officer when he grew up.

Now he faced a life in prison.

Carl's stomach pitched when he thought about it.

"Prison," he told his son so many times, "ain't
no place to be."

In 1983, Carl was arrested with an ounce of heroin and about half an ounce of cocaine. He spent
six years in North Florida correctional institutions.

Later, after he was released, Carl didn't shield
Eugene from the realities of prison life, about the
migraines and loneliness and physical brutality.
There wasn't a hint of bravado in his tone when he
recounted to Eugene the time he had to throw another inmate through a plate glass window.

"I didn't want him making the same mistakes I
made," Carl said.

And yet the cruel pattern was being repeated
before his eyes.

After prison, Carl found work at the Christian
Resource Center, a small ministry in East Tampa.
He did janitorial jobs and coached the summer
camp programs for kids. Though Carl was never
the churchgoing type, he was grateful to the min-
isters for giving him a fresh start.

With Eugene in trouble, Carl turned to them
again.

Two days after Eugene's arrest, sweat beaded
across Carl's forehead as he hurried to the ministry and knocked on Pastor Herman Moten's door.

The pastor listened quietly as Carl explained
the situation. He agreed with Carl's decision to
turn down the activist's offer.

"We're sitting on a powder keg already," Moten said.

Carl didn't want the case getting lost in the shuffle of the heavy caseload of a public defender. He wasn't even sure Eugene was safe in jail. He envisioned Eugene dying a mysterious death in his cell.

The pastor picked up the phone and began calling around for the names of some good criminal lawyers in town.

The cheapest estimate they got from a lawyer was $17,000. One told them fees could go as high as $30,000. All of them wanted money up front.

Carl made less than $100 a week coaching summer camp and some extra on the side for cleaning carpets. Eugene earned more than his father as a lifeguard at a city pool. A fancy lawyer was out of the question.

Carl walked out of the pastor's office feeling desperate.

It was a feeling he thought he buried years ago.

* * *

Eugene was raised in the crowded comfort of his grandmother's apartment. Everyone in the neighborhood knew Mary Robinson. She moved into College Hill in 1952, not long after it was built. Miss Mary relied on the Scriptures and a green switch from a sapling to keep her eight children in line.

Her youngest daughter was Linda, a quiet child with light almond eyes. Linda got pregnant in the 10th grade by her steady boyfriend, a handsome baseball standout at Hillsborough High named Carl Williams.

Eugene was brought home from Tampa General in a plastic bassinet.

Carl and Linda never married, but Carl visited his son nearly every day, bringing little toys when he could.

After he graduated from high school, Carl worked as a security guard for Maas Brothers. Five years on the job passed and he began to see his future: an old man standing around a fancy department store watching other people buy things. Then, opportunity knocked.

"I saw an easy way to make money," he said. Dealing drugs.

Carl didn't drink alcohol or use drugs. But the cash he could make in a day equaled a week's pay at Maas Brothers. He moved up fast, from street dealer to supplier. For once he was in a business where he could use his wits. The rewards rained down: TVs, VCRs, a motorcycle, two cars and a horse. He paid for a sister to go through accounting school.

In 1983, Carl was convicted on drug charges.

Carl would call home from prison and Eugene would hurry into the kitchen near the phone, trying to pick up bits of the conversation. Carl told stories of going to lockup because of fighting. "Don't tell Shorty," Carl would say, using the nickname he had for Eugene.

Eugene and his mother shared a tiny upstairs bedroom in Mary Robinson's apartment. Linda worked as a summer lifeguard at a city pool for several years, and she taught Eugene how to swim. But when Eugene was in the fifth grade, Linda began drifting away from the apartment for days at a time. Eugene's grandmother told him his mother was out of town on business.

It was a story Eugene would tell others long after he knew the truth.

At 60, a graying Mary Robinson found herself with a house full of kids. She was raising three other grandchildren besides Eugene. She made the boys iron their own clothes and rake the patch of dirt in front of the apartment. It was the only way she knew to encourage some order amid the growing chaos of the neighborhood. Gunshots were a part of the night's percussion. The police were always cutting through her yard with someone in handcuffs, their radios crackling under windows so often they become a part of dreams.

Carl was released from prison when Eugene was in the sixth grade. Not long after, Carl gained legal custody of Eugene.

Carl groped along, operating on instinct. "I didn't know *what* I was doing," he said. "I didn't know how to cook. We *ate up* McDonald's."

Carl scrubbed floors and eventually was promoted to supervisor at a janitorial company. He wanted to start his own company and hoped to bring Eugene into the business when he was old enough. The company would be called C and E Janitorial. Though he lived in a squalid section of public housing, he used part of his paycheck to spoil Eugene at the Malibu racetrack on Friday nights, blowing $25 on video games.

"I wanted to be his father *and* his friend," Carl said.

Carl watched out for Eugene like a hawk. Eugene's friends—all of whom lived without fathers—called him a daddy's boy.

But Carl could not be at his son's side all the time.

One afternoon when Eugene was 13, he was walking through College Hill, wearing a new sweat suit and a pair of high-tops. Two older teenagers came up beside him. One stuck a gun to his head.

"Give it up," the gunman ordered.

Right there on the sidewalk, Eugene stripped out of his sweats and sneakers. Terrified and humiliated, he walked home in his T-shirt and socks. He cried when he saw Carl.

At that moment, Eugene learned what a gun could do. It gave power to the powerless.

"People think just because they got a gun they bad," he would later remark. "I guess so, 'cause you can't do nothin' to nobody who got a gun."

The next summer, while working as a summer custodian on a school campus, Eugene was caught showing a gun to some students. He told the campus police officer he had found it behind the portable classrooms. He was charged with carrying a concealed weapon. A juvenile court judge sentenced him to 30 hours of community service.

Carl brushed off the incident.

"You can get a gun out here like soda water," he said.

* * *

Eugene's years at Middleton Junior High were sprinkled with disappointments and signs of trouble. At times he seemed on the verge of detonating. But then he would mystify everyone with an almost childlike act of kindness. He brought his favorite janitor—an older woman who had been at Middleton for years—a giant bunch of balloons on the last day of school.

For the longest time he was a poor student who kept his head down in class, rarely removing his books from his black gym bag. He was suspended for being disruptive. School held nothing for him.

On the days he skipped, he would return to Middleton for his free lunch, and then leave again.

"Bump it," he'd say, "I'm gone."

He'd walk to a girlfriend's house—Eugene began having sex when he was 14, often ignoring Carl's advice to use condoms—or he'd hang out at a park with friends.

Carl was frequently at school in parent-teacher conferences. Because of poor grades and emotional immaturity, Eugene had to repeat eighth grade. He wasn't embarrassed about it. He knew kids who were 17 and still in junior high.

At Middleton, Eugene entered a special program for students with academic problems but who still showed promise. He was given the gift of Herman Broxton, a tall, gentle teacher everyone called "Coach" because he coached the Middleton track team.

Broxton helped Eugene set goals and urged him to think independently. He noticed a student who could still be saved. "There was a softness about him."

But right away, Broxton saw Eugene's magnetism for troublemakers. "He was torn between two sides." Broxton said, "to be with us or to be with them."

A month after entering Broxton's program, Eugene and a friend were caught trying to break into a Tampa pawnshop. The alarm sounded and they ran, but a K-9 unit helped capture both boys. Eugene gave the police a fake name.

He was charged with burglary, possession of burglary tools and opposing an officer without violence. Under juvenile guidelines, he was sentenced to community control, a form of probation. Carl grounded him for a month.

Just when Eugene's downward curve seemed unstoppable, he took control.

His attendance at school improved. He brought his F's up to C's. His eyes brightened. He talked of wanting to be a police officer. He won the Turn-Around Award for being the most improved student in Coach Broxton's class, and Carl was selected as the most involved parent.

Eugene and Broxton made a bet over who could outdress the other at the awards ceremony. They shook on it.

Broxton couldn't believe his eyes the next day when Eugene walked down the crowded corridors of Middleton in a white tuxedo with tails.

Carl had spent $64 on the tux rental, a big chunk out of his $119 paycheck that week from his janitorial work. But he had always told Eugene, "If you need anything, if you want anything, ask me, and we'll find a way."

Eugene rode with Coach Broxton to pick up the cake for the awards party. In the car, Eugene looked over at Broxton and said, "You know, Coach, this has been a pretty good year for me."

Broxton thought to himself: We got hold of him.

That summer, Broxton was watching the news when he heard about a 16-year-old from College Hill who was charged with trying to kill a police officer.

When he heard the name, he cried, "That's Eugene!"

* * *

Crickets and the sound of footsteps in the gravel hung in the August night. Lisa Bishop was walking around the back of an Ybor City warehouse, investigating a possible burglary.

Suddenly, the rat-a-tat of gunshots perforated the air. Lisa threw herself against the wall of the building.

She realized the gunshots were at least a block away.

Eugene had done this to her.

Technically, she was fine. A department psychologist had okayed her return to duty. As much as Lisa was trying to regain her confidence, she was shaken. She realized she had taken the increasing violence of her job for granted. Nobody messed with the blue shirt and shield, right?

Partially, she blamed herself. She heard through the grapevine that some officers criticized her for not reacting more quickly when she was pinned on the hood of the car. Others wondered how she

could let her defenses down so far that someone
could surprise her so easily. Besides, what was she
doing alone in Ponce de Leon, which had the
highest crime of any of Tampa's public housing
projects?

Other officers wanted to know why she let Eugene run.

"Why didn't you just blow him away?" they
asked.

Deep inside, she wondered if she had it in her
to be a cop. She felt she had been tested and had
failed.

To her disappointment, she was assigned a new
zone to patrol, "to let things cool off," her sergeant told her. She missed the old neighborhoods,
where people knew her. "Yo, Miss Bishop,"
they'd call out, waving.

She felt isolated and disconnected in her new
zone, which was to the west of her old Oscar 8,
and much quieter.

Five seconds had affected every part of Lisa's life
—her job, her husband, her children, everything.

Morgan, her 7-year-old, came home distraught
from summer camp one afternoon.

"Mommy," the little girl said, "somebody at
camp told me somebody tried to kill you."

Lisa sat her daughter down. "You know Mommy's job," Lisa told her, trying to explain in simple
terms what happened. She didn't mention the gun.

Even before the Eugene incident, Lisa and her
husband rarely talked about her police work. In a
way, she was relieved. It kept her home separate,
almost sacred. It's not that Lisa was a *Redbook*
wife who pulled baked hams from the oven; the
closest she came to cooking was dialing Little
Caesars.

Lisa met Mike when she was 27 and a single
parent. A month after their wedding, Lisa was
sworn in with the Tampa Police Department. "Instant family, instant cop," as Mike, an engineering
technician with an environmental engineering
firm, put it. He never liked her being a cop, but
what was he going to do, make her choose?

As time passed, Mike noticed his wife toughening. He missed the old Lisa. She didn't need to lean on him as much as she used to. She seemed like a cop all the time. Once, when they both pulled their cars up to a gas station at night in a high-crime neighborhood, it was Lisa who automatically started scanning the parking lot and made sure her off-duty gun was within reach.

In Mike's eyes, Lisa was always working or tired or being paged by the department. Sometimes he wanted to hurl her beeper 10 miles. He resented her job—its pull on her, its danger. Everything. So they stopped talking about it.

But the Fourth of July forced Mike to confront all the reasons he disliked her job, after three years of trying to ignore them.

"I had been sweeping under the rug...the possibility of her going out and not coming home," he said.

Lisa and Mike tightened their grip on their daily chores, nearly tripping over the silence.

\* \* \*

A vacant apartment on a U-shaped street in Ponce called the Horseshoe was used as a 24-hour crack house and shooting gallery. The Horseshoe was known as an easy place to score drugs, especially heroin. People would make their buys and then disappear inside Apartment 1712.

The floor was littered with syringes and homemade devices for smoking crack. Urine and feces were dried on the floor. In the upstairs bedroom, a sad halo of condoms and butane lighters surrounded a children's Masters of the Universe mattress. In a gesture of vanity, someone had propped a mirror at the foot of the soiled bed.

Even a little girl who chased her cat into the apartment knew enough not to touch the dirty needles.

"People get too old too quick out here," Officer Gil Mercado said.

Every time the X-ray squad tried closing a crack house, a new one emerged. Most of the officers knew the war on drugs was little more than a political tag line. But they did what they were paid to do.

A month after Eugene's arrest, on a sweltering night in August, Gil and another X-ray officer were staked out behind a building in College Hill, watching a knot of dealers hawk their small plastic bags of crack and grass.

Sometimes a chase broke out, and X-ray got lucky. The officers mostly caught buyers—skeletons who were too weak to run, outsiders who didn't know the lay of the land or white suburbanites who drive around the projects with ground-down teeth and saucer eyes.

A ring of sweat soaked through Gil's navy shirt, making an outline of his bulletproof vest. In their dark shirts, Gil and his partner were hard to spot. But somehow a petite woman with short braids saw them. Eyes locked, and she abruptly turned in the opposite direction. Gil's partner recognized her. He had once issued her a trespass warning, a tactic used by the police to keep people from coming into public housing to buy drugs.

"Ma'am, we need to speak with you," Gil called out.

The woman broke into a run, but Gil easily caught up with her. She was tomboyish, with short hair and a men's warmup jacket zipped over her frail body. Her eyes were tired. She held a rolled-up towel in one hand.

Inside, Gil found a homemade pipe with fresh cocaine residue. Most of the rockheads snapped off part of a car antenna and shoved a little steel wool inside for a filter.

Gil searched the woman and discovered a small plastic bag in her front pocket, containing one piece of rock cocaine. She was handcuffed, taken to the sector office and later driven to central booking.

Gil didn't recognize her. If he had, he would have remembered her as the quiet woman who sat next to her son at a table in the sector office the day after the Fourth of July.

Gil had just arrested Eugene's mother.

* * *

Although Eugene told everyone his mother had a job that took her out of town, the reality was that Linda Evans was a phantom in her son's life because of crack. She was arrested for the first time when Eugene was in fifth grade. Over the years, Linda racked up four more drug-related convictions. Always buying, never selling. Just enough to get high.

Criminal records list her alias as "Shorty," as if it were an elaborately-plotted code name. Actually, Shorty was just the affectionate nickname Carl gave her in high school, the same name he later used for Eugene.

Barely 5 feet tall, Linda wasn't one for stylish clothes or keeping her hair in fashion, especially as she got older. She still had a taut, compact body from working all those summers as a lifeguard at the city pool. Her job applications revealed the same neat script as Eugene's.

Linda moved around. She sometimes stayed at Carl's apartment. Eugene once told Carl: "If you want to give me a present, you and Mama stay together."

But Carl could not explain that he had stopped loving Linda a long time ago. He just wanted to help her.

After she was arrested in August by the X-ray squad, Eugene was in one Hillsborough County jail, and his mother was in another.

A letter was waiting for Lisa in her box at the police station.

*Dear Mrs. Bishop:*

*Mrs. Bishop you got to believe I never had thought of hurting you. I'm not that kind of person as much as to take someone's life. I would rather take my own life before I will take or try to take anyone else life.*

*Mrs. Bishop there is a guard down here each time I look at her she reminds me so much of you and it just brings tears to my eyes to know that I almost took your life even though I wasn't intent to hurt you.*

Eugene's letter revealed a childish side of Eugene, one Lisa was surprised existed beneath such a cold act of calculated violence. But she would not show him any lenience.

"He's got to pay the piper," she said.

Shirley Williams, the assistant state attorney prosecuting the case, warned Lisa that going to trial was risky. Eugene had been indicted by a grand jury of first-degree attempted murder of a law enforcement officer. If they went to trial and a jury found him guilty of that charge, by law the judge would have to sentence him to a minimum of 25 years to life.

But if a jury returned a conviction on a lesser charge, a judge could sentence Eugene as a juvenile, to as little as probation.

The trial was a gamble. A plea bargain would at least assure Eugene of doing *some* jail time.

Lisa decided she would take her chances in court.

The prosecutor was pleased. She had a personal stake in this case.

Before going to law school, Williams was an agent with the Florida Department of Law Enforcement. And she was engaged to marry a Tampa cop. As far as she was concerned, when Eugene held the gun to Lisa's head, he held it to the head of all police officers.

She wanted to see Eugene get the maximum time in prison. Twenty-five years to life.

They were going to trial.

\* \* \*

Carl told Eugene he should write the judge just before he was sentenced, after his trial was over. But Eugene misunderstood and wrote the letter right away.

On the outside of the envelope addressed to Judge Diana Allen at the Hillsborough County Courthouse, Eugene drew a cuddly cat holding a sign that read, "Please Mrs. Allen. I begg of your forgiveness please."

Inside, the letter began:

*How are you fine I hope, me not too good cause I really miss my people at home.*

*Deep inside my heart is hurting. Being a police officer was my dream and now look what I'm into. I didn't pull the trigger or try to kill someone that's not my way. I would never do something like that it was I had a*

*bunch of low life peoples who wanted to pull
me down to there level 'cause they saw I was
doing better then they.*

A few days later, Judge Allen received another letter.

*Yes, it's me again. How are you fine I
hope. Me I'm trying to be strong for my love-
ing people.*

*I will get on my knees and begg and plea
for your forgiveness and Miss Bishop forgiveness and after this is over I'm going to
take her out for dinner and Miss Allen if you
give a chance I can get so close to Miss Bishop's heart until it will just be unbelievable.*

*Trouble is so easy to get in but so hard to
get out of.*

Eugene imagined a lady judge wearing black robes, a gavel nearby as she read his letters. He would not learn until later that Judge Allen did not always read mail from defendants awaiting trial. She read some of his letters, and forwarded the others to the court file, unopened.

In jail, Eugene suffered from headaches and sleeplessness. A county psychiatrist prescribed an antidepressant for him. Between the drugs and the junk food he bought from the jail canteen, his face took on a moonlike puffiness.

Each Friday, a movie was shown on a TV at the end of a hallway. The inmates viewed the screen by lifting up the food slot in their cell door and peering down the corridor. One of the movies Eugene watched was *Coming to America,* about a pampered African prince (Eddie Murphy) who ignores his father's wishes and journeys to New York City.

Because of good behavior, Eugene was moved to the juvenile pod at the Hillsborough County Jail, an octagonal-shaped, brightly colored space without bars. As opposed to the traditional linear jail, a pod helped cut down on fights, extortion and rape. Eugene was allowed the freedom to socialize with other inmates, all of them under 18.

"They sit around here talkin', 'When I get out of here, I'm gonna steal me another car,'" Eugene said. "I'm like, 'What's wrong with y'all, man, this ain't enough?' I guess they just want to be known."

Even though a public defender had been appointed for Eugene, Carl still was scrambling for ways to raise money for a private attorney. Fancy attorneys, Carl observed, always seemed to shave years off the sentences of white criminals who could afford the steep legal fees.

Back in the neighborhood, he put the word out. He needed money.

Some drug dealers from Carl's past started visiting him. They offered him a chance to get back in the business. They knew he was vulnerable. They heard he was considering doing some deals— short-term, large quantities—to raise money for his son's legal fees.

A member with the Tampa Police Department who had known Carl for 15 years heard through the grapevine what Carl was considering. Jobless men with expensive cars were seen hanging around Carl's apartment.

The officer drove to College Hill to find Carl. He had a piece of advice for his old friend:

"Don't go back."

\* \* \*

For one rare night in late October, police work was put aside. It was Halloween in Ponce.

The X-ray squad had transformed a boarded-up apartment building into a giant haunted house. Hand-carved jack-o'-lanterns were perched on the moss-covered roof. The officers arrived at dawn to shoo out the bums and sweep away the drug paraphernalia. Using plywood and 2 by 4s donated from the housing authority, the cops built coffins and elaborate graveyard scenes. For weeks, they planned their costumes, which they bought with their own money. Boogaloo, a small-time drug dealer and graffiti artist in the neighborhood, helped with sign-making.

In 1987, a few of the X-ray officers decided to hand out candy to kids one Halloween at the Ponce resident office. A planning committee of police and residents later formed, and the haunted house grew into an annual tradition.

For one night of the year, blue police uniforms were traded for a Freddy Krueger mask or an Elvira wig.

Officer Gil Mercado stood at the entrance of the haunted house, acting as doorman and daddy as nearly a thousand kids lined up, waiting their turn to enter the dark, humid corridors, where chain saws buzzed and cobwebs hung.

Gil's partner had her 9mm Glock slipped down into the waistband of her Levi's as a 3-year-old boy named Pooh clung to her neck. Pooh's older sister and a friend screamed with delight as they stepped inside the faded green haunted house.

"Feel my heart," the little girl said, placing her friend's small hand over her chest.

From the doorway of the haunted house, Gil looked out across Rivera Court at the sea of children. Cockroaches crawled on them as they slept at night. The free lunch they ate at school was their only hot meal of the day.

But on Halloween, with their faces painted like witches and tigers, the burdens of their childhood were invisible.

Suddenly, *pop-pop-pop.*

The sound of gunshots rang out in a distant corner of Ponce. The officers outside the haunted house tensed and held perfectly still. The children, though, were oblivious to the familiar sounds of guns. What made them shriek were the cardboard bats that flew in the trees and the plastic fangs worn by middle-aged cops.

A boy ran up to Gil, scared by a goblin in the haunted house.

Gil lifted the child up in his arms. "You all right, my man?"

For hours, Gil chaperoned groups of children, inside the haunted house. They clung to his legs and pulled at his shirt. They would not let go.

"Hold on to each other," he shouted, and together, they plunged into the darkness.

* * *

As Eugene's trial drew near, he wrote a letter to his attorney. It was written on yellow legal paper in his childish print:

*People look at me and tell me you might as well give up 'cause I'm going to prison they tell me. I would rather not get on the stand but if I have to I'm prepared to do so. I'll be real shy and nervous but I'll do it.*

*Right now, you have my life in your hands and I'm depending on you.*

Charles Scruggs, a quiet man who listened to classical music in his law office, was Eugene's court-appointed attorney. Eugene originally was assigned a public defender, but a conflict of interest arose (the public defender knew some of the witnesses involved in the case), and Scruggs was appointed by Hillsborough County.

There was something about the mild-mannered attorney that made Carl hopeful. Scruggs treated Carl with respect. He never drove to the projects—he considered the neighborhood dangerous—so Carl visited Scruggs' Hyde Park law office on several occasions, discussing his son's case among the antiques and Oriental rugs.

The attorney was realistic about Eugene's case. Police officers, he said, "were that thin line between us and anarchy," and Eugene had stuck a gun to one of their heads.

Scruggs was eager to negotiate a plea for Eugene, but Shirley Williams, the prosecutor, wouldn't consider it. They were going to trial. Scruggs' only hope was to convince a jury that an eighth-grader had done a horribly stupid act while intoxicated, but attempted murder it was not.

He wrote a reply to Eugene's letter.

*Your letters keep saying things like "My life is in your hands." Be assured that I'll do my best, but remember, I'm not a magician.*

\* \* \*

The day before the trial, Mary Robinson sat in the sixth row of her beloved St. John Progressive M.B. Church. She was a plain figure in a flock of fancy hats. Years ago, when she worked the all-night weekend shift as a nurse's aide at Tampa General Hospital, she'd come home at dawn and get her children dressed for Sunday school. Church always revived her.

"Sometimes when you go to church, you just want to go right back," she said.

When Eugene was a boy, Mary would iron her grandson's Sunday clothes and take him to St. John's. She'd take his hand and lead him into her favorite pew, settling on the velvet cushions in the cool lilac air. When the collection plate came by, she'd dig into her purse and give Eugene some coins to drop in. That boy had a smile.

As he got older, Eugene stopped going to church, but Mary never missed a Sunday.

Today, she needed something extra. She prayed hard. She gently rocked her body along with the mighty gospel choir dressed in their brilliant red robes. It was one of her favorite hymns.

*Come where the drops of mercy are bright*
*Shine all around us, by day and by night.*

\* \* \*

Eugene swore—to detectives, his lawyer, his family, to Lisa Bishop—that he was not the sort of person who would ever intentionally harm someone.

But Shirley Williams knew another Eugene.

She worked at home over the weekend, preparing for the trial. Inside one of the many file folders spread out on the kitchen table was her trump card.

A Tampa police officer had given Williams a crumpled note. It was written weeks before the Lisa Bishop incident and left on the windshield of a car owned by a woman in College Hill. The woman and Eugene often argued.

*Don't think I have forgotten about you*
*punk no bitch! I am going to put that .45 pis-*
*tol on your ass. I'll come to your houes.*

The note was signed with the name Eugene.

Williams had sent the note to the Florida Department of Law Enforcement crime lab for handwriting analysis.

Bingo. It was a match.

# Writers' Workshop

## Talking Points

1) Good writers use the five senses—sight, sound, touch, taste, and smell—but invest them with their own intelligence. Study the first sentence in the second part of "Metal to Bone": "Apartment 27 smelled like years of sweat and Lemon Pledge and perfect bacon." Like poetry, this 13-word sentence is precise, economical, and pregnant with meaning. How might editing some of the details affect it? What if Hull had written it this way: "Mary Robinson's apartment smelled like sweat, furniture polish, and bacon."

2) In *The New Journalism,* Tom Wolfe identifies three other techniques of realism besides recording of status details. They are 1) scene-by-scene construction, "telling the story by moving from scene to scene and resorting as little as possible to sheer historical narrative," 2) recording dialogue in full, and 3) "third-person point of view, the technique of presenting every scene to the reader through the eyes of a particular character, giving the reader the feeling of being inside the character's mind and experiencing the reality of the scene as he experiences it."

Hull employs each of these devices throughout "Metal to Bone." Find examples of each device and study how they are constructed.

3) Notice how skillfully Hull puts people on the page, not as sources or as talking heads, but as fully-rounded characters. Consider this evocative, sensitive description of Carl Williams: "Carl's skin was black-gold and his eyelashes curled over his eyes, just like Eugene's. His beard needed trimming, and the T-shirt he wore was faded and too small, but there was something proud and impenetrable about him." What is the effect?

4) "Metal to Bone" contains many extraordinary scenes, remarkable for their sense of people, sense of place, sense of drama, their attention to detail, and ear for dialogue. Examine and discuss the next to last section in which Eugene's grandmother sits in her church on the eve of her grandson's trial.

5) Can you figure out at which scenes Hull was an eyewitness and which she reconstructed? Discuss how the reporting differs in each case.

6) Does the writer have to be present at a scene to write it? How can writers ensure they are faithfully recording what was said, what happened?

## Assignment Desk

1) Hang out at a public housing project for several days and write a story about a love affair, a family reunion, the death of a child or an elderly person, stories, that is, that reveal the project as a neighborhood.

2) Write a one-paragraph description of a person in one of your stories, combining physical description and your assessment of character the way Hull does with Carl Williams.

3) Look at the quotes in your stories. Do they advance the story? Do they reveal character? Do they resemble dialogue? Could you have said it better? Paraphrase several quotes; which is more effective?

4) Write a scene that you witness personally. Reconstruct a second scene that you did not see first-hand. List the sources for everything in the reconstructed scene.

# Metal to Bone
# Day 3: Betrayals

MAY 4, 1993

*Everyone thought they knew the real Eugene. His grandmother knew the boy who ironed his own clothes. His father knew the son who helped him keep score at baseball games. But Lisa Bishop only knew the Eugene who was cold enough to nearly take her life on a dare. The trial begins.*

Technically, it was a crime without injury. Not even a scratch.

But on the first day of trial, on a crisp morning in December, Judge Diana Allen looked out at a crowded courtroom lined with news cameras. This case had become a flash point for public outrage, symbolizing the absolute derailment of law and order.

Eugene Williams sat at the defendant's table, oblivious to outrage and symbolism. New loafers from Payless pinched his feet. The dark turtleneck he wore was creased from being folded in a store package. His seventh-grade cousin had taken a bus to the mall and picked out the new clothes. Eugene's attorney, Charles Scruggs, was relieved when he saw the outfit; a suit wouldn't have seemed right on a 16-year-old accused of first-degree attempted murder of a law enforcement officer.

On the eve of the trial, Scruggs visited Eugene in jail. Eugene was relaxed and grinning. Scruggs reminded him he faced a possible 25 years in prison, "day-for-day, minimum mandatory." He told Eugene the jury would convict him if he appeared lighthearted. Scruggs left the jail puzzled. Here was a kid who wrote childish letters with animals drawn on the envelopes, but had the ability to hold a gun to a police officer's head. Eugene seemed completely disconnected from his act of violence. He thought if he wrote Lisa Bishop a letter of apology, everything would be fine. Eugene might be 16 years old, Scruggs thought, but emotionally, he was a child.

On the first day of his trial, Eugene wore a mask of somber concern.

"Is the state ready?" the judge asked, looking ashen and stern behind her oak bench.

"Yes, your honor."

"Is the defense ready?"

"Yes, judge."

On the Fourth of July, 1992, Officer Lisa Bishop was answering a call in the Ponce de Leon housing project when Eugene surprised her from behind and put a gun to her head. A bystander, William Merrell, lunged for the gun, and Eugene fled. A day later, he confessed. Those facts were undisputed.

But the state charged Eugene with attempted murder, so it would have to prove he intended to kill Lisa.

Eugene said he never meant to harm her.

The main piece of state evidence was a scrappy Colt .25 semiautomatic pistol. The other crucial piece of evidence was intangible. It was the sound of a click Lisa heard as the gun was held to her head.

Shirley Williams, the prosecutor, walked to the clerk's desk and picked up a small clear bag. She held it by the corner so the jury could see.

"A lot of your testimony is going to depend on this little gun," Williams said, passing it before the jury. "Every possible source of the click noise was in preparation for firing this gun."

Eugene didn't aim the gun at Lisa's arm, Williams said. He held it to her head, the most vulnerable part of the body. He took an executioner's stance. His purpose was murder.

"What would have happened if Mr. Merrell had not grabbed the gun from the defendant's hand?" the prosecutor asked.

She looked at each of the jurors—four white women, one white man and one black man. Williams made sure she had their attention, drawing them in with her pause.

"Maybe it's sad that a 16-year-old did something like this. But it's even sadder that Lisa Bishop could have died out there."

Eugene's attorney removed his tortoise-shell reading glasses and walked over to the podium in front of the jury. Scruggs wasn't one for theatrics. He was a country gentleman who listened to Mozart and liked to hunt quail. His opening argument was straightforward. He praised Lisa for her cool reaction. He wasn't about to lessen the heinousness of what Eugene did.

"It was a stupid and dangerous thing to do," Scruggs said, as he faced the jurors. "But it was not attempted murder. They have charged him with pulling the trigger of the gun. You will find no proof."

Eugene's father, Carl, sat just behind his son and laid a hand on his shoulder during a break. "This is the hard part now," Carl said, forcing a smile.

Months of exhaustion hung on Carl. His beard was ragged. His sweatshirt was wrinkled. There was no way he could have known that the trial was not the hard part.

In the end, the trial would revive his faith in courtrooms and judges. It was his son who would let him down.

Carl knew none of these things as Judge Allen called for the first witness. He leaned back in the hard wooden bench in Courtroom 11 as the prosecutor rose from her chair.

"The state calls Officer Lisa Bishop."

* * *

The door in the back of the courtroom swung open and a small figure in a blue police uniform passed through. Her French braid was threaded with a red ribbon. She had a gutsy walk as she made her way to the witness stand. Sliding into the seat next to the judge, Lisa shivered slightly. She was nervous and cold. She looked over to Eugene.

It was the first time she had ever seen his face.

He didn't frighten her. She turned away and tried to focus on the prosecutor's questions, giving a measured recital of her night in Ponce.

Lisa pointed to a diagram on a portable black-board and explained precisely where the attack had occurred. There was Ponce, shrunken and neatly sketched in chalk, revealing none of its bleakness for the jurors who looked on sleepily.

Lisa sounded official when she spoke, (she said "23-hundred hours" instead of 11 p.m.), but her steely demeanor cracked when the prosecutor asked her to recount what happened.

"I remember hearing feet," Lisa said, haltingly. "Someone had bent me over. I remember feeling a body against me. A hard object was pressed to the back of my head near my ear. I felt that if I moved the gun would go off."

"What happened next?"

"I heard a click."

Her body shivered, as if an electrical current had been sent up her spine. Lisa rubbed her bare arms.

"What did you think the click was from?" the prosecutor asked.

"The sound of a trigger pull."

No further questions.

Eugene's attorney stood up from his table. From her rigid perch in the witness box, Lisa watched him as he approached. She had never testified at a trial before, but she knew this was the part when the defense attorney would pick over her testimony as if it were a carcass, as if it were *her* fault someone put a gun to her head. Her green eyes lost all their softness as he stood in front of her. She reared her chin back slightly, in defiant preparation.

But Scruggs surprised her.

He didn't waste time casting shadows on her testimony of the attack. He was interested in the noise that night in Ponce, when the air was filled with gunshots and fireworks, and the tiny silver sound of a click could be easily imagined.

The click that could put Eugene away for 25 years.

"The sound was right there next to your ear?" Scruggs asked.

"Yes, sir," Lisa answered, with a clipped certainty.

"How would you characterize the click?"

"I can hear it now," she said. "It echoes."

Careful not to badger, Scruggs pressed further, asking Lisa to explain the sound. Did it sound like the single action of a trigger pull, or like a slide being pulled back and a round being racked into the chamber?

Lisa didn't hesitate. She made certain she was being understood.

"It sounded like the single action of a trigger pull."

As Lisa left the stand, she walked down the carpeted aisle, passing her lieutenant, her stepmother and her partner. She scanned the crowd for Michael, her husband. Lately, the tension between them had grown, much of it because of her job. The Eugene incident had just made matters worse. As she and Mike were scrambling to get the kids ready the morning of the trial, Lisa asked him whether he planned to come watch her testify.

"I'll try," he told her.

As she walked through the courtroom, she didn't see him.

* * *

Lisa heard a click. Where did it come from?

Two weapons experts testified that the click could have been caused a variety of ways:

A safety mechanism can click as it is being switched on or off. (The gun Eugene used had two safeties.)

A louder slapping can be heard as the slide is pulled back and a bullet is being loaded into the chamber.

No expert witness could say for sure where the click came from.

There also was the question of how the bullet got into the chamber of the gun.

Eugene told detectives he thought the gun was unloaded. When his friend handed it to him, it was in two pieces, the magazine and the gun. The magazine was empty, Eugene said, but he didn't check the chamber.

The first person to touch the gun after it was dropped on the sidewalk was a Tampa Police sergeant. Although crime analysts prefer evidence to be left untouched, the sergeant thought the gun was unsafe on a public sidewalk. He picked it up, and upon discovering a bullet in the chamber, ejected the bullet from the gun.

So the main piece of evidence had been disturbed at the crime scene.

Williams, the prosecutor, believed the testimony from the firearms experts proved Eugene had prepared the gun for firing. When the gun was found on the sidewalk, both safeties were off, and a bullet was in the chamber.

But Scruggs suggested that the bullet could have been loaded into the chamber before Eugene received the gun. And the clicking noise Lisa heard could have been confused with the Fourth of July fireworks.

There were so many variables. The dry testimony led one juror to doze.

Aside from all the mechanical possibilities of the gun, there also was the human element added to the mystery. At what point did William Merrell interrupt Eugene's mission?

Merrell testified he heard a click just before Eugene put the gun to Lisa's head. Scruggs was polite with Merrell, but he was persistent with his questions about sound.

"Was there a lot of noise that night?" Scruggs asked Merrell.

"Yeah."

"Would you describe that night in the projects as loud, confusing?"

Merrell shrugged and said he guessed so.

Merrell looked uncomfortable sitting in the witness stand. For months, he had tried to put the Fourth of July behind him. Merrell never did ask the police about reward money for saving Lisa's life. As much as he needed money to move his family out of Ponce, he wasn't the type to ask for help.

He had seen Lisa a few times since the incident. She considered him her guardian angel. Once, she showed up at his apartment with two other police units. She extended her hand, and then withdrew it, breaking into a smile. "Hell, gimme a hug," she said, embracing him.

The whole thing made Merrell feel queasy. Some of the young agitators who hung out near his corner eyed him with suspicion for helping the police. And now he was testifying for the state. To make matters worse, Merrell lived next door to one of Eugene's friends, a 22-year-old with an arrest record that included strong-arm robbery.

When Merrell finished his testimony, he quietly stepped down from the witness stand and caught a city bus back to his job.

* * *

During the noon recess, Eugene's family sat on the stone benches just outside the courtroom. Mary Robinson, Eugene's grandmother, took a Goody's powder for her headache. Even with her hearing aid turned up, most of the testimony came across as a dull roar.

One of Eugene's aunts was walking down the terrazzo hallway of the courthouse when she noticed Officer Bishop talking with one of the state's witnesses.

As the aunt got closer, she saw Lisa handing cash to the witness.

She turned and hurried back to find Carl.

"Are you sure?" Carl asked, incredulous. "You *sure* it was Miss Bishop?"

Carl looked around for Scruggs.

Not only had Lisa handed money to a witness, but a sergeant who also was a witness in the trial gave money to William Merrell. In the middle of a crowded hallway of the courthouse, two police officers had given cash to two witnesses.

Judge Allen's tone was arctic as she ordered a bailiff to bring Lisa back to the courtroom. The jury was still out of the room.

"I'll remind you you're still under oath, Miss Bishop," the judge said, as Lisa stepped up to the witness stand.

She asked if Lisa gave cash to a witness during the lunch break.

"Yes, ma'am," Lisa said.

"What on earth were you doing?" the judge asked, irritated.

"I gave him $5 to take a bus or a cab home," Lisa said, looking shaken. "Nothing more, nothing less."

"The appearance of what you did is totally improper," Judge Allen scolded.

Then the judge glanced at the empty jury box and said, to no one in particular, "it just occurred to me someone from the jury might have seen the exchange."

Lisa told the judge that another witness, a sergeant with Tampa Police department, was the only person she thought observed the transaction.

He, too, gave money to a witness.

Judge Allen cocked her head in disbelief. She ordered the bailiff to bring the sergeant into the courtroom.

"I gave him bus fare to get back to work," he explained, apologetically.

"It's not your place to be paying state witnesses," the judge chided.

She ordered the jury back in. Carl leaned forward. He knew a mistrial could be called. Scruggs and Eugene watched the jurors take their seats. Scruggs whispered in Eugene's ear. Williams sat at the prosecutor's table, her face completely without expression.

"Did any of you notice anything concerning the witnesses during the lunch break?" Judge Allen asked the jury.

The jurors looked puzzled for an instant, and then each of them shook their head no.

"Are you satisfied, Mr. Scruggs?" the judge asked.

"Yes, your honor," he answered.

Outside the courtroom, Lisa was embarrassed and angry. I don't need to bribe a witness, she thought. Someone had held a gun to *my* head, remember?

* * *

Shirley Williams had her trump card. It was the threatening note Eugene left on someone's windshield a few weeks before his arrest in July. A state crime analyst confirmed it was written by Eugene. Since the note had no direct bearing on the Lisa Bishop case, Williams could introduce it into evidence only if Eugene took the stand and denied he would ever intentionally try to hurt another person.

The note, Williams believed, revealed a violent young man.

She drew in a breath as the last witness of the trial was called by the defense.

The TV cameras in the back of the courtroom followed Eugene's short walk to the witness stand. Carl watched from the second row. The only sound was a bailiff clipping his nails. Eugene sat down, blinking nervously and struggling to stretch his top lip over his protruding teeth. A stylish side part had been razored in by the jail barber, as requested. He had gained nearly 25 pounds since his arrest, and the extra weight did not match his childish face.

Scruggs spoke to Eugene in a fatherly tone. "Now, speak to the jury, Eugene," he said.

Eugene gave a fitful explanation of what happened on the Fourth of July.

He testified he had seven or eight drinks throughout the night. He said he was high when one of his 14-year-old friends gave him a gun and motioned toward the police officer, daring him to put it to her head.

"I didn't say nothin' to her," Eugene said, his eyes focused on some imaginary spot on the back wall of the courtroom. "I stuck the gun to her head and she froze."

"Why did you do that?" Scruggs asked.

"I was just wantin' to feel a part of the little crew I was with," he said, shrugging and blinking, "trying to be seen, trying to be the big man."

"You never squeezed the trigger?"

"No."

"And you never engaged the slide back?"

"No, unh-uh."

"What did you hope to accomplish with doing that?"

Eugene paused, and shook his head hopelessly. "Nothin' really, just trying to be seen, be a big man."

Scruggs turned back toward the defense table. He hadn't even made it there when the prosecutor shot out of her seat to begin cross-examination. Shirley Williams was still on her way up when she asked her first question.

"How many people had a gun that night?" she asked sharply.

Eugene named three names, none his.

"Everybody had a gun but you?" Williams asked, her tone disbelieving.

"That's right."

"Do you recall telling Detective McNamara you had three to four drinks that night?"

"No," he said, his eyebrows arched in surprise, "not really. No, ma'am."

"When you had the gun to the back of Lisa's head, where was your finger?" Williams asked.

"On the trigger."

"You never pulled the trigger?"

"No."

"What did you think was going to happen when Officer Bishop got up from the hood of the car?" Williams baited. "You didn't think she might empty 17 bullets into you? Did you ever think that one of you was going to get shot that night?"

"I really didn't think about it," Eugene answered, softly.

"I have no more questions," Williams snapped, after five minutes of cross-examination.

She returned to her table, tossing her pen down, looking both disgusted and resolute. She never got the chance to introduce Eugene's threatening note into evidence.

The jury would never know about it.

\* \* \*

Lisa arrived at the courthouse early the next day. A corona of TV camera lights circled her. In uniform, she looked like a docudrama cop, with her perfect green eyes and shiny gun at her hip.

But the stress of the last several months had taken its toll. Dark crescents hung under her eyes. She seemed almost frail as she filed into the courtroom with her father on one side and her lieutenant on the other.

Eugene's family took their seats. Carl sat off by himself, his elbows propped on his knees. Fatigue had settled on him.

Closing arguments were brief.

It took the jury three hours to reach a verdict.

Eugene was led from a holding cell in the court-house back into the courtroom. He sat next to Scruggs.

The side door of the courtroom opened and Judge Allen swept through. She smoothed out her black robe and took her seat behind the bench. The low chatter in the courtroom evaporated.

"You have a verdict?" the judge asked the jury foreman.

Lisa's father wrapped his arm around her shoulders.

In silence, the foreman handed a slip of paper to the clerk, who handed it up to the judge. Eugene and his attorney stood up. The judge looked at the thin strip of paper. Eugene watched her hand it back down to the clerk.

"The jury finds the defendant guilty of a lesser charge of aggravated battery of a law enforcement officer with a firearm."

Eugene, smiling a lopsided grin, turned to his father. Carl cast his arms around Eugene's shoulders before a bailiff led him away. He would be returned to jail until his sentencing, five weeks away.

Lisa swept up her purse and keys from the wooden bench where she was sitting and rushed from the courtroom.

\* \* \*

On Dec. 23, five days after Eugene's trial ended, nearly every law enforcement officer in Tampa wanted to rip the black robe from the honorable Judge Diana Allen.

She released Eugene from jail.

The hearing that morning was brief. Scruggs asked the judge whether Eugene could await his sentencing at home instead of in jail. Carl stood next to Eugene, with one hand on his son's shoulder and the other holding a certificate he received for his volunteer coaching.

"I do have pretty good control over him," Carl said, looking up at Judge Allen, who nodded as she listened.

"Do you have anything to say?" she asked Eugene.

"If you give me a chance I will do better," he offered, softly.

For months, Judge Allen had watched Carl in her courtroom. He rarely missed a hearing. The judge believed that parental involvement was imperative to juvenile rehabilitation, and Carl's presence was a promising sign that Eugene could turn his life around.

And yet the judge knew she was taking a risk if she let Eugene out of jail. "We take risks every day," she would later say.

Judge Allen looked at Eugene and Carl, and then began scrawling on a piece of paper. "I'll grant the motion," she said.

Carl slapped Eugene's back and smiled brilliantly. Judge Allen glanced up at Eugene.

"You can't leave the house unless you're with this man right here," she said, pointing to Carl, who was still grinning. "I'll also allow him to leave the house with his mother."

Judge Allen did not know Eugene's mother was in a North Florida prison on a drug conviction.

Shirley Williams was stunned at the judge's decision. The state had vigorously opposed Eugene's release. She picked up the phone. Someone had to tell Lisa.

"This is a slap in my face," Lisa told Williams.

Lisa felt sick. A 16-year-old put a gun to her head, and then he's allowed to go home for Christmas. What kind of message does this send? Is it open season on cops?

The evening news reports suggested a would-be cop killer was let out of jail for the holidays. "Eugene Williams trades his jail cell for the comforts of home," one reporter announced.

In her College Hill apartment, Mary Robinson hummed as she washed her greens and started her casseroles for Christmas.

"The boy's comin' home," she said, her voice dancing.

* * *

Eugene spent Christmas day in Mary's cramped apartment, visiting with relatives. There was a

Christmas tree and plenty of good food. Carl bought Eugene new clothes and a Minnesota Vikings cap.

While in jail, Eugene had learned his girlfriend from Middleton Junior High was pregnant with his child. The girl had written him letters, and provided him with great comfort during the months he awaited his trial.

But when Eugene was released, he wanted to forget about the girl and the baby, "I don't need to be botherin' with that right now," he said, smiling in that sheepish way of his.

Carl later heard from the girl's mother that she had lost the baby. "Something about falling off a ladder," Carl said.

After months of working only sporadically, Carl was trying to get his janitorial service going. Keeping an eye on Eugene 24 hours a day as the judge ordered was difficult, unless he brought Eugene with him on jobs. So he had a talk with Eugene, his son.

"I can't sit here and watch you all the time," Carl said. "You can go to the game room, you can go to your grandmama's. But I'm gonna feel bad, just like a fool, standing in front of the judge, if you mess up."

Carl gave Eugene his freedom.

As far as Officer Gil Mercado of the X-ray squad could tell, 1993 did not bring peace or good tidings or prosperity around the projects.

Lately, Gil was wondering how much longer he could take the job. The faces were beginning to look the same. He was tired of baby car thieves taunting him they'd be out of juvenile detention within 21 days and back on the street.

One 14-year-old who bailed out of a stolen Oldsmobile was cheered on like a gladiator as he ran through the streets of Ponce, with the entire X-ray squad on his heels. Gil finally tackled the kid, who had stolen enough cars to fill up a GM dealership. He didn't care that he was arrested; he was embarassed he got caught in front of the crowd.

"You lucky I had a cramp," he told an officer.

He sat in the holding cell at the sector office, as Gil filled out the arrest report. "He's 14," Gil chided, not looking up. "Baby thinks he's a man."

"Man, I didn't hurt nobody," said the boy, who was the father of two children. "How long I gotta stay here? Man, I'm tellin' the judge. Y'all f--- heads try to hammer me for grand theft auto. Go get someone for murder."

Gil had grown weary. That bone-deep weariness.

On the night of Jan. 11, with two hours left on the shift, the X-ray squad was doing surveillance on a house near Ponce when the sound of screeching tires jolted them from their stakeout positions.

Two officers on bicycles saw it first: two juveniles driving a shiny red Chrysler LeBaron convertible, fishtailing down a street. The car came to a stop at the edge of a vacant field. Just as the officers were within 50 yards of the convertible, a bystander had shouted "Nine," a warning that the police were near. The car screeched off.

The officers followed the car for less than a block before it slowed and both occupants jumped out.

The car began rolling backward at the officers. The passenger got away, but the driver was not fast enough. He was caught and handcuffed.

Inside the convertible, the shell of the steering column was on the floor, cracked open when the car was stolen. The stereo was gone.

Gil arrived at the scene to take the suspect back to the sector office. Gil took out his notepad.

"What's your name?" Gil asked, beginning a line of questioning he could recite in his sleep.

"You know me," the boy said. "I'm Eugene Williams."

\* \* \*

Carl reached the sector office in four minutes. It was nearly 1 a.m. Cpl. Chuck Blount was waiting for him outside, smoking a cigarette under the giant oak tree. The sky was a dark bowl of stars. Chuck felt nothing but dread as Carl walked toward him.

Quietly, Chuck told Carl that Eugene had been caught driving a stolen car. There was an odd beat of silence, and then Carl's voice filled the night.

"Lord, have mercy," he cried, "I can't take this no more."

Chuck led him inside the sector office. Eugene was sitting in the holding cell, wearing handcuffs and the new Vikings cap Carl had bought him.

"Gene, you promised me," Carl screamed, his grief giving way to anger, "you promised me. You know you're going to prison?"

A string of excuses began to tumble from Eugene. They all began with "Daddy." But they could not penetrate Carl. He just stood there under the cold fluorescent lights and stared at his son.

When Eugene was led out of the sector office at nearly 3 a.m., a waiting TV camera filmed him walking toward a police car that would take him to jail.

"Eugene, can you tell us what happened?" the reporter asked, holding a microphone toward Eugene, who shielded himself with his ball cap. "I thought you were supposed to turn over a new leaf."

Carl was off to the side, watching. Suddenly, he spun around. He cut across the darkened playground behind the sector office. His strides grew longer and faster, taking him further away from Eugene. He unclipped his beeper from his pocket and smashed it to the ground, shattering pieces across the concrete basketball court.

By the time Eugene was in the back seat of the police car, Carl was a small figure at the opposite end of the dewy field.

He got in his car and drove. By the time he let off the gas, he was 80 miles down the interstate. The sign said Orlando.

\* \* \*

In an interview with a detective after his arrest, Eugene claimed that on the night of Jan. 11, he walked from his apartment in College Hill to Ponce, and then to Robles Park Village, a public housing project about two miles away. He ran into his friend Ricky, who was driving the red convertible.

Eugene and Ricky seemed to find trouble with magnetic ease. They were together when Eugene was arrested for trying to burglarize a pawnshop in eighth grade.

Carl knew Eugene was friends with Ricky, and he knew Ricky had been in jail for auto theft before. But Carl dismissed the crimes as if they were foolish capers. "He's not a bad kid, really," Carl once said.

True enough, in high-crime neighborhoods such as Ponce and College Hill, stealing cars ranked rather low on the scale of illegal activity.

But Carl didn't know the extent of Ricky's criminal activity.

Ricky, by his own estimation, had been in nearly 40 stolen cars.

On Jan. 11, Eugene said he was walking along when he saw Ricky in Robles Park, driving the red convertible. Eugene climbed in and asked to drive. The boys were cruising through Ponce when the police saw them. Eugene denied shifting the car into reverse and trying to hit the officers.

Eugene was charged with grand theft auto. For causing the car to roll backward, he faced a more familiar charge—aggravated assault on a law enforcement officer.

He was returned to jail where he waited for his sentencing in the Lisa Bishop case.

* * *

Eugene's cold act of violence touched every part of Lisa's life. She began to carry a small .22 pistol in her cowboy boot when she and Mike went out at night. If Morgan, her daughter, rode her bike to the convenience store at the end of the block, Lisa would telephone the store two minutes later to make sure Morgan arrived safely.

While she was on patrol one night, a group of teenagers who recognized her had threatened her: "Next time, that gun won't go click."

Like many crime victims, Lisa blamed herself for not reacting differently during her assault. When Eugene had her on the hood of the car, she froze. A friend told her about the Green Berets in Vietnam, about how they were trained to react instantly. Even if they were sound asleep, they would wake up swinging or shooting if disturbed. Lisa didn't know whether the story was true, but the Green Berets and their quick reactions haunted her.

When she tried to imagine Eugene's face, she couldn't. Gradually, he had lost his status as a person.

But Lisa wasn't ready for what she learned on the morning of Eugene's sentencing on Jan. 29.

She arrived in Judge Allen's courtroom and sat next to Shirley Williams at the prosecutor's table. As she took off her coat and laid it across the back of a chair, Williams handed her something. It was a copy of Eugene's presentencing investigation report, a confidential document about Eugene's past.

Lisa couldn't believe what she was reading. She flipped back to the beginning of the form to see whether she had the right report. The one she was reading said the defendant had been arrested five times and charged with eight felony offenses.

Eugene's juvenile record showed that his first brush with the law was in 1989, when he was charged with assault. He broke another boy's teeth in a fight. In 1991, he was charged with carrying a concealed firearm. In the winter of 1992, he tried to burglarize the pawnshop. In July, he attacked Lisa. And then the grand theft auto charge.

Eugene's journey to this courtroom began long before the Fourth of July. He was no newcomer to crime, as Lisa believed. He wasn't a lost kid who caved in to peer pressure one mistaken night.

Lisa glared at Eugene, who stood less than five feet from her in the courtroom. She swallowed hard to fight back her anger and tears.

*You son of a bitch,* she thought. *What would you have done if Mr. Merrell had not reached out for that gun?*

Lisa tried to focus on Williams, the prosecutor, who had a peacefulness Lisa envied. Lisa did not want to come unglued. She was furious. She kept staring at Eugene.

*You have taken up so much of my time,* she thought.

Eugene stood in front of the judge, with Carl on one side of him and Charles Scruggs on the other. He was dressed in jail clothes. Lisa rose from her chair and moved next to Williams. They all stood there, inches apart, waiting.

So much hung in the balance. Judge Allen could sentence Eugene as a juvenile or as an adult. His punishment could be as lenient as community control, or as harsh as seven years in prison.

Carl knew that Eugene had embarrassed the judge. Although she knew her decision would be sharply criticized by the city's police officers, she let Eugene go home for Christmas. And Carl figured the judge must be angry with him. Her one condition to Eugene's release was that Carl be with his son at all times.

Judge Allen quietly read the presentencing investigation report, compiled by a probation officer.

The report contained a family's well-tended garden of secrets.

Judge Allen placed the papers aside and spoke.

"No one asked (Eugene) at trial—and I won't ask him now—what he intended to do if Mr. Merrell had not pulled the gun away from Miss Bishop's head."

Judge Allen noted that it was clear Eugene's sense of judgment was underdeveloped. She wondered aloud whether he might suffer from a disorder such as fetal alcohol syndrome.

"Did his mother drink when she was carrying the child?" she asked, looking at Carl and sounding truly curious.

"Some," Carl answered, startled by the question.

The judge asked to hear from Eugene.

"I know I let y'all down," he told the judge, who regarded him with detachment as he softly spoke. "I know you stuck your neck out and let me go home for the Christmas holidays. I didn't go lookin' for trouble, it just happened. I'm real sorry for what happened."

The judge looked at Lisa. "Officer Bishop?"

"I would ask the court he be sentenced to the maximum you're allowed," Lisa said, her voice laced with anger. "I wonder how sorry he would be and what kind of apologies he could offer my family were I not here."

"This whole offense has torn my world upside down," she said, "personally and professionally. In my personal life, I have become very cold. It's created a disturbance in my home life."

Shirley Williams began to speak, but Lisa stepped forward.

"Your honor," she said, lifting her chin and clasping her hands. "Is he sorry for what he did or is he sorry that he got caught?"

There was a drawn-out silence as Judge Allen looked down at her papers. Eugene cast his eyes downward.

"I'm declining to sentence him as a youthful offender," the judge said, finally.

Strike one for Eugene. He would not be going to a boot camp for juvenile offenders, as Scruggs had proposed. He would be going to prison. Carl's shoulders sagged.

"For the aggravated battery on a law enforcement officer," the judge continued, "statute 775.08236, I'll sentence him to five years in a Florida state prison, with three years minimum mandatory for the firearm and because the crime involved a law enforcement officer, those minimums to be sentenced concurrently. That five years will be followed by 10 years probation, followed by $455 in court costs, psychiatric evaluation and 250 hours of community service work."

The bottom line was three years. Eugene was going to prison for at least three years. Carl stood there, not moving, holding the diploma his son earned for attending school classes in jail. He brought it to show the judge. She never asked to see it.

The lawyers snapped their briefcases shut, the clerk pounded documents with a rubber stamp and the judge looked down to sign the paperwork. Carl hung there. Even after everything, he clutched that diploma as stubbornly as he clutched his belief in Eugene.

Eugene was taken from Carl's side by a bailiff who guided him to the inkpad, where each finger was rolled and printed, one at a time, on a sheet of fresh white paper. Handcuffs were snapped around his wrists.

The sound was an unmistakable click.

## EPILOGUE

On April 16, 1993, Eugene appeared in court on his car theft charges. He pleaded no contest to grand theft auto and aggravated assault of a law enforcement officer. Judge Allen sentenced him to a 5-1/2 years in prison, to run concurrently with his previous sentence. He is currently at the Hillsborough County Jail, waiting to be taken to the Reception and Medical Center in Lake Butler, where incoming Florida inmates are processed before being sent to their designated prison.

There is little trace of the boy arrested last July. Eugene's voice has deepened, he has grown nearly three inches and gained 47 pounds. He recently wrote Judge Allen a letter asking about the possibility of his record being expunged when he is released from prison. He still believes he can be a police officer some day.

Carl also gets a letter once a week.

*Dad:*

*I just don't know how to thank you for all you have done for me. I know you're probably saying stay out of trouble but after this experience believe me I will stay out of trouble 'cause I'm going to try and find me a job to occupied by time 'cause you can believe one way or the other I'm going to get that 300 ZX car unless you have an objection about it.*

Carl Williams is trying to leave public housing and rent an apartment in north Tampa. His janitorial business is growing, and he still coaches baseball in the evenings near the projects.

Linda Evans, Eugene's mother, was released from a north Florida prison on April 16, the same day Eugene was sentenced for auto theft in Hillsborough County. She returned to Tampa.

William Merrell still lives in Ponce de Leon with his girlfriend and three children.

Officer Gil Mercado hopes to transfer off the X-ray squad this year and onto another specialized squad. A letter of commendation was placed in Gil's personnel file following Eugene's speedy arrest. "Gil Mercado is going to be a future leader of the TPD," his supervisor noted in his most recent evaluation.

Officer Lisa Bishop has been transferred from her beloved midnight shift to days. Though she objected, her supervisors felt she needed to work in a less stressful atmosphere. Her new schedule has at least allowed her more time with her family. The tensions between her and Michael have eased.

Lisa rarely thinks of Eugene, although she refuses to leave her back exposed, even while having dinner at a restaurant. Her back is always against a wall.

# Writers' Workshop

## Talking Points

1) "Technically, it was a crime without injury. Not even a scratch." So Hull begins the final installment of her series. The point, she says, was not lost on some journalists who read the piece and wondered why the big deal in these days of drive-by shootings and serial killers, why so much time and attention was paid to a "crime without injury." Debate the question.

2) Once again, Hull displays her gift for isolating the revealing detail as she describes what Eugene Williams wore on the opening day of his trial: "New loafers from Payless pinched his feet. The dark turtleneck he wore was creased from being folded in a store package. His seventh-grade cousin had taken a bus to the mall and picked out the new clothes."
Consider the reporting that went into those three sentences.

3) Bill Blundell, 1982 ASNE non-deadline winner, believes in the importance of building the dimension of time into your story. "You look at the past and you also anticipate the future. You don't just deal with the present. You go for different viewpoints." Study how Hull conveys the passage of time in her series.

4) Hull says the inspiration for her series was a brief but well-reported police story about the incident. Search your paper for stories that hold the promise of a more extended treatment. Discuss what sets them apart.

5) One of the most striking aspects of this series is the voice, which is deeply empathetic and gives the reader a deep understanding of its characters. Novelist Joyce Carol Oates has said, "Content yields to form, form to voice. But no one knows what voice is; only when it is absent; when one hears nothing."
Hull's voice—empathetic, authoritative, honest—dominates "Metal to Bone." Here is an example:
"Months of exhaustion hung on Carl. His beard was ragged. His sweatshirt was wrinkled. There was no way he could have known that the trial was not the hard part.

"In the end, the trial would revive his faith in courtrooms and judges. It was his son who would let him down."

Look for other examples of the writer's voice in this series and other stories you admire.

6) Examine how Hull compresses the trial into a series of dramatic, informative scenes. Notice how she uses dialogue to pace the narrative. Discuss the various roles of dialogue in a story.

## Assignment Desk

1) Take a police brief and examine whether it has the potential for a narrative. Who are the potential characters? What is the central conflict? What are the various sources: people, records, observation? What are the windows into the story?

2) One way to inject voice into a story is to turn the tables on yourself. Interview yourself. Ask the tough questions: "What do I think about this character? What's this story really about? How do I feel about this?  How does my reporting support my opinions and feelings?"

# Anne Hull: Detective
# Bringing a mug shot to life

**CHRISTOPHER SCANLAN: How did you come to write this story?**

ANNE HULL: The crime occurred near midnight on July 4 and our first story was on July 6 or 7. I frequently look for story ideas in the Metro section, and this one just leapt out at me right away, because no one died. Which meant everyone was alive to tell the story, if they were willing to cooperate.

**What was it about that story that attracted you?**

Whenever a crime story happens in a public housing project, I feel like it's always treated in a certain way. Very telegraphic, nothing that reveals any soul of the neighborhood. An intern happened to write the first story, and he actually went to the neighborhood and captured a little bit of the soul of this neighborhood, which gave me hope right away. He contacted Eugene's grandmother and got a couple of really nice quotes from this woman, and that fueled my interest. There were some details in there that were remarkable.

Eugene was a police Explorer, which is a great irony. Here is the kid who tries to take the life of a police officer, and yet he's in a junior police program himself. He's a lifeguard, paid to protect people and save lives, and he's a person who just tried to kill a police officer. It gave a side of this kid that was not cold and callous. Here's a person who had held a loaded gun to a police officer's head, and the initial story said that the gun misfired. And forever, people seem to think that the gun misfired, but as we found out in

■ Anne Hull, feature writer, *St. Petersburg Times*.

■ **Born:** June 8, 1961, in Plant City, Fla.

■ **Education:** Florida State University, 1979–80; St. Petersburg Junior College, 1980–81.

■ **News Experience:** *St. Petersburg Times*, 1985 to present.

■ **Awards:** Florida Society of Newspaper Editors, first place, features, 1994; American Association of Sunday and Feature Editors, first place, general excellence, 1994; Nieman Fellow, 1994–95.

day three of my series, at the trial, there was no proof that the gun was ever fired. The police officer heard a click, but there was no proof that the gun was discharged.

**Why did this initial story have such resonance for you?**

I had just read a book called *Clockers* (a novel by Richard Price). My favorite part of the book was the neighborhood, this housing project in New Jersey. I used that as my point of reference as what the story could be. I knew that we had the same sort of story in our own back yard. I was conscious that this was going to be a story essentially about a neighborhood and a family and a crime. There were just so many wonderful elements: This crime that happened on Independence Day, a female police officer, this kid had a father.

**Is it unusual for a book to spark a story?**

Not really. Movies, music, or even a word in a poem, can spark stuff with me. I'm improvisational and things just kind of come to me. I'll be inspired by listening to John Coltrane, or reading poetry. I get a lot of ideas from poetry because of the economy of the language. Certain words can set off certain things in my mind. Every time I went into this neighborhood, I heard a sound track in my mind: this powerful song called "Tennessee" from an album by Arrested Development. It has to do with the historical sadness of being black in the South. I might see a tree, but a black person might see a lynching. There's a sadness to this neighborhood, a weeping, mourning, wailing, desperate sadness. It's something that I've felt, and I think there are shades of it that have ended up in the writing months later, although it wasn't conscious.

**Did you know from the beginning it was going to be a series?**

No. I had latitude and the luxury of time to kind of pursue the story for a couple of weeks. I probably took two weeks just sending out letters, calling the people involved, the primary characters, meeting them, and after a couple of initial interviews, I figured this was going to be something that I needed time on. I had to go to the attorneys and get their cooperation. That was key up front, because Eugene was a juvenile. I called the attorney, and we met, and he was unclear about what I was going to do, and I was kind of unclear about what I was going to do, but the one deal that we made was that the story, whatever story I was going to write, would not be published until their case was resolved. That immediately relaxes everyone. If you can offer that sort of—I don't want to call it a deal, but that sort of agreement, that's great.

**Did you negotiate this from the beginning with an editor?**

Not really. It was in a transition period with editors, too. So I was doing the story basically with no leash for a couple of months.

**Did your editors know you were even doing it?**

Yeah. They knew what I was doing. But we didn't know it was going to be a three-day piece until I actually sat down to write the story.

**How long did you spend on this story?**

Six months.

**Did you do any other stories during that time?**

Yeah. I covered the hurricane (Hurricane Andrew, which devastated south Florida). I was down in Miami for a good two weeks covering the hurricane. But from late October 'til February or March, I did nothing but this story

**You have this unique gift for collecting details about people. Officer Lisa Bishop doesn't just wear boots, she wears "size 4, steel-toe" boots.**

Well, think of that combination: The Terminator meets a ballerina. And that's who she was. I do think those details can help explain the sum of a person.

**Do you consciously look for these kinds of details?**

No. That's the one thing that's always come easy. I've always been observant and curious. I see brands. Maybe it's from covering fashion. That was my first job. Details are everything in fashion.

**How did you find out that she wore a size 4 steel-toe boot?**

I asked her because I noticed she had small feet. And I said, "Are those steel-toe boots?" A lot of it is just conversation. It's not conscious reporting. They think it's chit chat, but it's my job. I'm writing down everything.

**But you learned some intimate details, too. Like the marital troubles that are common among cops. And that wonderful detail of Lisa stripping off the bulletproof vest before she hugged her sleeping kids. How do you establish rapport with your subjects, so that they will tell you these things, or you will learn these things?**

Time. People establish rapport after time. Lisa is not particularly articulate when she's being asked questions. In conversation, she's great. So I didn't really play reporter with her too much. I just was there with my notebook. I stopped the, "how do you feel about...?" The good stuff never comes that way, never, ever. I just hung with her. I'd say something, and then she'd either validate it or give some contradictory statement. I just don't think you can ever study someone too much, or be around them too much. The story was so little about actual questions and answers. It was more about hanging out with people. It's observing, which is just as important as the words that come out of their mouth.

**What does "playing reporter" mean?**

I think of the people on the courtroom steps holding a microphone and their blank note pad, asking an attorney how he thinks the trial went. I freeze in those situations. I don't ask the right questions. But in the company of someone, I'm just very comfortable.

**How would you describe your interviewing style?**

Very casual. Lots of eye contact. I tend to give my two cents, and say, "Oh, yeah, I know what you mean. That happened to me once," because that makes people comfortable. But you can't do too much of it. I'm never afraid to put my feelings in the notes. It's not just what they say. It's how I think they look, how they say something. We're paid to react and gather information, so why shouldn't we include some of our own observations in our notes? I'm not saying get on a soapbox, but I trust what I see and hear.

**You talk about "characters" in your story. Why do you think of the people in your stories as "characters" as opposed to sources?**

To get people to read about this subject. There had just been a series of very violent crimes committed by juveniles, and we'd run a lot of mug shots of young black males. I wanted to bring a mug shot to life, and let them learn about the life behind this photograph, and the path that swept this person to the crime.

**Why did you want to do that?**

To engage and entertain readers. To put them in a neighborhood that they don't know anything about and teach them about this place. There's a lot of stereotypes that exist about public housing projects, and I wanted to be instructive, but to also lift them out of their lives. I know a lot of journalists really bristle at the word "entertain," but that's what storytelling is about. And I think important social lessons could be learned about these characters, and why they made certain choices in their lives.

**Did you have any difficulty, as a white, middle-class reporter, being accepted in this black housing project?**

I know some reporters who won't go into that neighborhood. I was perceived as an outsider at first, and I did become more comfortable, and people did know me, but I never was foolish enough to think I was a part of the neighborhood. The family grew to trust me, but it took awhile. Of course, they're very suspicious of the white reporter coming into the neighborhood right after a crime, like a vulture, scavenging details, and then leaving and never coming back again. This is a neighborhood that's so used to TV trucks coming in with their cameras and never coming back.

I did these ride-alongs with the cops—the X-ray Squad—which is a very small, self-contained group of police. I became known as someone with the police at night. There were many arrests and conflicts and altercations with the residents, stopping cars, and I was always seen with the police, so I was perceived as an outsider when I was hanging around with the police. During arrests, I tried to stay in the background, because I didn't want to be aligned with the police.

I was always conscious of "whose side am I on?" and I just tried to stay in the background as much as possible.

**Whose side *were* you on?**

No one's side, really. I completely sympathized with both sides.

**How did you earn their trust?**

Constant presence helped my case. What seemed like an obstacle at first, but turned out to be a blessing, was that no one in the neighborhood I wrote about had a telephone. That forced me not to sit at the desk and make calls. It forced me to drive to the neighborhood. I was always in the neighborhood. When I was there to interview Carl, I'd go over to the grandmother's house and knock, and just say, "How are you doing?" I don't think I was in the office much at all during two or three months of reporting. I was riding with the police at night. And I couldn't even call Lisa because she worked all night. I'd occasionally page her in the middle of the night, but she slept all day. I didn't ride with Lisa too much—probably six or seven times. I rode with X-ray a lot, because it's a way to get to know some of the people in the neighborhood, to watch them do their jobs. The more you ride with them, the more they drop their cool, and the more they become themselves, the language gets rougher, their treatment of suspects gets rougher. The real them starts to come out. They've become comfortable with me. I don't think you can ever hang around someone too much.

**Why did you spend so much time in the project, whether it was by day doing interviews or at night riding with the X-Ray Squad?**

The honest answer is it was fun. It was dangerous. I would probably be a cowgirl, if I weren't a journalist. I like that drama and that excitement.

**What was the value to your story of immersing yourself in the project?**

The neighborhood was the anchor for the story. I just knew it. It was a sense from the beginning. And I couldn't get enough details. Understanding the neighborhood would perhaps, in the end, help understand Eugene's actions that night on the Fourth of July.

**What was the focus of your story?**

I could tell someone it was about community policing, juvenile crime, poverty, all the social issues, but I thought all the time that the heart of this story was this neighborhood, this threadbare, dusty, desperate place where a lot of crime happens.

**How did you begin the actual writing?**

Along the way I kept index cards of some incredible moments that happened. This is one of my favorite scenes in the series, and to me, it was an important moment in the series. It was Halloween in the public housing project, the one night of the year all the cops stopped being cops, and they dressed up. They created a haunted house out of what most people perceive as a haunted house anyway.

All the kids came, and the barriers were dropped on that day. I'll never forget the scene of the kids rushing up to Gil and holding onto him, and the way he took them in his arms, and they all went into this dark, haunted house together. It still gives me chills, thinking about it. I wrote on an index card the next day: "Halloween, haunted house, feel my heart," which is what a little girl said, and she placed another little girl's hand over her heart.

**And did you use the index cards during the writing?**

I would refer back to them. I needed to remember this excitement, and these little note cards helped me key into that scene. I can still smell the air when I look at this little card. I remember what that night was like.

**How do you organize your stories?**

At some point, you've got to figure out what shape the story is going to take. How many days. What the story essentially is about. And I think there is a slight problem with the story in that I basically retold a crime, and I didn't explain why

Eugene did this. I think there's some truth to that, but I would also argue that I don't know why, and I don't think he knows why, and none of us know why. And that's part of the frustrating thing about the crime. There's no answer.

My biggest challenge was organizing this bulk of material. I am not an organized thinker, an organized writer. I'm very improvisational. I'm disciplined in that I work hard, but not in the way my mind works. So Tom French (*Times* reporter and ASNE finalist for non-deadline writing in *Best Newspaper Writing* 1987 and 1989) was instrumental in helping me erect the story. I had to break it down into scenes, which I'm naturally kind of good at, but scenes have to fit together, and there have to be peaks, and there have to be waves. And that was the hardest part of the story, making the outline. That was like math work, for me. It was like sitting in geometry class. I always keep a time line. This is something Tom taught me. And then I do an outline.

**What's in the time line?**

The crime happened at 11:56 p.m., July 4. Preceding that, though, I know what Eugene did all day, and I'll have Eugene's time line. And then I'll have what Lisa did prior to the crime. She went to the family picnic. Eugene went to a family picnic. So I have all these mini-chronologies, and one major chronology. And then I'll have an outline of where I want things to go.

I build around key scenes that explain who someone is, or where they came from, or why they did something. I think scenes can really be explanatory and instructive. And because I tend to spend a lot of time with someone, there's always action for the story, and I'm always there for that action, interaction with people. Watching them do something.

**"Metal to Bone" is such a wonderful phrase, so graphic, so sensual. How did it come to you?**

I really tried to concentrate on what this crime was about, and it all came down to this barrel of a gun at the bottom of a skull. I read police reports. I interviewed Lisa. I interviewed Eugene. I wondered what it felt like to have a gun shoved up to your head below your ear. I tried to go one step beyond and say, "Give it a sensation." Lisa explained it to me, but it was cluttered. So I just scrapped it and left it at "Metal to Bone."

## Do you draft without notes?

I do believe the heart of the story is sort of in your head and you can just write it. But when something takes as much time as this story, you do forget things. I always read through my notes a couple of times during the process, just to refresh myself.

## At what stage did you write the first nine paragraphs of the story?

When it was all over. They needed that for design. We needed something to let readers know what they were getting into. I wrote it in three hours.

## What was the value of doing that, for you, for the reader?

I'm a micro person. I see details. I lack in analysis. That forced me to sum up the whole story. If you're going to ask a reader to give you so much of their time, you need to tell them what they're about to step into.

## You use quotes very sparingly. Why is that?

Quotes should be the best things they say, and not just filler. When you use quotes, it needs to be a conversation, a dialogue, that that character is having with another person, not with me.

## I wanted to ask you about the letters you quote from in your series. You varied the documentation so that the letters were a really interest-

**ing element, and you sprinkled them in the narrative.**

I got Eugene's letters from his attorney's case file. Making the inroads with the attorneys was very important, because Eugene was a letter writer, and he wrote several letters to his attorney, and they really opened up who this kid might be. There are some really good clues in these letters. The attorney let me look at this file throughout this entire process, and that was a real benefit. Whenever Eugene would send a letter, Mr. Scruggs would just put the letter in the file. Every month or so, I would go through the file.

**Why did you use the letters from Eugene?**

I think Eugene was the weakest link of the story, and I struggled with him so much to bring him more to life. He is basically a 15-year-old kid—which to me is the hardest age to interview, kids of that age. And he's not very articulate when he talks, although he can write, and his letters were very helpful.

**How much of the series is a reconstruction?**

The whole first day is reconstructed.

**How do you know when you have enough to do it?**

You get the bulk of it through interviews, and there were police documents available, there's a criminal investigation file at the State Attorney's Office. Having interviewed everyone who was a part of that crime, you just feel like you have enough.

**How do you recreate a scene?**

A hundred questions. You need to go back to someone and make them rebuild what happened, whether it's a car accident or a conversation.

This is something Tom French has taught me. When you're recreating, you know, you take someone step by step. You ask them literally every move they made. Was their TV on in the background? What time of day was it? Did so and so have her fan on? Every little detail you can possibly find out, you ask about.

How did you feel? What did you say? What were you wearing? And what did he say? And where were you sitting? What was the air temperature like? What time of day was it? And that's just stuff that's hard to do on the first go, because you don't know what scenes you want to build on.

Some of it's natural, but I've had the benefit of just incredible mentors, and Tom French was probably one of the strongest influences in my life. I've sat next to him for six years and I've watched how he's done things.

**How has he influenced you?**

I really grew up in his shadow, you know. I watched how he worked. How he talks to people. Everything I do, from fact-checking to really spending time on my pitch letters is stuff I learned from him. He's not traditional, and he's emotional, emotion-based. He has taught me how to recreate scenes, and he's taught me that it's okay to recreate. You don't need to see it. All of history is recreation. A deposition is recreation, yet we think that's official. So that's been an invaluable lesson, and it's given me confidence to recreate scenes. Neville Green (former *Times* news features editor who is now the managing editor of the Tampa edition) has been an important mentor, too.

**What have you learned from Neville?**

Neville's very untraditional. He gets to emotional cores, which a lot of editors don't. He's kind of like Tom that way. "Yes, but why this, or why that?" He always has many questions. And I use all his questions and go back and ask that person, "Why this?" and "Why that?"

**What were the literary influences of your series?**

The pacing of the neighborhood, and the crime, and the gritty language, came from *Clockers*. The sweetness of some of the characters came from Alex Kotlowitz's *There Are No Children Here*. The dialogue was influenced by Elmore Leonard, the way he'll use slang and never explain what it means—I don't think you need to explain some words. Maya Angelou's speech at the Clinton inauguration. I was writing when that came across. I almost started crying when I heard that speech. It crossed the wires that afternoon, and I kept it on my desk the whole time I wrote.

**Why?**

For the economy of her images, the power of images. She used a reference to dinosaurs—"who left dry tokens." It makes you stretch and push. Don't go for the ordinary words. Pick something else. You know, look at each word, and use another word, especially when it comes to verbs. That's something we all should do, but reporters don't have the confidence to maybe look like a fool and try a new word. Some words don't work, and they are forced or clichéd, but take a risk.

**How conscious are you of readers when you are writing?**

I'm asking them to give me a lot of time, so I sprinkle rewards throughout. Descriptions. It can't be all work for them.

**How do you revise?**

It's building for me. It's adding. Building paragraphs. And making sure certain images last in someone's mind.

**Let's look at an example of revision by comparing the lead of Part Two as it appeared in an early draft with the published version. In the**

**draft you wrote, "The apartment was hot and dark, but so clean it smelled of Lemon Pledge." The published version reads, "Apartment 27 smelled like years of sweat and Lemon Pledge and perfect bacon." Why did you change it?**

Because that's exactly the way that place smelled, a conglomeration of all those things. I guess I thought harder. Lemon Pledge means, "Here's a person who's neat and clean and cares about their environment." But what else does it smell like? It's more than Lemon Pledge. Sweat, all the years of toil that have gone into the place; and she was a marvelous, maternal woman who cooked for the neighborhood. Those three images I thought were important, those little status details.

**How do editors help you?**

You need trust.

**How can the editor hinder you?**

By not showing enough enthusiasm. Listening is a key quality. I really need someone's eyes to jump back at me. It validates all the work I'm doing. It says, "Yes. We are onto it. We've got it. Let's go."

**Did you learn any lessons writing this story that you apply now?**

When I hear someone relating an anecdote, I really make them flesh out that anecdote right then and there. It just saves legwork.

**If you had to pick a metaphor to express your view of yourself as a writer, how do you see yourself?**

A detective. Finding out about people's lives.

**How do you check the accuracy of what you've written?**

I go through line by line and say, "How do I know this? Where do I find it?" and I go back to my notebook and find out where it came from.

**You take a lot of time describing your characters, thinking about how you want to describe them. Could you read your description about Carl and talk a bit about why you choose to say what you do about the people in the story?**

"Carl's skin was black gold and his eyelashes curled over his eyes, just like Eugene's. His beard needed trimming, and the T-shirt he wore was faded and too small, but there was something proud and impenetrable about him." Carl and Eugene are two characters who came to this story burdened by many stereotypes. They were poor, they were black, they lived in a public housing project. Carl really has skin that's so black it's nearly metallic. And I liked the use of the word "gold" because it's a precious metal, and it somehow elevated him.

**You write with such authority. Can you talk a bit about the development of that voice?**

My editor, Chris Lavin, encouraged me to go back and put a little more of myself in there. "Don't be afraid; you've spent four or five months with these people," he said. "We need perspective. Just don't rehash this trial. What does it all mean?" And what he meant was, you've spent months in this neighborhood and with these people. You know the material. Take a leap.

I went back through the story, and put in some of the lines that were a bit judgmental. I really went scene by scene, paragraph by paragraph, and said, "Now, is there anything else I can say that would give a summation of what I'm trying to say?"

**Why didn't you put it in originally?**

Because I was holding back. I didn't have confidence in myself, number one, and I had never written a narrative with this sort of voice. I didn't trust myself. That's not something we do on our everyday jobs, but there's a little more leeway to do it in these. That's the synthesis that you have to do, and that is the key to success of these things, the "what's it all about, Alfie" paragraphs.

And when you start doing some of that, that's when lines like "Gil couldn't remember the last time he dealt with a father" emerge. That's when there is the freedom within me to say, "It was a land of tired women." It opened up some kind of channel.

**What do you mean?**

When I did some of that layering, when I was encouraged by my editors to go back and put a little bit more of me in there, I was unshackled as a writer. I just felt more free to write. Not to report, but to write.

# Chris Lavin: Editor
# Trusting the writer

*Chris Lavin edited the "Metal to Bone" series. Lavin is Sunday Features and Discovery editor at the St. Petersburg Times. He has worked as a writer, writing coach, and editor at the Rochester (N.Y.) Times-Union and the Finger Lakes Times in Geneva, N.Y. Before returning to editing in 1992, Lavin traveled throughout Florida writing news, features, and projects. He has a degree in anthropology from Hobart College.*

**CHRISTOPHER SCANLAN: What was your role in editing "Metal to Bone"?**

CHRIS LAVIN: It was really just constantly reminding Anne to trust her own instincts. Heavy lifting in editing is when your hands are on the keys, and you're actually doing some of the synthesis for the reporter.

I never had to do word one of that. Our conversations were across a table, looking at sections of the story that worked and that didn't work. And reminding her of things she would say to me in conversation, analytical things, that didn't find their way into the story.

**Through this revision process, what were you telling Anne?**

I never used the word "bad." I just said, "We can do a lot better." I've seen editors who, as a tool, will be aloof, distant, and doubting; you figure you'll milk the most out of the writer's energies by making them scared. I don't like that technique. I like to be hard-assed about my judgments, but I like to say I'm with you up until I have to say, "It's not working."

**How many drafts did the series go through?**

Each piece went back maybe three or four times. And it was remarkable; she had to basically reinvent the stories each time. And each version came back with more energy, more of Anne, better thinking. Her energy never seemed to fade. It built as she trusted herself more.

**Anne gives you a lot of credit for strengthening the voice. That quality is one of the most special about the series. How did you do that?**

The best writing I've seen is written with confident authority. And I had seen Anne do it before, and she hadn't done it in this piece. When I read it, I said, "Geez, it's just missing Anne."

**Missing Anne?**

Yeah, all the things that she came back excited about were not in there. It needed the arrival of a journalist on the scene. If you're profiling somebody, you're writing your view of that person. Don't just try to have some false omniscient voice that has no life to it. Readers are pretty smart. They can figure out what your judgments are and what they might or might not buy. I just kept saying, "Here, here, and here, I need to know what *you* think. Otherwise, it reads like a court transcript, and who gives a damn." I knew what had happened and when they played out flat in her version, I asked her why. "When you told me about it, you told me this way. Why can't we just write it; shorten this eight inches of court stuff to a really nice paragraph by you and the facts that you need to get in, and move on."

**Now, you say you knew certain things, but they weren't in the draft, so you knew from discussion?**

Yeah. I needed to know what we had. As an editor, you can't say, "We have great stuff," and then deliver mediocre or bad stuff, because that's your currency as an editor, your judgment.

**What do you do to know the story?**

Talk a lot to the reporter, but just have them tell you the story. I really hold back at that point. When they tell me something, I don't say, "God, that will make a great lead."

**Why not?**

They may have something better in mind, or in their notebook, that they're forgetting to tell me. I don't want to make those judgments for the writer, particularly with somebody like Anne. I know she's more surprising than I am as a journalist. I want to give her every chance to surprise me, to come up with the thing that I won't think about as an editor, that she's more familiar with. I have 15 stories in my head. She has one.

**How else can an editor help a writer?**

Blunt honesty. Utter support. You can't say, "Oh, that's a great idea. Go for it," if you really don't think it is, or if you have doubts. You have to share your real feelings, so the reporter knows exactly what they're dealing with.

You also have to believe in reporting. Reporters are the source of good ideas; editors sitting around a room are the source of predictable ideas.

**How can an editor hinder the reporter?**

By seeing the reporter as a minion who is there to do the bidding of an editor. I've always thought editors who talk about "their staffs" and "our productions" versus what Anne does, or what Tom writes, aren't giving enough homage to the people who actually do the work, who are out there on the street, exposed to danger in some cases, boredom in other cases, while we sit in the office and have relatively long, but predictable, days.

**Let's turn this around. How can a writer help an editor?**

The best reporters I've worked with have an understanding of the environment in which the editor works. There is this war for resources, performance, achievement. And a good reporter will realize that there are times in the business when you do things to gain credits, that sometimes the opportunity to do the Pulitzer piece is through the side door.

**Do one for the club?**

Sometimes that sort of flexibility can lead you in unpredictable directions.

**How can a writer hinder an editor?**

It's usually rigidity. I don't expect people to jump when I say jump. That's just not a good relationship. Most of my problems with writers have been with the sort of insecurity that they can't overcome. Working on longer pieces, particularly, that really get into the person's mind, you feel more like a psychologist and diplomat than you do a boss.

**What are the attitudes that you hope the writer will bring to the table?**

Join in the collaboration. Don't see it as a butting of heads. Speak what's on your mind, call me an idiot if you think so, in a closed office environment. But don't shut down. Question your editor, but be willing to question the basic assumptions of your own work, too. The best reporters here are very fair, and they question their own biases, and they're nervous, like Anne is, about what they don't know. Anne seeks out advice from any reporter around who might be better at something than she is. Her greatest gift is that she constantly looks for people who are very good at things, and schools herself on that.

Try some things you're not comfortable with. I always want to shake people and say, "Go do this piece you haven't done in three years. Go into a court file and get a feel for it." We're in a business whose great blessing is no need for routine. Keep moving.

**How do you read a story for the first time?**

On a very long story, I read a printout, because then I can make notes in the margins as I go along. And then quite often I read it again, but give the writer my reaction to the first version. Sometimes I put notes in it, but I like the writers to keep their hands on the keys as much as possible, so the fewer notes I can send them, the less my worries start finding their way into their copy.

**You don't want that?**

No. We're heading down the road to failure when my words start ending up in your story. Or not failure, but less valid work. I really believe in reporting, and I trust that. When I write a long note in which I know what I'm doing is planting pretty direct seeds about what that section should be like, or what you might want to use for the kicker, then I know at that point I'm dictating.

That's why it was such a good experience for me to work with Anne. She went back at it and at it and at it. It was her own work. And sure, it might not have gotten quite there without the editing and the support of her friends and the senior editors, but it was her own work. There was no one else's hands on the keys and no one saying, "Do it this way."

You ask yourself why you're an editor sometimes. It's this sort of experience, where somebody puts themselves out on the edge and you support them a bit, and they make a leap. It was the single best experience—not because of the award, just as an editing experience. The best one I've had in the business, really.

**You started at the *Times* as a writer. You're editing now. Are you able to do any writing?**

I keep trying to do book reviews and short stories, and I'm going to try to do at least one major story a year, because you just forget how isolating it is to be a writer, and how many facts play in your mind for so long when you're working on a really good story. Sitting down and writing a rough first draft is not an indictment. Sometimes it's just mental fatigue. If you're really a good writer, you're just thinking these things all the time to the point of distraction.

### Do you think all editors should write?

Editors have a lot of busy work and tough decisions, but the real work of a paper is done by the people out there gathering good information and presenting it well.

If every editor at this paper was required to write a feature every year, one that had to be good enough, well-written enough for the front page, and one able to withstand the scrutiny and the editing of a Page One story, it would be a better paper.

# Craig Dezern

## Finalist, Non-Deadline Writing

Craig Dezern has worked for *The Orlando Sentinel* for seven years, most recently covering Walt Disney World. A native of Louisville, Ky., Dezern earned a bachelor's degree in journalism from Western Kentucky University. In 1991–92, Dezern was a journalism fellow at the Yale Law School, where he earned a master's degree.

From its opening scene to the final haunting line, "The Miracle of Philip Chandler" is a riveting, poignant chronicle by a storyteller in complete control of his material. Avoiding the sentiment so common among "medical miracle" stories, Dezern keeps readers enthralled with a narrative that is part suspense tale, part primer on brain injury. Its strengths include a simple yet elegant chronological structure, meticulous pacing, and a lean prose style that is a textbook argument for the heart-wrenching power of understatement.

# The miracle of Philip Chandler

DECEMBER 26, 1993

Eve Chandler plots her life in palm-sized note-
books of pink paper. In a tight script, she records
every phone call she makes, every call she receives. Each visitor is remembered in ink; every
occasion, special or mundane, remarked upon.

Now, Eve sits with her husband, Jim, on a
brown couch in the family room of their ranch-
style home in Pine Hills, just west of downtown
Orlando. She balances a notebook on her knee and
looks out over the swimming pool, turning green
with algae and disuse. Eve draws a breath. On a
fresh sheet of paper, she starts another entry, a list:

*Jason Gunn*

*Charles King*

*Manuel Arroyo...*

Nine names in all. They will be her son's pallbearers.

It is Tuesday afternoon, July 20. In a hospital
room in Sanford, Philip Chandler's heart is slow-
ing. The intensive care nurses, their raspberry uniforms a shock of color in the silent room, stare at
a video screen displaying the teenager's vital
signs, willing his reluctant heart to beat faster.

Sixty beats a minute would be healthy. But
Philip's heart is easing him out of this world.

Forty beats a minute...

Despite 72 hours of aggressive emergency
medicine, he is getting worse.

Thirty beats a minute...

It won't be long now. Maybe a few hours,
maybe one more day.

Twenty beats a minute—each one a tiny drama
in which it is never certain that the muscle will
squeeze hard enough to pump blood.

Philip lies deep in a coma, a machine breathing
for him. Nurse Judy Constable looks down at his
pale form, his thin arms drawn up, his head too

heavy for his neck, his brown eyes staring wide at nothing.

*Why, he's a little bird,* she thinks.

## THE CRIME

The smack of the screen door woke Eve at 8 o'clock that Saturday morning. Philip was home. The smell of pancakes drifted from the kitchen, where Jim was cooking his favorite breakfast.

Philip had spent the night with his best friend, Jason Gunn, but he was eager to get moving again, making the most of these hot summer days and his new drivers license.

He needed a haircut, and he wanted to play a game of basketball with his friend Manuel. Jim pulled $7 from his wallet to pay for the cut, and Eve handed him $7.50 of his allowance. Philip was off again.

Well, almost.

Eve stopped him with a reminder that he hadn't washed the clothes he would need for work that afternoon. The Little Caesar's uniform, reeking of tomato sauce and spices, was still out in the garage where he had taken it off the night before.

Eve let him get by with putting the clothes in the washer.

"I'll dry them for you, but you still need to clean your room before work." Philip hugged her and Eve kissed him goodbye.

Her son stepped out the door into the steamy blast of a July day. It wasn't even noon, and already the temperature was passing 90, the humidity right behind. Eve waved from the porch as he drove off in Jim's red Mustang, then she ducked back into the air-conditioning.

Jim went to the grocery store while Eve busied herself in her home office, sorting through papers and catching up on letters.

She was alone at noon when the phone rang. It was Manuel, asking where Philip was.

Getting his haircut, Eve told him. He should be there soon. "Manuel, noon," she wrote in her notebook.

Then another call, this time Philip's friend Charles King, who wanted to know if Philip could give him a ride to work. Eve said she'd ask and made a note to remind herself.

"By the way, he's supposed to go to Manuel's. Have you heard from him?"

Charles said he hadn't.

"Oh well. He went to get a haircut. He probably had to wait longer than he thought."

But when Manuel called again at 1:20, Eve began to fret.

"Philip's not where he's supposed to be," she told Jim when he came through the door minutes later. She sent him out looking while she started phoning Philip's friends, thinking maybe this once Philip had changed his plans without calling.

Jim's 35 years as a police officer told him it was too early to worry—teenage boys were seldom where they were supposed to be. But his 16 years as Philip's father told him different. Philip knew how they worried about him. He had left movies before they had ended to avoid breaking curfew.

With a bad feeling, Jim drove first to the barber shop. Then he traced the route to Manuel's house. He drove over to Rosemont, where another of Philip's friends lived. He looked for the flashing lights of a patrol car that might indicate an accident.

But he was just marking time. If there had been a wreck, he knew, someone would have called already.

To clean his room, get dressed and make it to work a little early, the way he liked to, Philip would have to get home at 2:30.

That's when Eve began to panic.

"Be careful!" she had called out as Philip left for work the night before.

"I can take care of myself, Mom," he said, as always.

"I'm sure you can, Philip. But if somebody has a gun, you're going to do what they tell you."

By 2:31, Eve was ready to call the sheriff's office, but Jim doubted their fears would be taken seriously after only three hours. They should wait a little longer.

Eve took out her pink notebook—now covered with line after line of anxious phone calls she had made—and wrote one final note:

*I'm really worried. This is not like Philip. He always calls if he's going to be late. I'm afraid something bad has happened to him.*

An hour later and seven miles away, three women were stopped at a traffic light on East Colonial Drive when they saw the strangest thing.

Something—maybe a hand—was reaching up from the trunk of a small red car in front of them, squeezing through a hole at the back window where the center brake light was missing.

What was going on? Was somebody stuck in the trunk?

As the women watched, they saw a girl in the back seat switch places with one of the teenage boys up front. He began punching down into the hole, putting a lighted cigarette there.

One of the women memorized the license plate so she could tell the police.

But the teenagers were laughing and waving at them, the other women said. It was just a stupid prank. The light changed and they drove on.

\* \* \*

Jim and Eve were married in Eola Park on Sept. 30, 1973, after a 43-day courtship.

As a friend led them through their vows, Eve grasped the strong, masculine hand she'd first admired from a neighboring pew at Tabernacle Baptist Church in Pine Hills.

Eve brought out the laughter in Jim. In turn, he was the strength she craved. Every morning, Eve stretched up to kiss Jim goodbye and watched from the porch as he drove off to work. And every day, she made a mental calculation of exactly how long they had been married.

By Day 180; she was at her doctor's office trying to find out why she wasn't pregnant. Eve, the youngest of 16 children, soon learned that she could never bear any of her own. She was devastated.

Eve began another calculation, counting the days until she and Jim had been married three years and could qualify to adopt a child. As soon as they could, they registered at the Children's Home Society and were approved in December 1976. But don't expect any news for one year, maybe more, the social worker told them.

Then on April 13, 1977—a Wednesday, Eve remembers—a phone call interrupted her soap opera: "How would you like to have a little boy?"

"Yes!" Eve said, barely hearing the woman's admonition that the baby had been born prematurely and still had medical problems.

The baby weighed just 4 pounds, 11 ounces when he was born, with his umbilical cord wrapped twice around his neck, so tight the doctor had to resuscitate him. Alone, never seen by the high school girl who gave him up for adoption, the baby spent the first three months of his life at Orange Memorial Hospital.

Two bouts of neonatal meningitis nearly killed him. When they didn't, the nurses took to calling him the "Miracle Baby."

Eve and Jim called him Philip Clayton Chandler.

His eyes were crossed, his feet turned in and he squalled as a nurse placed him into Eve's arms for the first time. Eve cried, too.

On the way home, they stopped at Walgreen's to buy bottles and formula. Then Eve called her own mother.

"Mama, Guess what!"

"You got a baby."

"Yes! How did you know?"

"I could tell by your voice. I can't think of anything else that would make you sound that happy."

Eve worked with Philip, turning his feet out each time she changed his diaper, looking into his face and making eye contact to straighten his eyes. Jim handled the 4 a.m. feedings—it was faster and easier to feed Philip himself than it was to wake Eve.

After two weeks, Eve went back to the Children's Home Society.

"Where's Philip?" the social worker asked. "You were supposed to bring him back in."

"This is Philip on my lap."

The woman looked again, trying to reconcile the smiling, chubby baby in Eve's lap with the sickly child who had left the hospital only two weeks before.

Philip grew tall and skinny, and every year Eve hung a new picture until the dining room wall was covered with a dozen 8 by 10s. Every one of them showed a happy boy with a smile so broad it took over his whole face, sending his thick eyebrows arching above his dark eyes.

From the start, his parents told him he was adopted, but with his angular face and dark, curly hair—so different from Jim and Eve—that almost seemed unnecessary.

They enrolled Philip in Heritage Preparatory School, an intimate private school run by Tabernacle Baptist Church. He was not an outstanding scholar, not a jock or a class leader. But he always had plenty of friends who liked him for acting goofy and for being the one person they could tell their troubles to. Philip was a good listener, and he always cared.

Sometimes, when the little kids passed Philip in the hallways, he would playfully grab them, holding on until they declared he was King of the School. His teachers knew him for, among other things, talking out of turn.

Jim taught Philip to play basketball, the way he played it when he helped Apopka High School take second place in the state tournament in 1954. And when Philip turned 14, his dad started teaching him to play guitar. Philip's long, delicate fingers seemed made for the instrument, though he favored Metallica over his father's country tunes.

Soon enough, Philip and his friends had formed a band they called Straitjacket. Sometimes they practiced in the Chandlers' garage. Jim and Eve didn't mind. They liked having the boys around.

As Philip grew, Eve's friends would sometimes fuss at her, telling her she doted too much on the boy.

"You can spoil a child with things," Eve would say. "But you can't spoil them with love."

The afternoon Philip disappeared, Bob Ware, the pastor of Tabernacle Baptist, fell to his knees. "Eve and Jim can't take this," he prayed. "Please let him live long enough to acknowledge that he remembers them."

\* \* \*

As she talked, Eve kept her chair turned toward the dining room window, her attention on the street outside.

"Has he ever...," the deputy began.

Eve cut him off. "No, he has never run away. He has no reason to run away."

Philip was wearing a white T-shirt and white shorts, she told the deputy, imagining that every car she heard outside would be the red Mustang pulling into the driveway and bringing him home.

Describing her son to this uniformed stranger, who took notes of his own, made Philip's disappearance suddenly official, broadcasting her worry outside the comforting circle of family and friends. Eve cried, but Jim wore his cop face, talking officer to officer, trying to convince the deputy that it was not too soon to issue a BOLO—"Be On the Look Out"—for his son and his car, though it was only 4 o'clock in the afternoon.

Finally, the deputy accepted a photograph of Philip and left the Chandlers to wait.

At 5:40 p.m., a phone company operator called the Chandlers' unlisted number to relay a message: The Seminole County Sheriff's Office wanted to contact them in reference to a red Ford Mustang.

Eve sat by Jim's side on the brown couch in the family room as he dialed the police: The car had been recovered at the intersection of George Avenue and U.S. 17-92; it had been occupied by three teenagers, two of whom were in custody. The police needed one of the Chandlers to come to Maitland and identify the car.

The thought that Jim had been pushing aside all afternoon hit him again like a fist in the gut: *Philip is dead. Philip is dead.*

Jim and Eve drove to Maitland in numbed silence. Jim wanted to say something reassuring, but he couldn't. Philip was dead. There was no comfort to give.

It was nearly 8 o'clock, but still muggy when they stepped out of the family car, a huge white Mercury Grand Marquis. The red Mustang sat by the side of the road, caught in the swirl of the squad car lights.

A Seminole deputy told the Chandlers what he knew: About 6 p.m., three teenagers were driving up 17-92 in the Mustang when a patrol car pulled up behind them. The teenagers kept looking back, checking the rearview mirror so often that he finally called in the tag number. When he found out Orange County was looking for the car, he turned on his lights. After a short chase, the Mustang turned onto George Avenue and jumped the curb; the three teenagers ran. Deputies nabbed two of them—a 16-year-old boy and a 14-year-old girl. They sat hand-cuffed in the back seat of the patrol car.

There was no sign of Philip.

"Have you checked the trunk?" Eve asked.

The deputy said he didn't have the key. Jim walked over to the Mustang with the spare set. Eve walked with him, scared that Philip would be inside, almost as scared that he wouldn't.

She didn't breathe as Jim popped the lid.

Nothing.

But the trunk was a mess. Plastic bags, magazines and books were strewn about, the spare tire and lug wrench shoved aside, the mat rumpled and twisted.

Jim saw Philip's wallet in the mess. He picked it up. It was empty, his $7.50 allowance gone.

Jim tried to stay a detective, to notice details that might be helpful. Like the way the carpet by the rear window had been picked at all around the hole where the center brake light should be.

The Seminole deputy wanted to turn the car over to the Chandlers, but Jim stopped him.

"Somebody's been in this trunk. We need a homicide detective out here."

Jim walked back to the Mercury and slumped heavily in the driver's seat, feeling tired and older than his 58 years. He thought back to a case he handled early in his career. A little boy—9 or 10 years old—disappeared one day. He just didn't come home. Four weeks passed with no trace. Then, his body washed up on the shore of Lake Mann. Jim had to tell the boy's parents.

Eve sat in the car, too, calling friends on a cellular phone to tell them what she knew. She called all the hospitals in Orange County, describing Philip. She stared at the teenagers in the patrol car. They had told the deputy they found the car, key in the ignition, at a Sanford apartment complex, but Eve just knew they were lying. An image flashed in her mind. Philip, his legs drawn up, crammed in the trunk and gasping for air.

They had stuffed Philip in the trunk, and they knew where they dumped him. She looked at them with fury. And when she caught their eyes, they looked away.

"Where's Philip!" she demanded. "Where is my son!"

* * *

Carolyn Richter checked the clock in the security office—5:30. Her shift was almost over at the DeBary Campus of Daytona Beach Community College. It was time for a break.

She stepped out of the office, and that's when she saw it—a figure lying in a heap on the hot asphalt about 150 feet away. It was a boy, a white T-shirt pulled up over his face, no shoes on his feet. When Richter pulled the shirt down, she saw foam coming from his mouth. His eyes stared beyond her.

*He's dying,* she thought as she ran to call 911. Then she stood between the boy and the sun to shade him until help arrived.

Within minutes, paramedics had lifted the boy into the back of an ambulance. Richter held one of the intravenous lines that dripped cool fluid into his veins. The boy's chest heaved, his breathing erratic. Someone checked the pockets of his white shorts for identification. They found nothing but 50 cents.

The ambulance rushed him to the nearest hospital, Central Florida Regional in Sanford, calling ahead to alert the emergency room. He was admitted as John Doe.

On the examination table, the boy's face was flushed, his body hot to the touch. How hot, no one knew—the thermometer could measure no higher than 108 degrees.

Dr. Dennis Natale assessed the patient's vital signs.

Blood pressure was a low 62/40, indicating shock. His heart tripped at a dangerous 170 beats per minute. His pupils were unresponsive, his breathing irregular.

Natale noticed, too, the light whiskers on the John Doe's chin. A young man, perhaps no older than his own son of 17.

The heat was killing him, Natale knew. He was probably past any help they could give.

Even in a Central Florida summer, Dr. Natale had never seen a case of heat stroke this severe. *Was this a drug overdose?* Natale wondered. It looked like one.

The emergency room team had to get the boy's temperature down, his blood pressure up. One by one, the patient's organs were shutting down. His brain swelling. His liver malfunctioning. His kidneys failing. His heart could be next.

The nurses covered him with towels soaked in cold water. They piled ice on top of that, nearly slipping on the cubes that skittered across the floor. Intravenous lines dripped fluids into the boy's veins to increase his blood pressure and cool him more. They pushed a respirator tube down his throat and fed oxygen to his lungs.

For an hour, eight people worked the John Doe until he reached a precarious stability in his blood pressure and heart rate.

Then Dr. Natale noticed a clenching of the fists and a turning outward of the arms. It's a phenomenon called "decerebrate posturing"—a near-certain sign of serious brain damage.

*The insult to the system is too great,* he thought as he prepared to pass the case to the intensive care physician. *I don't think he's going to survive.*

The boy's body temperature was under control now, but he was bleeding profusely, and keeping his blood pressure up was a struggle. The heat had damaged the platelets, the blood's clotting cells. The liver, too, had been damaged and was no longer producing its clotting factors. Throughout the patient's digestive tract, tiny blood vessels broke—a normal occurrence, but now they bled freely.

Intensive care nurse Lynn Drysdale looked at the boy's face—his eyes open, his pupils pinpoints—and thought about her teenagers at home: *There's a mother connected to this child somewhere.*

\* \* \*

Eve let her mind go crazy, wondering where Philip could be. He had been thrown in a river. His body had been dumped in a ditch. He was lying by a road somewhere, needing her.

*If I just knew where my baby was. If I just knew where my baby was.*

It was 10:30 p.m., and the Chandlers were back home. Eve's friend Estella Penny came to comfort them, and Jim's sisters were on the way. While Eve was in the kitchen getting tea, Estella went to Jim on the screened porch.

"What's the chance of Philip being found alive?" she asked.

Jim shook his head.

"The Lord is good," Estella said. "We'll just have to pray about it."

They knelt on the floor.

At 11, Jim and Eve silently watched the late news on Channel 2. Philip's school picture flashed on the TV screen, and the anchorman called the disappearance a "strange case."

At the hospital in Sanford, a nurse watched the news, too. She thought the missing boy's picture looked familiar, and when the anchorman mentioned that Philip had left home for a haircut, she thought of the hair clippings on the T-shirt that the John Doe had been wearing.

By midnight, Jim's sisters had arrived from Auburndale, bringing husbands and children with them. The living room was crowded. They sat and talked about anything but Philip, a respite from grief, the way families sit at funeral homes and avoid mentioning the dead.

Eve couldn't stay still any longer. She withdrew alone to the kitchen and started a fresh pot of coffee, all she and Jim had put in their stomachs since the pancakes 16 hours ago. She busied her hands by emptying the dishwasher.

In the other room, someone laughed. And though Eve knew it was just a way to try to make the night seem normal, it made her mad. There was no room for laughter in her house.

She slammed the silverware drawer shut.

"Where is my baby!" She was sobbing. Jim and his family ran to her. She fell into his arms.

"If I just knew where my baby was! If I just knew where my baby was..."

This time, Eve didn't have to wait long for an answer.

No more than a half hour passed before an Orange County deputy knocked at the Chandlers' door. It was 2:30 a.m.

"He's been found," the deputy said. "He's in a hospital in Sanford."

The next few minutes were an elated rush of slipping on shoes, running to the bathroom and deciding who was going to ride in what car. During the half hour drive to Sanford, hope seeped through the cracks in Jim and Eve's despair, as if they hadn't heard the rest of the deputy's message: "Philip's condition is serious. You need to come right away."

Dr. Kevin Scanlon—tall and thin, just five years past residency—met them in the waiting room outside the hospital's intensive care unit. He was blunt, ticking off a list of medical emergencies threatening Philip: the soaring temperature, the coma, the liver damage, the internal bleeding, the erratic heart rate.

As she listened, Eve prayed silently that Philip had passed out immediately and had known no pain.

Eve didn't want to listen but had to hear the doctor's words: "Very, very serious....In a very deep, deep coma."

With the last of her hope, she demanded, "How do you know that's *our* son in there?"

But minutes later, when she saw him, there was no doubt.

Philip lay in a narrow bed in Room 6, in the corner of intensive care. The respirator covered his mouth. Two tubes carried fluids in. A catheter carried fluids out. His face betrayed no thought, but his body was twitching and tense. Blood poured from his nose and mouth, turning the white towel beneath his head to crimson as quickly as the nurses could change it.

Eve wanted to hold him, but she couldn't reach around the tubes and machines that kept him alive.

*Whoever did this is not human,* Eve thought. *They are the lowest form of life.*

In a small conference room nearby, Dr. Scanlon explained to the Chandlers that the next three days were critical. For those 72 hours they would do all they could to keep Philip alive, in case there was some slim chance of recovery. If Philip made it through the next three days, they would meet again to discuss how far the doctors should go to prolong his life.

The Chandlers nodded, but in their hearts they were certain there was nothing in Philip's bed but his mortal shell. *He's already with the Lord,* Eve thought as they began another vigil. *This is just the machines breathing for him.*

* * *

During the next three days, Philip's high school picture was everywhere. On the television. In the newspaper.

In a hotel room at Walt Disney World, a woman named Karin saw the story on the news. *How could one kid do this to another?* she thought. She looked at Philip's picture on the TV screen. Her son would be that age.

Eve wouldn't watch, wouldn't read, wouldn't listen to the talk in the waiting room. Each time she thought of Philip trapped in that tight, dark space, she could feel the heat, and the fear—so oppressive she couldn't breathe.

Jim got his information from the Orange County homicide detective handling the case. The third suspect—who dodged officers after the Mustang crashed—turned himself in and gave a statement. One cop to another, the detective gave Jim all the details:

Terence Jenkins and Michael Daymon, both 17, had stopped Philip as he came out of the barber shop, threatening that they had a gun. They had forced him into the back seat of the Mustang. Sometime later, they shoved him into the trunk of the sports car, forcing the 5-foot-11 teenager into a space 5 feet by 3 feet, and just 1 foot deep. Somewhere along the way, the boys stole his shoes.

Then they picked up one of their friends—a 14-year-old girl—and just drove for hours during the hottest part of the day. When the afternoon temperature peaked at 95 degrees, the detective told Jim, the heat was magnified to 130 degrees in the trunk.

Terence Jenkins told investigators that he and his friends had stopped the car at the community college to open the trunk so Philip could get some air. When they saw his condition, they dropped him in the parking lot and fled.

Daymon and Jenkins were charged with attempted murder, kidnapping and robbery. The girl was charged as an accessory. They were all in jail.

Jim buffered the information for Eve. Even so, she cried whenever they talked about Philip's ordeal. She prayed silently that he remembered nothing.

Together, Eve and Jim moved into a hospital room next door to the intensive care unit. Room 343 had two beds, but the Chandlers rarely slept. It was a place where they could go and close the door. Sometimes they had to get away, even from the friends who crowded in night and day, once filling three waiting rooms and spilling over into the halls.

Every hour, they visited Philip, though Eve found it hard to look at him sometimes: "Philip, I'm so sorry this happened to you. You didn't do anything wrong. This wasn't your fault."

In case Philip couldn't hear, Jim took his son's long fingers into his own rough hand. Eve ran her fingers through Philip's mess of curly hair. "I love you." Doctors and nurses bustled in and out. "The Lord is with you."

Each time, before they left, Eve leaned down to Philip. "Aren't you going to give me a hug?" she would ask.

They were careful about what they said in Room 6, concerned that Philip could hear and understand. But in their own room, Jim felt the bitterness creeping in.

"Why did God let this happen? Why doesn't He listen to all these prayers?"

Pastor Bob Ware did his best to offer spiritual comfort. It was OK to ask those questions, he told them. Christ asked the same on the cross.

Ware reminded them that 16 years ago at Tabernacle Baptist, he put his hand on Philip's head, saying, "Lord, we got this child as a gift from you, and today we're giving him back to you, to do with as you please."

Back at church, Ware met with the youth group, about 50 children and teenagers, many of whom had known Philip for years.

"If you have anything you want me to say at Philip's funeral, write it on a piece of paper and give it to me. I'll keep it and try to say it."

But the teenagers refused to write anything down, insisting Philip would not die.

"You're wrong. Philip is not going to get well. I'm sorry. Philip won't be with us unless God performs a real miracle."

Indeed, as the 72 hours drew to a close, there was no change. Tests showed no function in any part of the brain. Dr. Scanlon rubbed his knuckles on Philip's sternum—"deep, painful stimuli," in medical terms—and got no grimace or frown. No reaction at all.

It was time to talk with Jim and Eve again. They were drawn and pale and exhausted. Jim had collapsed once by Philip's bed. Eve's angina was coming back, and pains would clutch at her chest. Still, they had to talk about life support.

In the hospital conference room, Dr. Scanlon
told them that neurological recovery seemed remote at best. They could expect a cardiac arrest
within two days, if not hours. What did they want
him to do if Philip's heart failed?

Philip had a living will, they told him. He did
not want to be resuscitated. What about donating
his organs? Philip had an organ donor card. They
would like that. Dr. Scanlon said he would notify
the harvesting team.

This time, Dr. Scanlon hugged them as the consultation ended.

\* \* \*

Philip has too many friends, Eve realizes, as she
makes her list. She writes 15 more names in her
pink notebook. They will be honorary pallbearers,
she decides, with seats up front at Philip's funeral.

Now another thought tugs at her mind. She
calls Pastor Ware and asks him for a favor. She
wants him to call the Children's Home Society to
ask the adoption agency to find Philip's birth
mother and tell her what has happened. Philip always wanted to meet her.

Then she calls Estella and arranges for her to
pass Philip's birth mother off as a friend, should
the woman want to attend the funeral service
anonymously.

Eve and Jim pray and read the Bible. Jim reads
the book of Psalms: *Commit thy way unto the Lord;
trust also in him; and he shall bring it to pass.*

Eve relies on Matthew 11:28: *Come unto me all
ye that labor and are heavy laden, and I will give
you rest.*

There is no rest now. It's time to go back to the
hospital to sit with Philip while he dies.

That night, July 20, Jim's sisters sleep in the
intensive-care waiting room, wanting to be there
at the end. But it doesn't come. Not that night or
the night after.

In Room 6, a strange thing has begun to happen. Philip's heartbeat has picked up just a bit.
The nurses, in their raspberry uniforms, see it on
the monitors. Jim and Eve are not excited. Philip

is not getting better, just lingering, like Jim's aging mother in her nursing home.

Eve is no longer keeping notes. She's too exhausted from staying up past midnight and waking up by 6 a.m. But she calls her twin sister, Lula Hayes, in Georgia every day, and Lula chronicles the news:

*07/23/93—He had a good night; temperature is 100 degrees; oxygen level at 60 percent. He is leveled off. Heart rate is erratic; removed respirator to see if he could breathe on his own, but he took two breaths and struggled, so it was put back on him.*

*07/27/93—Losing weight; feeding tube through nose—blue milk shake (Mother told him that it is blueberry, which he loves). Mother talks to him lots. Still has fever, fungus in lungs caused by antibiotics; bruise on upper part of leg; 5 cuts on lower part of leg; bruises on upper part of arm.*

*07/29/93—Sonogram revealed pancreas is swollen; gall bladder has sludge in it, but not stones; blood in stool; blood transfusion today; temperature is down to 102.7 degrees; fever is caused by breakdown of central nervous system; EKG revealed a heart murmur, neurological damage is irreversible; will do another EEG; heart is fine now—stabilized.*

The doctors still give Jim and Eve no hope. Philip may be stabilizing physically, they say, but his coma is too deep, has lasted too long. At best, Philip will live out his life in a coma, fed by a tube and turned in his bed to prevent sores.

Quietly, though, the intensive care nurses have begun questioning that prognosis. Their shifts are 12 hours long, and from their station, they can see through the glass wall of Philip's room. Sometimes, they think, for just a second, Philip catches their eyes with his own. There is a brightness there, an awareness they have trouble defining. "He's looking at you, not looking through you," they tell each other.

One morning, nurse Cindy Ernest walks into Philip's room and, she is certain, he follows her with his eyes. "What do you think?" they ask each other, certain of what they are seeing. Certain, too, that they are seeing what they want to see. They don't trust themselves, and they don't tell the Chandlers.

Jim and Eve have their toughest decision to make, and they don't need to have it complicated.

On Saturday, July 31, the Chandlers are given papers to sign, granting permission to remove Philip from the respirator. Philip is being weaned from the machine, but doctors aren't sure if he has enough activity even in his brain stem to control the coughing needed to keep his lungs clear of mucous. Within 24 hours, Dr. Scanlon and a neurologist tell the Chandlers, they'll find out if Philip will die or if he will exist in a vegetative state.

"Don't believe it," Estella tells Eve. "He'll recover."

Eve tells her to stop. She doesn't want to hear such talk. Either way, this will surely be the end of Philip.

Three of Philip's friends have come to visit. Eve makes them go in, one at a time, to tell him goodbye.

Charles King, a tall lanky boy with a flop of brown hair, stands crying.

"I can't do it."

"Yes, you can," Eve tells him, feeling cruel. "You'll feel better later."

Jason Gunn, whom Eve calls her second son, understands. But Isaac Alvarez is stubborn, trying to be tough as he clenches his square jaw and tells Philip it has been good knowing him, like a soldier saying goodbye to a buddy in an old war movie.

Then, Isaac's face brightens as he comes out of the room. "I just know he's going to make it. I know he's going to make it."

At 1 p.m., Jim and Eve sign the papers, then go to their room to wait with Estella. At 1:15, a nurse comes to the door to announce, "He's breathing on his own."

"I'll be right back." Eve runs from the room to see him.

"Looks like he's making it," Eve tells Estella. Then she permits herself a smile, a private imagining that Philip could get better.

For Jim, though, this is the worst day since Dr. Scanlon told them Philip's heart was failing. There is no sign that Philip will come out of the coma, and Jim knows he wouldn't want to live this way. With death, there is grief, but it's followed by healing. But with Philip in a coma—perhaps for a natural life span—the only thing that could follow grief would be a cruel hope forever nagging at his mind.

The rest of that afternoon and into the evening, they spend 10 minutes in Philip's room every hour. Eve reads poetry to him. Jim holds his hand. Best of all, with the respirator out of the way, they can finally hug Philip properly.

Each time she leaves, Eve leans down to his blank face and tries to get his glassy eyes to focus on her own. "Philip, can you give me a hug?" Then she gathers his limp form into her arms.

At 12:30—Sunday morning now, two weeks since Philip left for his haircut—Jim and Eve go in to say good night to their son. It is time to try to sleep. They are alone in the room, and the intensive care unit is still.

Eve leans in, and one more time she asks, "Philip, can you give me a hug?"

Slow and shaky, but with a purpose, Philip lifts his arms from the bed and drops them around his mother's neck.

It is eerie, like being hugged by a dead man. Philip's face is still emotionless, his eyes fixed at something far away.

"Jim, did you see that?"

"Do it again."

Eve asks for another hug. Philip responds the same.

She is ecstatic, laughing and crying. This is the miracle she prayed for, but didn't dare hope for.

"Jim, can I please call the nurses?"

No, Jim says. This moment is for them. He thinks of all the stories of faith and answered prayer that people have shared with him in the past two weeks. Now, Jim thinks, we're becoming one of those stories. His hopes soar, too. Surely God wouldn't carry Philip this far only to drop him.

Jim steps in and asks his boy for a hug. Only after he gets it does he tell Eve to call the nurses.

"Philip just gave us a hug," Eve exults in the hospital silence. "He really did!"

## THE TURNING POINT

One bed, three chairs, a wheelchair for trips to physical therapy, and a four-drawer chest stocked with T-shirts, shorts and socks. Speckled gray wallpaper, speckled blue carpet, a plaid privacy curtain to pull around when the nurses change his clothes, and five cans of ULTRACAL to drip through his feeding tube. Outside the window, a water fountain splashing without sound.

This is Philip's world, his room at the Florida Hospital Rehabilitation Center.

Propped up on pillows, his bed at a slant, Philip stares, unblinking, toward the calendar on his wall. "TODAY is 13, FRIDAY, AUGUST." He is alone in the room, and behind the pale mask of his face a thought laps like a wave at the edge of his mind.

A thin arm reaches up from the bed, slow and wavering as if it were moving underwater. Philip draws a shaky hand across his mouth to check for saliva. He doesn't want to lie here drooling.

Then he bends each leg and flexes each arm just a bit. They all work. Reassured, he stares toward the calendar again.

On the wall, below a television that he doesn't watch, is a school picture of himself—blown up to grainy poster size—that he doesn't look at. He is 5 feet 11 and 140 pounds in the photograph, a skinny high school junior, holding an electric guitar.

A mirror, hanging beside the photo, shows Philip today—103 pounds of translucent skin and knobby limbs. Not talking, not walking, Philip is like a Polaroid photograph himself, one just beginning to develop. The medical experts can't tell the Chandlers how closely the final picture will resemble the son they knew.

Eve, though, expects an image as perfect as before.

This is the end of his first week in the rehabilitation center. Inside this quiet, contained space—down the hall and around the corner from the bustle of the rest of the hospital—doctors and therapists are trying to figure out how much of Philip is left inside this rag doll body.

Eve is not waiting to be told.

"Good morning, Philip," she announces, sweeping into the room with Jim right behind. "Wake up, you lazy thing!"

Philip's eyebrows dart up.

"Where's my hug?" He reaches up to her and she talks into his ear. "Make one of Jason's funny faces. Here comes a funny face." She sticks her tongue out at Philip, and his smile widens.

She notices he is wearing a restraint, a flannel vest of blue plaid that ties to the safety rails on the sides of the bed.

The day nurse, Benita Brewer, bustles into the room and starts talking before Eve can ask.

"Let me tell you what's going on with Philip. He's trying to get out of this bed. That's great, but we don't want him to fall."

He tried to brush his teeth this morning, Benita tells Eve and Jim, and in the shower he tried to wash his hair. Eve exclaims over each accomplishment, but Philip doesn't react. He has reverted to his favored posture, lying on his right side, knees slightly bent, hands at his chin, head bowed down. Still, with his parents nearby, he wears a faraway smile, like some vague but happy thought is drifting across his mind.

Once Philip is dressed, they sit nearby. Eve begins sorting the day's mail, another stack of get-well wishes and testaments to prayer. Eve has started keeping notes again. She pulls out a pink pad and writes the name of each sender. At home, she'll file the card alphabetically, with the others.

"Dear Mr. and Mrs. Chandler," Eve reads to Philip.

"You will not recognize my name, for I have never met you....When I heard the news that Philip was beginning to come out of the coma, I fell on my knees, crying like a baby and praised the Lord for his kindness, love and mercy. I truly feel in my heart that the Lord is answering our prayers and that Philip will have a FULL recovery."

Philip's breathing sounds congested. She reaches for a tissue and puts it to his face.

"Blow your nose," she says. "Good!"

Then she brushes his hair so she can take a picture. "Smile," she says. Philip's eyes lock on his mother. For just a second, he comes into focus, resembling the schoolboy holding the guitar.

\* \* \*

On Monday morning, Jim and Eve meet with the team of 14 doctors, nurses, therapists and social workers who are working on Philip's case. They have observed Philip since he was moved to the head-injury unit at Florida Hospital nine days after coming out of the coma.

Jim is nervous. This reminds him too much of the daily briefings with Dr. Scanlon in Sanford, where the news was always worse than Jim expected it to be.

In 10 minutes, the experts at Florida Hospital lay out all they know about Philip's condition and the prognosis for his recovery. It's not much.

There isn't a lot of medical literature about brain injuries caused by heat stroke—almost no one with a temperature as high as Philip's has survived.

Early tests show diffuse damage to his brain caused by a lack of oxygen. Locked in the trunk, Philip got so hot that the protein in his brain cells was altered, allowing fluid to pass through the membranes and causing the brain to swell, creating pressure on the blood vessels. Meanwhile, his blood thickened, pooling in his torso.

No blood, no oxygen: Permanent brain injury.

Though the dead brain cells can never be replaced, some of the injured cells might begin functioning again on their own. Philip's progress may be dramatic from week to week, even from day to day.

Already they have seen some hints that his personality is returning. Philip cannot talk, but he smiles, especially when fussed over by the young women therapists. He laughs silently when his buddies visit. He sticks his tongue out for "yes" and shakes his head for "no," though he answers simple questions correctly only half the time. And during a recent workout, he kicked at his therapist to let her know he was tired. These are all encouraging signs, but this "spontaneous recovery" won't continue. How extensive is the brain damage? When will Philip talk? How much will he recover? The doctors don't know.

Eve does.

It is a miracle that Philip did not die that first night. It is a miracle that he came out of the coma. God, in answer to prayer, has directly intervened to change the course of natural events. The miracle will continue, she knows.

The experts tell Eve that Philip won't be home until November. Won't they be surprised, she thinks.

Jim is more guarded. Some nights, as he sits silently by Philip's bed, each breath is a small sigh. God has performed a miracle, surely. But maybe this is as far as it goes.

Events in the next week seem to bear out Eve's expectations. There's a new notch on the yardstick of Philip's progress every day, another picture for Eve's scrapbook, another note on pink pages.

Thursday, during speech therapy, Philip's chapped lips mouth his own name.

Later, Jim and Eve fuss over him, pulling up the white stockings that help his circulation, coaxing him to practice taking deep breaths so he can talk again.

"What time is it?" Eve asks. "Show me with your fingers what time it is. Can you see the clock?" It's on the wall about 10 feet away, a round schoolhouse clock.

Philip keeps his head down, but his eyes sweep the wall. He holds up his index finger.

"Yes, it *is* 1 o'clock! I think you knew! How about that. He can see pretty good if he can see that."

"And tell time," Jim adds.

But Eve is already out the door, rushing to tell Benita and the therapists.

Friday, though, caps the week with a turn that Eve finds so exciting she insists the hospital issue a news release.

In the morning, a therapist performs a test to see if Philip can swallow without choking. As soon as he can, he'll supplement his 2,300-calorie daily tube feeding with solid food.

Philip passes. Hospital food is his dubious reward. It's also a victory for Jim and Eve, who had been skipping lunch and delaying dinner because they wouldn't eat in Philip's room as long as he couldn't.

For lunch, Philip is served boiled chicken, mashed potatoes, carrots and tapioca pudding.

He goes straight for the chocolate chip cookie.

Eve starts calling friends to tell them of his latest accomplishment, like a mother with a new baby. But in the late afternoon, the strain shows.

Eve pulls a chair beside him and, closing her eyes, leans her head on the rail of the hospital bed. She has a caffeine withdrawal headache that the decaf served at this Seventh-Day Adventist hospital won't cure. With her glasses off, Eve suddenly looks her 49 years. She stares now, too, her unfocused gaze looking past the door, her fingers methodically rubbing his hand. No longer the cheerleader of recovery, she's an exhausted mother with nothing to manage right this minute.

She looks at Philip, silent in his bed, and she wonders what he is thinking. *Is he happy here? Does he miss his friends, his school? Is he remembering what happened to him?*

Philip is exhausted, too. But at 5 o'clock when Jason Gunn and Isaac Alvarez come into his room, he struggles to straighten himself in the bed. He reaches down to the rumpled sheets, trying to cover his stockinged legs, brushes at his bed-head and tugs at the hideous plaid vest until his parents understand he doesn't want to wear it in front of his friends.

Isaac, all dressed in black, pulls up a chair and sits so his head is on the same level as Philip's. Talking low so the grownups can't hear, he starts nearly every sentence the same: Remember...

That night they climbed the church roof and drank Dr. Pepper until the cops ordered them down? Philip laughs, silently. That time they got their teacher off the subject with an irrelevant question and kept him off the subject until class was over? Philip laughs again. Earlier this summer when they watched *A Few Good Men?*

"I want the truth!" Isaac demands, imitating Tom Cruise's big line in the film.

"You can't handle the truth," Philip mouths, imitating Jack Nicholson's reply. He laughs again, his mouth wide open, his head bobbing.

More friends arrive until they surround his bed, and all you can see is one foot sticking out from the covers. Two of the boys are fascinated by his feeding tube and the monitor that beeps with every drop.

"Hey, Philip. It sounds like a microwave."

"Yeah, you're done, man."

Philip laughs.

* * *

The next Monday, August 23, is the first day of school at Heritage Prep, and the same friends who gathered around Philip's bed sit in the auditorium of Tabernacle Baptist and plan their schedules. The juniors, Philip's classmates, take Algebra II, Spanish II, Chemistry, Chapel, American Government, English and Choir.

The juniors make plans to get the best lockers, talk about the woeful condition of the football team and catalog who among them has a restricted license and who has the real thing.

Under the wan fluorescent lights of a therapy room six miles away, Philip says "Mom" for the first time since his coma. Eve cries.

Everything is going to be all right.

* * *

Philip hasn't talked for a month and a half, Eve jokes, and he has a lot to say.

Actually, Philip says little on his second day of speech, and it's no wonder. Every word is a rough approximation, a patchwork of syllables that he struggles to produce.

His speech therapist works with him. "What's your name?"

Philip takes a breath, deep and deliberate. He keeps his right hand on his T-shirt, as if he needs to feel his chest swell to confirm the accomplishment.

Then he breathes out, and the wind of his exhalation nearly drowns out his answer: "Vilub... Shanlur."

"Tell me how you're feeling today?"

"Egg...zell...ent."

Philip has trouble coordinating his diaphragm, vocal chords, tongue and lips. That explains the monotone and slow pace of his words. Philip has other problems, too. There are times he hesitates, as if he can't find the right word. Other times he answers a question by repeating the end of it:

*Do you want to eat lunch now?*

*Eat...lunch...now.*

Philip's difficulty isn't purely mechanical, his therapists suspect. More tests should tell them if this will be part of his permanent brain injury.

Eve isn't hearing any of this. Finally Philip can communicate, that's the main thing. She worries about his monotone—he was always such an animated speaker before—but she's sure this is just a phase in regaining his speech. He's even reading now, big words like "occupational therapy" and "neuro lab" on the chart of his daily activities. "You are amazing," she tells him.

\* \* \*

The television is on, the sound low, when Jim and Eve enter the room on a Wednesday night, Philip's third day of returned speech.

Inspirational messages flash across the bottom of the screen. *Welcome to Florida Hospital....The world is a looking glass and gives back to each person a reflection of his attitude....It's not what happens to you in life. It's how you respond to it....*

Eve turns off the set. "It's rude to watch TV when people are visiting. Isn't it, Philip." The fluorescent light gives a green cast to the sheets on the bed where Philip rests. Mom and Dad settle in, enjoying the peaceful lull of day's end.

Philip's voice, a novelty still, comes as a surprise. "Mus...tang."

What did you say?

"Mus-tang."

He wants to know what happened to the car.

A friend sold it for them, they explain, because they didn't want to see it again. Jim and Eve answer carefully, not sure exactly why he is asking.

"I'm...glad," Philip says.

"I...would...have...given...them...the...car."

Eve's eyes meet Jim's. Philip remembers.

Jim gets up to close the door. Under those lights both bright and cold, Philip begins to answer the questions his parents have been afraid to ask.

Jim grasps his son's hand. "Did they point a gun at you?"

Philip points his finger at his temple and begins to cry, noisy sobs that make the room seem close. Jim's hand tightens around Philip's. And, for the first time since Philip left the house that day, the Chandler family grieves together.

Eve strokes his hair. "Were you scared?"

"Yes. They...made...me...get...in...the...trunk."

Each word so slow, each word an indictment of what they did to him. Eve feels like she's back at the Mustang that night, staring into the empty trunk with her sickening knowledge. She can see Philip there in the suffocating heat, smothered by darkness. He's suffering alone. Her chest hurts at the thought.

She prays, holding Philip in her arms. Did he pray in the trunk? Philip nods.

Did he remember putting his hand through the hole in the back? Yes.

Did he want to stop talking? He didn't have to tell them this. Did he want to stop talking? No.

"Where...did...they...find...me?"

Jim and Eve tell him about the parking lot, about Carolyn Richter, the security guard who dis-

covered him and who came to visit him in Sanford. She put a holy card, bearing the picture of a
saint, under his pillow when he was in intensive
care. Philip starts crying again.

"Do you remember riding around for a long
time?" Eve is hoping he passed out quickly.

"Yes."

"Which one had the gun?" Jim wants to know,
because no weapon was ever found.

"The...smaller...one."

They are in jail now, Jim tells him. They are in
jail where they can't get out, and they are charged
with attempted murder and kidnapping. They
can't get out.

"Don't...want...to...testify."

Jim and Eve stay with him until he sleeps.

* * *

August ends. Philip is walking now, a therapist
under each shoulder as he moves down the carpeted hallway like a marionette, picking up each
heavy basketball shoe and dropping it to the
ground. His friends are busy with school and visit
less often, though one night they pack the room
with 29 people—the whole junior class and then
some. Philip is more attentive, his eyes finding the
person who is talking to him, though his gaze
wanders if the conversation drags.

He is up at 7 a.m. for breakfast, a shower and
morning therapy. And though doctors are testing
for problems with his memory, he greets every
nurse, therapist and doctor by name. Eve arrives
by 10 a.m., but she is confident enough in his
progress to slip out in the early afternoon, running
errands and taking care of the house. Jim is back
at work as an Ocoee police detective, but reports
faithfully by 4:30 to spend the afternoon with
Philip.

There are once-a-week outings with other patients who are recovering from head injuries.
Philip goes to Pizza Hut (his choice) and Red
Lobster, reading his menu, ordering for himself,
remembering to put the napkin in his lap and prac-
ticing his eating protocol: *small sips, small bites,
chew well, sit up straight.*

And Philip has a new visitor now. Her name is Karin.

\* \* \*

"This is the Children's Home Society."

For 16 years, Karin had waited for this call.

She never even saw the baby. She tried in the delivery room that Tuesday afternoon in 1976. She had lifted her head through the fog of sedatives, but a nurse pushed it back to the pillow. The next morning, a different nurse handed her some papers to sign and told her the baby was a boy. He weighed 4 pounds, 11 ounces. He had respiratory problems.

The nurse left her alone.

The next day, they sent her back to her family in South Florida to finish high school. Karin knew she'd done the right thing. Still, she left the adoption file open to her son, hoping one day he would care enough to find her.

Her life had gone on—a marriage, a daughter, a divorce. Still, Karin would look at boys and think: *He's the same age as my son. He's a teenager now. Is he a good kid? Is he in trouble? Does he have his father's curly hair?*

Since his last birthday, she'd been thinking about him more and more. Finally she realized why. He was 16 now, her age when she got pregnant.

Karin held the phone in the long fingers of a trembling hand, so thrilled. This could mean only one thing. Her son wanted to contact her.

"I've got some real disturbing news for you," the woman said, and Karin started crying.

Her son's name was Philip Chandler, the woman said, and he was dying. He had been kidnapped, locked in the trunk of his car...

Oh, God! That was my son? She remembered the TV report about Philip when she was at Disney World.

Karin could visit Philip at the hospital in Sanford, if she wanted, the woman said. His parents didn't mind. She was invited to the funeral, too.

She'd think about it, Karin said, and hung up.

She thought. *Should she see him in a coma? Or would it be better never to see him at all? How would she tell her daughter, Tara? How would his adoptive parents react? Why were they calling her now?*

This was not her life. It was a made-for-TV movie.

Over the next few days, Karin fretted—quietly, so Tara would suspect nothing. She told only her mother what was happening. *She'd lost him once. She didn't want to lose him again.* Before Karin could reach a decision, Philip came out of the coma.

She didn't know what this meant. With so much going on, she would be a distraction. But Eve insisted that she come for a visit.

Finally, they made arrangements for Karin to meet Philip on Wednesday, Sept. 1.

Karin drove to Orlando with her boyfriend. She still didn't understand why Eve was taking this chance, introducing a complete stranger into the taut fabric of their lives. And though the letters from Eve had assured her that Philip had been wanting to meet her for more than a decade, Karin thought he might resent her for giving him away.

To make matters worse, Eve had given them wrong directions. Karin was nearly frantic when they finally arrived at the hospital, 45 minutes late.

Karin knocked at the open door. Philip looked up from his wheelchair at the long-limbed young woman with dark hair and dark eyes, the high forehead, straight nose and forthright chin.

She looks just like me! Philip thinks. Before anyone can say a word, he throws his arms out to her.

"You're Karin, aren't you," Eve says, and they all laugh.

There are awkward pauses that afternoon. Philip still speaks little, and Karin fills the space in her low, direct voice. They look through pictures of him as a child. They talk about Tara, who can't wait to meet him. Karin tells him how lucky he is to have such good parents. How happy she is it all worked out.

"Philip," Eve says, "wasn't there something you wanted to tell Karin?"

Karin leans in, smiling expectantly. She puts her hand on Philip's chest and he takes it with the long thin fingers so like her own. She feels his chest heave as he struggles to expel a complete sentence.

"Thank...you...for...not....having...an...abortion."

Karin's eyes tear. "You're welcome."

Karin calls Eve once or twice a week and visits Philip again a couple of weeks later, bringing her daughter with her.

While Philip is in therapy, they watch videotapes of his progress, Tara amazed at how big her big brother is. "He's got the longest tongue," she says, seeing him in speech therapy. "He's got huge hands."

When he comes back to the room, Karin sits by the bed and looks through a photo album with him, asking him about his friends. Philip just stares at her, infatuated.

"We don't want to tire you out," Karin says.

"You...don't...tire...me...out," Philip assures her.

"You know, I'd like to come more often. It's just I have to work and all."

"I...understand."

"I just talk and talk and talk. I don't want to keep you awake."

"You don't," he says, and pulls her close to hug her.

But he is worn out from therapy, barely able to keep his head up. Karin hugs him goodbye. Tara, too.

"You want me to take your shoes off?" Karin asks. "You'll let me do that."

She and Tara tug at the basketball shoes.

"Big feet," Tara says.

* * *

Philip falls back to the black bedspread and looks up at a teenage boy's proper vista—posters of bikini models and rock groups pinned to a corkboard wall.

It's Sunday morning, Sept. 11—64 days since he left the house for a haircut.

"Home," he sighs. "Finally."

But not for good.

Philip is just stopping in to get dressed for church, his big post-coma debut.

Tabernacle Baptist is packed. "Stand up, stand up for Jesus," the choir sings. As the song fades, Philip walks in—Eve at one elbow, Jim at the other.

He gets an ovation from the congregation, a football and jersey from the Heritage Prep team. Three local television stations videotape his entrance, and the preacher dedicates his sermon—titled "Why Do Christians Suffer?"—to him.

"Philip, just so all these young ladies can see you haven't lost your good looks, can I get you to stand up one more time?" Pastor Ware booms from the pulpit.

Philip grips the pew in front of him and, with Jim's hand steadying his back, pulls himself up. A royal blue suit hangs from the peaks of his shoulders. Jim's white shirt loops around his neck. His curly hair is tall today, threatening to overwhelm his delicate features. His expression is resolute. His lips are pressed together and pushed out, deepening the cleft in his chin. There's a slight squint to his eyes and a knitting together of his eyebrows. Philip looks defiant, as if he's daring to be alive in front of all these people who had thought he would die.

After church, Philip sits, tired but smiling, in the middle of a long table of family and friends at an Italian restaurant.

"You know," Estella Penny begins, "I never would have thought..."

"I know," Eve finishes. She is radiant with the day's success. "Doesn't he look good sitting there?"

But that evening, Philip's mood darkens. The Chandlers sit in the dining room, eating pizza before taking Philip back to Florida Hospital.

"I...want...my...old...life...back," Philip announces, out of nowhere.

"Philip, we can't change what happened to you," Eve tells him. "We'll never have our old lives back."

Philip sits silent.

"Remember how I've always taught you to think of others?"

"Others."

"Well, you're going to have to start thinking of others, not yourself. That's what your dad and I do. We're thinking about you and about others."

Dr. David Cox, the neuropsychologist, had tried to warn the Chandlers that this was likely to happen. Philip is more willing to accept his condition when he is in the hospital: *Of course my brain isn't working right—that's why I'm in this rehabilitation unit.* The familiar setting of home magnifies his new problems. *I'm home. That must mean I'm well.*

But he's not.

And each time he goes home—every weekend now—Philip leaves the quiet comfort of the rehabilitation unit with its handrails on every wall. He leaves the therapists who walk slowly beside him so he doesn't stumble, the nurses who show no embarrassment when he needs help getting to the bathroom, the doctors who listen patiently to every word no matter how long it takes to get it out. The world outside is loud and bright, with hard surfaces and uneven walkways. It is full of friends who talk too fast. They don't wait to see if he understands, they don't give him time to reply.

On the Monday after Philip's first weekend home, Eve helps Philip back into bed after lunch.

"Will...my...voice...be...normal?" he asks his mother.

"Yes, Philip, it will be normal. You have to be patient."

"I'm...running...out...of...time."

"Do you mean you're running out of patience?"

"No," he says in his monotone. "I...mean, I'm... running...out...of...teenage...time.

"Don't...cry,...Mom."


## THE STRUGGLE

Philip steps, blinking, into the bright afternoon, lets go of his walker and raises his arms high above his head. Victory. He is going home for good today.

It is the perfect gesture for the evening news, an image of triumph to wrap up the story. The cameramen move in. A crowd of Florida Hospital workers applauds Philip, providing a soundtrack.

*Walker, left foot, right foot.* The simple act of walking takes all his concentration. The noise, the cameras, the worrisome stairs up ahead, they all distract him.

*Walker, left foot, right foot.* A TV reporter pushes a microphone in his face. "What does this day mean to you, Philip? Can you tell me what this day means to you?"

*Walker, left foot...*

"Free...dom."

*Right foot.*

*Walker, left foot, right foot.*

It is Friday, Oct. 1, more than a month before doctors expected Philip to leave the hospital. Philip's story leads the local news:

"Philip Chandler is home tonight and doing better than his doctors ever dreamed...."

After the news, Jim and Eve and Philip sit in their garage with the door open. They look out past the shade trees, wave to their neighbors, feed the birds, talk to all the friends who call to say they saw Philip on TV, that they've been praying for this day, that he just looked so good.

Everybody loves a happy ending.

* * *

Philip's head smacks the pavement, hard.

"Philip! Philip, are you okay? Philip?"

Eve runs around the car. What happened? He just collapsed. He swung his legs out of the car, just like always, reached for the door frame and pulled himself up. Then he collapsed in the parking lot of the outpatient rehab center.

By the time Eve reaches him, the right side of his face has started swelling. His lip is bleeding, and a chunk of skin is torn from his knee.

"Philip, are you okay?"

She bends down to him. Philip's legs are folded under him, his right arm pinned behind his back. He doesn't move.

Eve pulls his head into her lap. She strokes his face. "Are you okay? Are you okay?" He's coming around now, sobbing. Eve cries with him. What happened? Did he lose his balance? Did he black out? Was it a seizure?

It is two weeks since Philip left the hospital, his second day at the rehabilitation center. There are no TV cameras around now.

Eve holds onto Philip, his blood staining her white blouse.

A therapist runs out with a wheelchair. She helps Eve straighten Philip's legs and lift him from the pavement. It's not hard. He still weighs only 115 pounds.

They take him inside and clean him up, then stretch him out on a therapy table. Philip lies there crying softly, embarrassed, frustrated.

After he rests, Eve drives him to the family doctor. Jim leaves work to meet them there. Philip is bruised, but there are no broken bones. His heartbeat, though, sounds irregular. It's worrisome. A cardiologist needs to check it out.

*Is this ever going to end?* Eve thinks as they leave. Jim's doubt creeps into her mind. Maybe this is as far as the miracle goes. She pushes the thought away and helps Philip to the car.

Philip seems shrunken in his wheelchair. His face throbs with pain, but worse is the humiliation of being pushed around like a baby in a stroller.

He's glad his friends can't see him like this.

When Philip first came home, everything had started out so well—like a holiday.

Friends came over, and Philip's den was noisy again with the sounds of teenage laughter and music being played too loud. The Orlando Magic's Nick Anderson dropped by and presented Philip with a pair of size 11½ sneakers, autographing the toe of each shoe.

On Tuesday, Jim and Eve were able to witness to all of Orlando about their personal miracle.

More than 200 people filled a Florida Hospital auditorium for a monthly worship service called "Joy in the Morning." The local news stations covered the Chandlers' appearance.

Eve could hardly believe she was in front of all these people. But as the cameras broadcast their testimony about faith in Jesus Christ, about forgiveness, about hope in desperate times, she thought that moments like this were the reason Philip was allowed to live. God has proved His power and mercy through her son. God is glorified through Philip's victory.

The next morning, Eve sent Philip to Heritage Prep to spend a day with his friends—the first day of kindergarten all over again.

She didn't want to let him leave her. He was anxious to head out on his own. Though she was exhausted from hovering over Philip for four days, she couldn't rest while he was gone.

Philip sat in the back of chemistry class, dressed sharp in purple jeans and a red shirt.

After the teacher assigned reading, Jason and Matt started cutting up with their friend, talking about the visit from Nick Anderson, discussing Michael Jordan's retirement and the negotiations over Anfernee Hardaway's contract.

Philip laughed and nodded and passed around photos. But Philip—the one who used to get in trouble for talking too much in class—didn't say a word.

As much as he liked being with his friends, he couldn't help thinking how different he was. *What do they see when they look at me? Do they notice the way I walk?*

They crowded around him when he went down the hall. *Do they think I'm going to fall? I'm so skinny. Do I look strange?*

And his voice. He has heard it so many times on TV—he sounds like a robot or something.

For four hours, he kept up appearances. Using his best balance, focusing on his friends when they talked to him, sitting up straight.

He went home wrung out and slept until Eve woke him for supper.

\* \* \*

Philip's blackout in the rehab parking lot has Eve on edge. A cardiologist finds an irregular heartbeat, maybe caused by a small seizure. He recommends a neurologist.

Until she knows what's wrong, Eve will hardly let Philip out of her sight. He must have someone watching out for him. But Eve can't do it by herself.

She uses money in a special trust fund to hire an aide, Lynn Pape. Lynn is not a nurse or a therapist. She's a motorcycle-riding widow who organized a benefit for Philip about a month ago. She doesn't really know the Chandlers, but when her husband, a city employee, was dying of cancer several years ago, Jim donated some sick days to him.

Lynn promises Philip a ride on her cherry-red scooter as soon as he is able in hang on tight. For now, they'll stick to the minivan.

They sing songs on the drive up to the rehabilitation center on Lee Road, starting every morning with the *Mighty Mouse* theme: "Here I come to save the day!" In the afternoon, when he's tired, she brings him a candy bar from the snack machines as a surprise.

And everywhere he walks, Lynn is right beside him.

October passes. Every night, Philip tells himself, there was progress today. Every night, he promises himself, there will be more tomorrow.

Karin calls often and brings Tara up for a weekend visit, weaving into the Chandlers' lives. But Philip's friends don't stop by as they once did. Philip sits alone in the den. He has thrown out his rock tapes and CDs, telling his parents a Christian shouldn't listen to that garbage. Now he watches movies on the VCR. Lately, it has been *Aladdin,* sometimes twice a day. He watches, mesmerized by the bright action and the hero who gets everything he wished for.

Eve hates to see Philip bored. She worries that his friends are forgetting him. They call and want him to come out to the movies or come to a football game. They don't understand when she tells them he can't. *He's home, isn't he? That means he's well.*

The doctors still aren't sure why Philip passed out that day, but they're nearly certain it could happen again.

*  *  *

On a Thursday late in October, about three weeks into outpatient treatment, Philip's case manager pulls him aside to talk. It's a chance for Kim Marshman to sound Philip out—without his parents there to speak for him. A chance to find out how much he understands about his own condition.

They sit together in a small room. Kim closes the door. There's going to be a conference this afternoon, she tells him, with all the therapists and doctors around a table talking about him. His speech, although still slow and strained, is not as halting.

"Can I attend the conference?"

"Absolutely. It's for you." This is good. Philip is at least curious about his condition.

Philip is using his best paying-attention look. His hands are flat and pressed to his thighs, his body curved forward and his head up. His mouth is set with a slight smile, held tight to keep it closed. He holds his eyes wide, his eyebrows up. When he blinks, it is hard and purposeful.

"So far, what questions might you have for the people in the conference," Kim asks.

"How am I doing?"

"Any specific areas?"

"In speech and memory group."

"What else might you want to know in the conference?"

"Nothing." He shrugs and holds his hands out, palms up.

Kim reminds him of the five goals he came up with when they first talked several weeks ago: to run, to walk better, to jump higher, to play basketball, to swim. All physical goals, she thinks, all related to the way he appears to others. It's typical of brain-injury patients to focus on their physical impairments, unaware of, or denying, the cognitive problems.

"What about school?" she prompts.

"What about it?"

"When do you want to go back?"

"Think I'm ready," Philip says. It's hard to tell if it's a question or a statement.

Kim says that next week a tutor will start teaching him while he's at the therapy center.

"What do you think will be a little bit hard for you?"

"Nothing."

"What about reading," Kim prompts. He is far below his grade level.

"I can read."

Maybe Philip wonders about a couple of the neurological tests they've done to see how fast signals move across his brain.

"I don't get things right all the time," Philip says.

"Why do you think that is?

"I'm not fast enough. My brain doesn't work like it used to."

"Why do you think that is?"

"Because of my injury."

Philip won't say "brain damage." He hates that. To him, it's an insult, not a medical term.

"You still have the thoughts, but the signals are a little slow. It's kind of like if you're going from your house to school and there's construction in the way. It might take you three times as long to get there, but you still do. It's like rush hour in your brain."

Kim pauses to see if he's getting it and then continues.

"I can't believe it. Almost everybody asks me one more question. How long am I going to be here?"

Philip smiles and obliges. "How long am I going to be here?"

"So glad you asked."

Four to six months. "Our crystal ball is a little fuzzy, so you might beat that time frame."

"I will beat that time frame."

"It's a deal," Kim says, shaking his hand.

"I'll hold you to it." The tight smile is replaced by a squint of determination.

"You're a hard worker," Kim says.

"Tisha said I'm an excellent worker."

"Wow, Tisha doesn't say that about a lot of people."

"If she had the perfect patient, it would be me." He points to himself and a sly grin spreads across his face. "Of course, she was on TV."

They laugh, and Kim compliments Philip on his sense of humor. It's a complex brain function and shows thinking on a higher level. And it can be an important tool when therapy gets tough.

"Of course, you don't have to be happy all the time. You can be sad."

"Mostly I'm happy all the time. But sometimes I get frustrated."

"One of the things I want you to remember is it's okay to get frustrated. You don't have to smile all the time."

Philip smiles at her.

"If you need somebody to yell at, you just come get me, and we'll come to this room and you can yell at me and I won't say a word."

"Okay," Philip says, but he laughs at the idea.

"I think you're doing really well. You've got a long, hard road ahead of you."

As he walks out, Kim shakes her head. Philip doesn't seem to understand his own condition yet. And she doesn't trust this perpetual good humor. The Chandlers, she suspects, don't show anger and frustration to other people.

Still, she sees no way for Philip to avoid those emotions. Brain injury is cruel. The better Philip gets, the worse he'll feel about himself. The clearer his thinking becomes, the clearer his perception of all he's lost.

Like his reading skills—by the time Philip reaches the end of a paragraph, he may have forgotten the beginning. He can't solve problems that have several steps. It takes him twice as long as before to remember a grocery list of six items, although when he does remember it, it sticks.

The key to Philip's trouble is attention—the foundation of memory and learning.

Attention is not just concentrating on information you want, it is ignoring information you don't. Philip, like many people with brain injuries, is overwhelmed at times by the sights and sounds around him—as if all the world is a crowded mall at Christmas time.

The doctors think there is a disruption along the neuro-chemical pathways that ferry information into the brain—the same pathways involved with speech. It's as if one light bulb has burned out, causing a whole string of Christmas lights to fail.

Philip has come a long way in a short time and will continue to improve for at least the next year, maybe longer. He should be able to continue his education, to hold down a job, to live independently.

But brain injury is not a disease. It's like an amputation. There is a part of you that's gone forever. No matter how well he does, Philip won't be the same person he was before.

Some day, Kim knows, he'll take her up on that offer to yell.

* * *

It's Lynn who catches it just a couple weeks later.

"I'm not a baby," Philip tells her. "I don't need you to walk beside me."

When he gets home that afternoon, Eve sits him down on the couch for a talk. "You've got to have someone walking with you because you could faint again."

Philip balls up his fists and pounds on his legs, so hard the sound echoes in the room.

"I get so frustrated because I want to be normal again."

He will be, 100 percent, Eve assures him. It just takes time.

"Those slime buckets ruined my life. The Lord told me to forgive them, and I have forgiven them. But I don't like them very much."

"Philip, I don't like them at all."

"I can't be bitter."

"Yeah, because you'd only hurt yourself and us. Those guys wouldn't even know you were bitter."

The following Sunday night, Jim finds Philip alone in his den—no music, no television—looking like he could use some company. Jim sits beside him on the couch, a new one with legs because the old one was too low for Philip to get up from.

For a while, neither says anything. They just sit together in the quiet.

"How could they do this to me?" He looks straight ahead as he talks. His lower lip quivers.

"There are just bad people in the world, and you ran into a couple of them."

"They should not see the light of day for a long time."

The conversation is punctuated by Philip's sobs and long silences.

Jim breathes in small sighs, his hand on Philip's shoulder. He lets the boy talk when he is ready.

"They took something away I will never get back. I will never forget what happened to me."

\* \* \*

It's a Monday afternoon in mid-November, and Philip is wandering through the house.

He blacked out again the night before, just collapsed in his mother's arms as he leaned down to hug her good night. He was out for just a minute, but he stared at the ceiling all night, too worried to sleep.

The neurologist thinks it may be a seizure. He prescribes medicine, but he also schedules follow-up visits. Just another thing to deal with.

Philip felt too tired to go to therapy this morning, so he is staying home with Eve. She's planning an early Thanksgiving dinner to honor the security guard who found Philip that July afternoon and five women who fasted and prayed for four days when it looked as if Philip wouldn't make it. They are all part of the miracle.

Philip wants so much. To drive. To go to school. To hang out with his friends on a Saturday night. To pick up his life right where he left it that morning in July.

Eve wishes she could make him see things the way she does. There will be a healing—100 percent. His voice, his thinking, his guitar playing will be restored. She believes this even if his doctors don't. Philip wants it all so bad that she must believe it for him.

She asks the Lord for that healing each time she prays. But mostly, she thanks the Lord that Philip is still around to pray for.

He'll walk into the kitchen to get himself a handful of M&Ms, and Eve will look up from the newspaper as though she's seen an apparition. It's miracle enough to have him walking through the house or calling girls on the phone. Or just sitting beside her on the couch where she and Jim planned his funeral less than four months ago.

On a pink notebook, Eve writes out what she'll need for dinner tomorrow night: *Call Publix, Call Black-Eyed Pea, Get corsages.*

Philip sits in his den and watches *Aladdin* for the 11th time, wishing he was out with his friends, maybe playing basketball at Manuel's or playing guitar in Isaac's garage. On the TV screen, Aladdin is flying away with the princess, all his dreams fulfilled.

What if he had three wishes, like Aladdin had? What would he wish for?

Philip imagines this for a minute, one eyebrow cocked in speculation. He holds out one long finger to begin counting off his wishes.

"To be normal again."

He holds out two fingers and thinks some more, longer this time. Then he closes his hand.

"That's really all I can think of."

# Lessons Learned

BY CRAIG DEZERN

It's a lot easier to write when your wife is eight months pregnant with your first child.

When I started writing "The Miracle of Philip Chandler," I had all the ingredients for a classic case of writer's block: a carton full of notes gathered over more than three months; a half dozen editors of increasingly weighty titles all but watching over my shoulder to make sure I didn't blow it; an emotionally exhausted family trusting me to tell their story just right; my own certainty that Philip's story was a rare opportunity.

A year before, I might have frozen, too overwhelmed by the possibility of the story to turn it into a reality. I might have labored over my writing until it became labored writing. I might have busted my deadline until I had no time to do anything but cram the story into the paper. I might have given in to the tension.

Fortunately, there was a lot more tension at home, where my wife, Cheryl, seemed ready to give birth at any minute. It was just the counter pressure I needed to put the situation into perspective. I didn't have the luxury of obsessing over the story this time.

After a week of preparation—making an invaluable timeline and a five-page outline—I began writing the story Nov. 1. The baby was due Nov. 12.

While secretly hoping the baby would be late, I figured I must write 1,000 words a day—100 lines on my VDT—to have a first draft finished before the baby arrived.

A thousand was an arbitrary mark. It was rigid. It was also freeing. I committed myself not to 1,000 great words. Just 1,000 words. Quantity first, something to show those editors hovering over my shoulder, something to work with later.

Instead of obsessively rewriting the introduction to the story, I cranked it out. Every morning, I allowed myself to read the previous day's work one time to find my place. I permitted myself 30 minutes of small fixes and reconsiderations of my outline. At the end of the day, I read the whole story once and noted any changes I needed. I did not take home a printout.

If I found holes in my reporting, I left blanks in the story to be filled in after the rough draft was complete. If I needed more details to make a scene come to life, I wrote myself the kind of pesky notes that editors always insert: "What kind of couch? Plaid? Floral?"

I hit the 1,000-word mark almost every day, and on Nov. 22 turned in a rough draft that was a hefty 17,000 words long. Four days later, Stanley Willis Dezern was born. (Pretty hefty himself at 9 pounds, 9 ounces.)

A few days later, when I came back to my rough draft, I found it was rougher than usual. But the structure was sound and there was an immediacy to the writing in several sections, the kind of energy that is killed when a story has been fussed over.

And because I hadn't driven myself crazy while writing the story, I was a better re-writer—more dispassionate, ready to sacrifice whole sections of the story for the greater good. And my rewriting made sense. Instead of playing with the same few paragraphs all day only to find out later that they didn't matter, I was able to do my rewriting in the context of the whole story.

The "Miracle of Philip Chandler" may not be the best story I've ever written, but it is certainly the best I've ever re-written.

More disciplined writers, often older reporters who can actually produce a story using a typewriter instead of a computer, follow this practice every day. I still struggle to join them, catching myself 20 minutes from deadline, rewriting my lead for the fifth time while the body of my story is still somewhere in my notebook.

That's when I remind myself what I learned: Let your rough draft be rough.

# Hank Stuever

### Finalist, Non-Deadline Writing

Hank Stuever was born and raised in Oklahoma City and earned a journalism degree from Loyola University/New Orleans. He began writing as an intern at *The Washington Post* Style section and then at the *Los Angeles Times* View section. He joined *The Albuquerque Tribune* in 1990 as a general assignment metro reporter and moved to the paper's feature section in 1993. He has won writing awards from the American Association of Sunday and Feature Editors and Scripps Howard, among others. He was also a finalist for the 1993 Pulitzer Prize for feature writing.

Stuever writes uncommon features that inform, illuminate, and entertain. He has a reporter's thirst for facts and the vision and voice of a writer willing to take risks. In "On the Beach," he takes an assignment that in less-stylish hands could have been a mundane perennial—a day at a water park —and uses drama, humor, and evocative details to take the reader behind the scenes as well as into the pool.

# On the beach

JULY 1, 1993

*Water slides, waves and a brush with death—it's all in a day at the Beach.*

Rome had baths, America has water parks.

**65°** The sun rises white and round like a Bayer aspirin behind the haze. This is the first day of summer and the Beach water park is still asleep. Tumbleweeds collect in the bone-dry water slides; in the Wave Pool, 700,000 gallons of mouthwash-blue water make like a mirror, pock-marked by the breeze. Yellow and blue inner tubes are stacked and piled around tall metal spindles. A tiny spider flails in the Lazy River. Today a boy will drown and be brought back to life through cardiopulmonary resuscitation, the park's first such incident ever. Today a storm will blow in from the west and knock down tents and send hundreds of sunscreen-slickened patrons running out of the park. But right now there is no hint of anything but a clear, chlorine day.

"You're late," Bucky Bomaster says in his deep voice. He walks across from over by the south concession stand. He is the chief maintenance man and the owner's son, smoking a Kool. He has dark-brown skin and platinum-blond hair and tight white tennis shorts—he is Dar, Ocean Castaway, citizen of Planet Jimmy Buffett. He is here first every morning.

I'm late, yes. I was putting on SPF No. 6, otherwise I'm toast. But now I am ready to go beneath and behind the Beach, to see how you move a million-some gallons of water by twisting valves and pushing buttons, "kicking on the verticals" and "turning the Blue Valve." Bucky goes through a door behind the Wave Pool. I can tell he is doing something very important when he kneels in front of a metal cabinet and turns and punches several knobs that apparently are connected to the whole park and serve vital functions.

What is all that?

This? This is the radio, he says.

He cranks it up and a day at the Beach begins.

**70°** "I was a bartender for 13 years," Bucky says, looking on a shelf in the garage workshop for a part to fix a broken water pump. "Everybody wants my job in the summer, but nobody wants my job in the winter, when I'm the only one out here."

**74°** Today will be Hoffmantown Baptist Church youth day. There also will be several groups of children from Albuquerque Parks and Recreation programs, and the normal Beach patrons—flabby dads on a day off with the kids; adolescents who get dropped off by their working parents. They are lining up at the front gate.

Underground behind the Lazy River, Bomaster points out two 20-foot-tall heat pumps that keep the water warm. We are surrounded by large pipes and pumps—slightly brighter environs than the set of *Alien³*. You can hear water gurgling all around us.

Brian Kadle, the park's "aquatic systems supervisor" (he's in charge of water quality and lifeguards), is busy running back and forth among the pumps.

Lifeguards practice saving each other in the pool.

"I'm going to turn the Blue Valve," Bomaster tells everyone on his walkie-talkie. He flicks a spent Kool onto the pavement. "By the time you get down there," Kadle responds, "we'll be ready."

The Blue Valve squeaks open and water is moved from the Wave Pool through the rest of the park, the circulation system of this body, and the front gate rolls up. "People go, 'Why does it cost me nine bucks to get in here,'" Bucky says. "Then you look at all this power going on and everything that's behind it and you realize it's a pretty big deal. If they saw it they'd say, 'Oh, OK.'"

**78°** While children run past the concessions patio and across the bridge into the play area, Bucky studies the control panels for the Wave Pool. It has eight settings: the Parallel, the Large Parallel, the Side Pipeline, the Challenger, the Split, the Double, the Peak and the Destroyer. You can set it variably. He dials up 1, 3, 5, 7. With a resounding, rhythmic ka-klung, the hydraulic pumps begin their best impression of the sea.

Hundreds of children and adults rush to rent yellow inner tubes to ride the waves. Almost instantly, there are bodies shooting down the slides and freshly Coppertoned tots splashing in the kiddie pool.

Somewhere in the Wave Pool, among the floating, tossing, bobbing heads, skin, bikinis and yellow rubber tubes—just 27 minutes after the park opens—Victor Baldizan dips underwater and does not come back up.

**80°** "Get back! Everybody please get out of the pool!" The little boy's limp form is pulled out of the water. 911 is called. The young lifeguards and emergency medical technicians begin CPR. "Please," a lifeguard tells the crowd. "Stand back."

No pulse.

"One-and-two-and-three-and-four-and-five."

Nothing. Some little girls, their hair dripping, hold their hands to their mouths and try to look around the crowd for a better view.

Victor Baldizan came to the Beach with the Parks and Recreation La Luz Playground group. He is 9. No one saw him go under. He was floating near the bottom—"No pulse"—and the guard saw him and pushed the emergency wave stop button—"And-two-and-three"—and jumped in to get him.

Still nothing. Several minutes now. His fingers and toes are grayish blue.

"Six years and nothing ever like this."

"No pulse."

"And-three-and-four-and..."

Sirens in the background.

"Oh please, please," says a woman watching.

"Wait."

"What?"

Angels? Something, anyway. "Oh God," says a young EMT as Victor takes a breath. The boy's body turns itself sideways. The toes twitch. A rescue.

"You guys did it," Brian tells the EMTs and lifeguards. "You saved him."

**84°** They carved out the Beach into a steep incline against Interstate 25 six years ago at a cost that some said was $6 million and others said was $10 million and everyone finally agreed on as being about $8 million.

This was part of the same mid-'80s golden slumber that dreamed the Renaissance, a real-estate nirvana that flopped.

The original investors—members of the Montgomery family of Montgomery Boulevard, etc.—lost millions the first year, 1987: The park opened a month late and the desert despised it, sending down summer rains over the Beach's steep, fragile earth, carving natural arroyos through it and beneath it, flooding the whole works, twice.

So, too, the banks, who foreclosed on the Beach twice in two years. So, too, City Hall, fining the Beach thousands of dollars the summer it leaked 100,000 gallons of water every day.

But what Mother Nature and the banks and water conservancy groups hounded, the people loved: You could grow up in New Mexico and not know a real wave. Until the Beach, you might not have a concept of unlimited chlorine. The park was never wanting for patrons.

In 1991, Jay Bomaster and Billy Smith took over the lease on the park and ran it not as a Disney World pipe dream but merely as a place to cool off. To date, they are the first to make much money off the place and keep it in working order. They run the Beach like a family: Jay and his son, Bucky; Brian, who has been employed here five seasons; and 88 employees, mostly teenage lifeguards. The older women sit in the office and chain-smoke, counting the money and telling jokes.

The crowds continue, as many of 5,000 people a day.

**71°** Dark clouds and wind, heading on 2 p.m.

Brian Kadle is sitting in his office in the back of the first aid shack near the Wave Pool. Even though the staff is shaken up about the near-drowning with the boy, now in intensive care at University Hospital and later to be upgraded to serious condition, the Beach remains open.

In the kiddie pool, among the "Smurfs" with their chattering blue lips, a lifeguard reports a "Code Brown" near the top of the slide and maintenance crews are dispatched to collect the offending dookie and disinfect the area.

Brian asks two lifeguards, meanwhile, to stand outside and monitor the approaching storm.

They watch for lightning, then count the seconds until you hear the thunder. Divide by four. If it's fewer than eight, you need to get people out of the water.

Brian loves the water park. He worked here the summer he was 18, when he had just become a lifeguard. He says he has the best-trained guards in the city. Today he can prove it because Victor Baldizan is alive.

We stand outside the back door and watch the kids float by in the Lazy River. Lightning. (Two, three, four, five...) When it's not summer, Brian goes to school and studies accounting. (9, 10, 11, 12...) Or he works odd jobs. (15, 16, 17, 18...)

"Well, last year," Kadle says of the winter interim, "I cleaned carpets." Thunder, low and distant.

Divide by four:

An eight.

"We need to get people out of the pool," he tells the guards. We step out by the lockers and watch the crowds evacuate the rides after a voice comes on the intercom. "This storm is big," Brian says. "Welcome to the Beach's Day From Hell, 1993."

**63°** The storm is sudden and rude, like a drunk at a baptism. Everything is called off. Within minutes, it is obvious that the Beach will have to close for this day, the first day of summer. For the employees, it truly feels like the longest day of the year.

Children who can't find their mommies are running around in a goose-bumped panic as dark storm clouds let loose a cold, dousing rain.

Lounge chairs and inner-tubes blow across the AstroTurf and carpet. Lifejackets collect in the corners of the now-choppy Wave Pool. People huddle under patio roofs. A giant concession tent blows down, its thick metal poles twisted and bent by the wind.

Bucky and Brian man the front gates, handing out rain-checks as the unhappy masses run to their cars. A lot of kids are left standing in the rain by the locked gates, unable to get their parents on the pay phones.

A day at the Beach is cut short.

"You had to come today," Bucky turns around and tells me.

**75°** The sun sets fat and forgotten like a tangerine Jujube melting on the windowsill. The water park is quiet. From atop the hill, in the glimmering evening light, the Wave Pool is a melting blue Sno-Cone. The water jets and slippery slides and Lazy River are at rest; the body, asleep. Tomorrow will be a perfect day. It will come with its own all-day cloudless sky. The lifeguards will bravely return to their perches. The money will be counted. The verticals will be kicked on. The Blue Valve will be turned.

The boy and girl in us all will get very wet.

# Lessons Learned

BY HANK STUEVER

My editors at *The Albuquerque Tribune* are always saying one thing to me: "Try something new." (Oh, and: "Is it done yet?")

My assignment was simply this: Do "something" for our Thursday entertainment tab about the summer crowds at the Beach, Albuquerque's only water park. It sounds like one of those dreadful tasks. The temptation is to just go down there, get the quotes, and glue it together with summertime clichés. But *The Albuquerque Tribune* isn't an average newspaper, and I get really interested in the very ordinary things people do with their time and money.

"On the Beach" follows my standard feature writing m.o.:

I called and asked what it was like behind the scenes. Who runs the place, who takes care of the details? Can I follow these people around? Are they interesting? May I speak to one of them? What time should I get there? What time do you get there? Great, I'll be there.

Then, research. The final version of "On the Beach" is missing a brilliant six or seven inches. I wanted more lines about the strange real-estate deals that brought the park to Albuquerque, the various bank foreclosures, the implicit go-go '80s morality. I looked up most of that stuff. Published or not, it always helps to know everything in advance. But play dumb. Dumb gets me very far.

Then, go. Maybe something funny or weird or tragic will happen. I have never found the act of "hanging out" while doing a feature story to be wasteful.

One of the obvious reasons this story takes care of itself is a series of extraordinary events that took place on what was meant to be another ordinary day. A drowning, a thunderstorm. Who can't write something good from a boy's life saved? I was kind of surprised that the park's owners didn't ask to me leave—especially after I used their phone to call in a brief to the city desk for the Home edition. Instead, they spent the rest of the day nervously bragging to me about their spotless safety record.

Then, synthesize. Digest. I had come back to the office, wet from the rain, thinking, "Well, so much for my sunny day story. A kid drowned and the storm closed the park. What now?" But the more I thought about it, the better it was. I never have to resort, in this piece, to doing the same old man-on-the-street quotes from small children, parents, and other "revelers," "patrons" or—yeesh—"sunbathing Beachgoers escaping the city's scorching heat."

Then, write. Play with sentences like toys. Pose them, stack them, knock them over, save-move, control-delete. Start over. Overwrite, so you'll have something to pare down.

You'll notice that I get away with using personal pronouns. ("I was putting on SPF No. 6, otherwise I'm toast," etc.) There are so darn many rules in the business and yet everyone's wondering why people have quit reading daily papers. Sometimes "I" can work, as naturally as a phone call to a friend or a conversation at the kitchen table—telling a story the way we all tell stories—and still be accurate, fair, insightful journalism. Writing is the act of getting an audience into the tent for the show.

I needed a chronological focus, but I'm bored with day/night/week-in-the-life stories that are structured around pointless clock watching: "2:03 a.m.: The ambulance arrives and the nursing staff is ready, blah-blah..." It occurred to me that temperatures are more vital to a summer day than what time it is. So, thanks to the local weather service, I had my (possibly hokey) transition device. With good reporting—a notebook full of details and a file folder full of alternately useful and trivial research—the writing gets itself done.

My editor, Scott Gullett, cut some lines here and there, and we ran a lifeguard-slang glossary as a sidebar, with the required breakout box of location, hours of operation, ticket prices.

Re-reading this or any article is always kind of a downer: I want more reporting in it, even more details, even more funny lines, even more narration. I want it to be better. I'm not sure daily newspaper writing can ever be better than pretty good. Is this my best story? Hardly. I look at it and ask, "What's this guy's deal with metaphors?"

One other thing about this story, and it's something I try for in all my feature stories, is a strong narrative voice. That's all journalists do, really—narrate life. My style has been known to come off as intrusive, bratty. People who pick their noses usually wind up in my story picking their noses. I'm not some incredible kick-ass reporter who gets the mayor impeached or blows the whistle on toxic dumping. On my best day, I'm a point-at-ass reporter. The *Trib* takes occasional delight in publishing such stories, which is why I love to work here. Readers, I find, love reading something beyond the standard schlock. Even if they hate it, they usually hate every word—sometimes twice.

# Joan Beck

## Commentary/Column Writing

Three decades before "family values" became a Presidential-campaign buzzword, Joan Beck was writing a syndicated column about children while raising two of her own. Her 40-year-career at the *Chicago Tribune* is studded with firsts: first woman to run a daily section, first woman on the editorial board, first woman with a regular op-ed column. Retirement hasn't slowed her down: She continues to write her syndicated column twice a week.

Beck works from a white two-story house on a quiet suburban street in the Chicago suburb of Lake Forest, Ill. Her office, off a spacious, airy kitchen, is lined with shelves brimming with books, award citations, and family photos. Boxes overflow with clippings, research materials, and letters from readers. One carton is stuffed with cards and letters she received in response to the column, included in this book, that paid a moving tribute to her husband, medical illustrator Ernest

Chicago Tribune

Beck, who suffered a fatal heart attack in July 1993. Another of her award-winning columns alludes to her treatment for cancer, diagnosed shortly after her husband's death. But Beck rejects any suggestion that she has shown courage in her determination to keep writing. It's what a writer must do. As she puts it, "You do not have any choice."

# Scare science may be hazardous to your health

MARCH 25, 1993

Can your cellular phone give you brain cancer? Are electromagnetic fields really dangerous? Must your local school system spend millions of dollars to get rid of asbestos used for insulation decades ago? Should the hole in the ozone scare us into changing our polluting ways? How necessary are all those environmental programs on which the nation spends $140 billion a year?

Questions like these reflect the current and growing concern about the complex relationships between science and public policy, public panic and explosively expensive costs.

The conviction is spreading that a combination of misunderstood science, dogmatic environmentalism, sensationalizing media, gullible public and scientifically naive legislators and regulators may be wasting billions of dollars, causing unnecessary fears and misdirecting the search for the real hazards in our lives.

One indication of that concern is the Heidelberg Appeal, a plea that originated to counter the environmental hype of the Earth Summit in Rio de Janeiro last summer. The document warns against decisions made on "pseudo-scientific arguments or false and non-relevant data" and has now been signed by more than 2,500 scientists, including several dozen Nobel laureates.

Papers published by the group assert, for example, that there is no proof dioxin causes cancer or birth defects in humans, that the dangers of asbestos when properly used are greatly exaggerated, and that the hazards supposedly posed by the ozone hole and the greenhouse effect are "largely hypothetical." Moreover, in part because of public anxieties about radiation and chemicals, this nation and others are spending billions of dollars on cleanup projects that contribute very little benefit to public health and take money that could be better spent elsewhere.

In other evidence of changing attitudes, Carol M. Browner, new head of the Environmental Protection Agency, is pushing for changes in federal laws that would ease some of the current absolute prohibitions against pesticides and other chemicals that seem to pose only very minimal risk, if any, to humans.

At issue, for example, is a provision in the Federal Food, Drug and Cosmetic Act called the Delaney Clause. It prohibits any use in food of any additive or pesticide residue in any amount if the substance has been shown to cause cancer in laboratory animals.

But since the provision was enacted in 1958, scientists have learned to measure chemical substances in ever-smaller amounts, easily as little as one part per billion or less—exposure that could not have been detected earlier and that many scientists now believe is not generally not harmful to humans.

Scientific doubts are also growing about the usefulness of tests that dose laboratory animals with extremely large amounts of a test substance to see if it produces tumors. If it does, the theory is that smaller doses may do the same in at least some human beings and that the substance is a carcinogen.

But the high dosage itself may be what causes the cancer, according to Dr. Bruce Ames, professor of biochemistry and molecular biology at the University of California at Berkeley, a world-known authority on detecting carcinogens. The overdosing can cause damage to the tissues that leads to chronic cell division—and that, not the test substance itself, is a major risk factor for cancer, he says.

It's easy enough to say that decisions about health and environmental concerns should be based on sound, scientific evidence that meets commonly accepted standards. But it's not that simple.

Scientific evidence may take years to accumulate—and may still be inadequate. It's impossible to expose large numbers of people to possible car-cinogens or other harmful substances to determine their precise dangers. Animal data are increasingly being questioned. Computer models and test-tube experiments are even less definitive.

Much of what we consider scientific evidence is based on links and associations—not clear-cut cause-and-effect relationships. That can lead to misconceptions and errors, as Ames has noted. "The number of storks in Germany has been decreasing for years," he has pointed out. "At the same time, the German birth rate also has been decreasing. Solid evidence that storks bring babies!"

Human beings may react differently to environmental factors, depending on their genetic makeup, age, dosage, lifestyle and other variables. What they believe is also influenced by their emotions and a need to find a reason or something to blame for an illness. Some Vietnam veterans, for example, are still convinced they were harmed by Agent Orange contrary to numerous studies. And a man set off a nationwide storm by charging on a TV talk show, without evidence, that his wife's brain cancer death was caused by a cellular phone.

This spring, the Supreme Court will rule on what standards of scientific evidence are permissible in federal court and what credentials expert witnesses should have.

The case, *Daubert v. Merrell Dow Pharmaceuticals Inc.,* involves the drug Bendectin, developed to relieve nausea in pregnancy. It was used by 33 million women and numerous scientifically acceptable studies judged it to be safe.

But among such a large number of women, it was inevitable some would have babies with a birth defect, unrelated to Bendectin. It was also predictable some of them would sue Merrell Dow, claiming the drug caused the prenatal injury to their child. Most of the cases quickly lost in court. But the legal costs and hassles led the manufacturer to discontinue the product, leaving women without an effective treatment for nausea in pregnancy.

At issue in the case now before the Supreme Court are questions about the quality and validity of science information that judges should allow to be heard and whether rules of evidence should exclude so-called "junk science" and unorthodox scientists.

Regardless of what the Supreme Court rules, similar questions will continue to plague all of us and, in particular, should trouble public policy makers, regulators and opinion shapers. For starters, all of us need to become more sophisticated about science, its accepted standards of evidence and its current limitations. Failure to do so is costing us dearly—in drugs we need but don't have, in billions wasted on unnecessary environmental cleanups, in pointless panics and in misdirected searches for answers to problems now going unsolved.

# Writers' Workshop

## Talking Points

1) Notice how Beck begins this column with questions about what appears to be a series of unrelated scientific controversies? What is the unifying feature?

2) One of Beck's greatest strengths as a journalist is the way she seems determined to let readers make up their own minds on controversial topics, rather than imposing her beliefs on them. A good example of this attribute can be found in paragraph three. How could this be rewritten in a less objective fashion? How would it differ from Beck's approach?

3) Beck asserts that attitudes about risk are changing. What evidence does she offer for this argument? Is it persuasive?

4) In paragraph 16, Beck cites an upcoming Supreme Court case that will deal with the issue of standards of scientific evidence. Is this a news peg that makes this column timely? Should it be higher in the story?

5) Beck deals with extremely complex subjects. But she is adept at leading readers through these challenging minefields of information with a style that seeks to simplify rather than confuse. One useful tool: short declarative sentences. "But it is not that simple." "Animal data are increasingly being questioned." "Most of the cases quickly lost in court." Find other examples.

## Assignment Desk

1) Imagine you have just been assigned to write a story on the subject of "scare science." Map a reporting plan: interviews, documents, books, etc.

2) Research what the Supreme Court ruled in *Daubert v. Merrell Dow Pharmaceuticals Inc.* Write a news story about its decision, focusing on the implications for scientists, regulatory officials, the public.

3) Review your stories for sentence length. Are you breaking lengthy sentences in half? Do you strive to write short, declarative sentences? Rewrite one of your finished stories and compare it with a previous version.

# It's time to kill flying 'Tinkertoy' and refocus NASA

JUNE 24, 1993

No one really wants to kill the space station.

It's like being the evil Klingon who shoots down the Enterprise, the idiot who denies humans the chance to go where we have never gone before, the dolt who can't feel the call of the final frontier or the seductiveness of the stars.

But it is time to call a halt, with clear finality, to plans by the National Aeronautics and Space Administration to construct a manned space station—and to former President Bush's visionary goal of landing a manned spacecraft on Mars by 2019.

The reasons are not just the soaring costs. The money involved can't be brushed off, of course. NASA has already spent about $9 billion on the space station and has little to show for it except some new scaled-back blueprints.

Under pressure from President Clinton, NASA has redesigned the old proposed space station named Freedom to pare down its costs. Current estimates put the price tag at $10.5 billion over the next five years—$16.5 billion by 2001. That is considerably less than earlier projections for more elaborate models. But in the wondrous ways of Washington, no one can be sure what the final price tag might be or how much it might cost to operate even an economy-sized version.

The space station design the president picked earlier this month combines elements of two of three scaled-down options NASA offered him earlier this month. It looks like what some of its critics are calling it, a "Tinkertoy in the sky," although backers insist it doesn't deserve the derisive label. But it won't support the soaring hopes and expectations that were built into the space station when it was planned by the Reagan administration.

Initially, the space station was to be assembled in space orbit by astronaut-technicians using materials ferried up by the shuttles. It would house wondrous experiments with plants and animals, would be used to grow flawless crystals and manufacture drugs with unearthly precision and would monitor the effects of weightlessness and life in space on humans and other living things.

Most important, it would be the next great step into the universe beyond Earth, the launching pad for manned space craft heading first to Mars and then, perhaps, beyond. It would rekindle the frontier spirit that is the heritage of Americans, give us new heroes, a new unifying pride, new incentives to excel, new claims to leadership in the world—and a serendipitous spinoff of new products and new technology.

But a reality check prompted by budget considerations throws doubt on most of these expectations.

The space station's lofty goal of boosting astronauts on to Mars could probably be done by 2019, despite the unprecedented hazards to humans and the 300-day trip each way. But the price tag would be at least $500 billion, a tough commitment to make in today's political climate. Scientifically, almost as much could be learned about the red planet with far less expensive and dangerous unmanned voyages.

The rest of the solar system is far more relentlessly hostile to human life than even the airless red rock of Mars. Unless scientists are drastically wrong about the nature of the other planets and the inhospitable voids between them, human beings will not be able to reach them any time in the predictable future. Certainly, it is wildly premature to build a station to launch manned vehicles into space without more certainty about when and how and where we could go.

Other arguments for a space station are equally weightless. Experiments with crystals and drugs on space shuttle flights show no clear advantage over Earth-bound production. Counting on serendipitous, second-hand benefits from technology is silly; space station money could pay for far more advantages directly.

The Soviets have had cosmonauts in a station in space for months at a time studying weightlessness and space technology; it has not won them great scientific glory, inspired them to new scientific or political heights or taught them much we haven't known.

The argument that because we have already spent $9 billion on a space station we must keep on supporting the project whatever its eventual cost or usefulness is a foolishness only the government could suggest. That killing the plan would cost jobs is true, but a painful necessity if progress is ever to be made in cutting back the deficit.

Even easier to counter is the argument that finally terminating the space station would mean the death of NASA. There are still plenty of space exploration projects for NASA to do, incredible discoveries about the solar system to be made with better telescopes, space probes and unmanned missions like the Voyagers and Magellan-Venus.

It's true that the space station is supposed to be a precedent-setting example of international cooperation in scientific endeavor. But our Japanese, Canadian and European partners are not uniformly enthusiastic about it, for good reasons. Surely it is possible for nations to work together on scientific projects that would be of greater benefit to people on the Earth, such as medical and environmental research.

It is a typical Washington mistake to keep stringing the space station along, cutting back on its funding and its functions, but not killing it cleanly. It is hard for space buffs—including me—to give up the dream of interplanetary travel in our lifetime. (Even my computer objects; at every pause in writing this column it switches to a screen-saver program that gives me the exhilarating illusion of speeding through space among the onrushing stars.)

President Clinton can't bear to pull the plug on the space station. Congress will have to do it, at least before the budget is finalized. Reality is not a magnificent, mind-boggling Star Trek adventure, but a bureaucratic boondoggle with huge cost overruns.

# Writers' Workshop

## Talking Points

1) In her lead, Beck assumes readers' familiarity with Kling-ons and the Starship Enterprise. But what about the millions of Americans who don't watch *Star Trek*? Is she doing them a disservice by not explaining the reference? How do you decide when background is needed?

2) Beck usually keeps herself out of her columns. But in paragraph five, consider the ironic tone in the sentences that begins, "But in the wondrous ways of Washington, no one can be sure what the final price tag might be..." If irony (as Cicero, the Roman statesman, observed) is saying one thing and meaning another, then what does Beck really mean here? When, if ever, might irony be permissible in a news story? Find other examples of Washington-bashing in this column.

3) The word "wondrous" resurfaces in paragraph seven when Beck is describing the dreams of the space station's designers. Does Beck intend this to be ironic? Might she have used a different adjective?

4) Notice, in paragraph 11, Beck's description of Mars: "the airless red rock." It is precise yet lyrical. Where would a writer discover that information about Mars?

5) Study the way Beck weaves in artful references to space travel with word choices that echo her subject matter, such as this line in paragraph 12: "Other arguments for a space station are equally weightless."

6) Beck's mastery of the subject of space travel is impressive. How many different news stories does she seem to know thoroughly?

7) Alliteration, the repetition of an initial sound in two or more words, is more commonly found in poetry, occasionally in prose, rarely in newspapers. Beck uses it twice in this column: "serendipitous spin-off" and "bureaucratic boon-doggle." Search for such wordplay in your newspaper and in your own stories.

## Assignment Desk

1) Rewrite this column by making Beck's enthusiasm for space travel apparent sooner. How does injecting her personal opinion up high affect the story? Does it damage or enhance the credibility of her argument?

2) Have you made alliteration one of the elements of your writing style? Play with words in your next story, have fun and then take a serious look. Is the wordplay effective? Does it appeal to the ear? Does it reflect the subject? Puns or alliteration in an obituary would probably be inappropriate.

# Don't blame leaders; AIDS prevention is up to individual

JULY 1, 1993

There's a life-death message in the final report of the National Commission on AIDS. But the report concentrates so hard on blaming political leaders for not doing more about the epidemic the message is lost between the lines of anger and frustration.

No cure for AIDS is in sight, the commission's report notes. A vaccine is years away. HIV continues to be a slow, inexorable killer, mostly of adults in the prime of life.

But, as the report should have stressed in language strong enough to burn into the brains of us all, you can generally protect yourself from getting AIDS.

The government isn't going to guard you from getting AIDS. It can't. President Bush couldn't. President Clinton can't. The White House's new AIDS coordinator, Kristine Gebbie, can't either, no matter how urgently AIDS groups pushed for that post to be created. Neither can the governors, mayors, members of Congress, corporate executives or community and religious leaders the commission's report blames for not doing more.

Most AIDS activist groups are much more concerned about people who already have AIDS than about preventing others from becoming infected. Most laws dealing with AIDS are intended to help and shield the HIV-positive, not to safeguard others. Protecting yourself from getting AIDS is something you have to do for yourself.

Doctors can't cure you if you get AIDS. They can only postpone your death, treat some associated illnesses and keep you feeling a little better as you slowly die. All the politically correct attitudes, all the anti-discrimination laws, all the political activism, all the red AIDS ribbons, all the support groups, all the finger-pointing can't change the basic facts about this epidemic.

The same sober assessment about the lack of substantial progress against the AIDS epidemic was sounded repeatedly in Berlin in June, when thousands of scientists met at the annual international conference on AIDS. The lack of encouraging scientific news included studies pointing up the limited benefits of AZT, the primary drug used to treat HIV infections and AIDS.

Prevention is now the only way to stop the epidemic from continuing to spread widely and rapidly throughout the world, scientists repeatedly emphasized at the Berlin conference.

HIV does not infect humans easily, like the common cold. It is not genetic, the result of an unlucky mistake in DNA coding. Its cause is known, unlike most forms of cancer. AIDS, like it or not, is an infection acquired by having sex with an infected partner (anal-receptive sex is particularly risky) or sharing a needle with an infected intravenous drug user.

Exceptions include babies of HIV-positive mothers, people inadvertently transfused with HIV-positive blood, accidentally infected health care workers and a few cases for which the cause has not been established.

The hard fact is that those who want to protect themselves against HIV infection and AIDS can almost certainly do so by not sharing intravenous drug needles with an infected person and by having sex only within an established monogamous relationship with a partner who is free of HIV.

Why is it so hard to push this message clearly and explicitly?

For one reason, it's widely assumed that changes in sexual behavior in the last three decades have made the message of premarital abstinence and marital fidelity naive and obsolete. Never mind that two generations ago, it was considered the social norm (whatever the exceptions in practice).

So those who are trying to prevent the spread of AIDS are relying on messages about "safe sex," which generally means condoms. Condoms can substantially reduce the risk of acquiring HIV

from an infected partner—as well as the chances
of getting other sexually transmitted diseases,
which in turn increase susceptibility to HIV. But
condoms have a high failure rate as a contracep-
tive, and the AIDS virus can much more easily
slip through microscopic holes in a condom than
can a much larger sperm. A woman can usually
become pregnant only about two days a month.
The sexual partner of a person with HIV is always
at risk.

Even so, an increasing number of schools are
making condoms available to students, sometimes
over the strenuous objections of parents who feel
the implicit message is that sex is okay and expected of teenagers and that more immature
young people—not fewer—will be at risk.

It is also difficult to shape messages about
sexual behavior so they will be acceptable to mi-
norities and to gays who are at higher risk of
AIDS than the population as a whole. But excessive sensitivity, exaggerated political correctness
and concern about seeming to blame the victims
can sometimes dilute the cautions too much.

We do need much more scientific research
about AIDS—and more money to pay for it, even
though AIDS research is now better funded than
work on other diseases which claim many more
lives. We do need support and good care for per-
sons with AIDS and HIV. We do need an end to
residual prejudice, discrimination and unjustified
fears of infected people.

We do need more treatment facilities for drug
abusers, although the high rate of recidivism is
discouraging. Needle exchange programs have ar-
dent backers, although critics are concerned about
supporting what is self-destructive behavior regardless of the risk of AIDS.

We do need more empowerment for women, in
the United States and especially in many Third
World cultures, so they can protect themselves
from the sexual demands of high-risk men and
from dangerous sexual practices.

But while we are working on all these difficult
things, it would help to broadcast clearly and

loudly the message of individual responsibility for avoiding HIV and individual power to do so, instead of blaming the government for not doing more.

# Writers' Workshop

## Talking Points

1) Beck gives a lengthy list of actors in the battle against AIDS in paragraph four.

"The government isn't going to guard you from getting AIDS. It can't. President Bush couldn't. President Clinton can't. The White House's new AIDS coordinator, Kristine Gebbie, can't either, no matter how urgently AIDS groups pushed for that post to be created. Neither can the governors, mayors, members of Congress, corporate executives or community and religious leaders the commission's report blames for not doing more."

Why do you suppose she included all these individuals or groups? What is the effect?

2) Beck raps AIDS activists sharply in this column. Examine the column and find other examples of her criticism against them. Discuss the validity of her points. What do you think is Beck's goal for this column?

3) Analogy centers on the partial similarity or dissimilarity of features between two items: an analogy between the heart and a pump, for instance. Beck employs analogies in paragraph nine: "HIV does not infect humans easily, like the common cold. It is not genetic, the result of an unlucky mistake in DNA coding. Its cause is known, unlike most forms of cancer."

What is the value of the analogy as a means of making complex subjects understandable?

4) This column focuses sharply on the need for prevention and the importance of personal responsibility to stop the spread of AIDS. A secondary theme is Beck's view of the efforts of AIDS activists to blame the death toll on the failure of government. Isolate the elements that relate to each of these themes. William Safire once observed that a column could be about one thing—or three things—but not about two things. Are there two columns here?

5) Consider the italicized phrase in this sentence in paragraph nine: "AIDS, *like it or not,* is an infection acquired by having sex with an infected partner (anal-receptive sex is

particularly risky) or sharing a needle with an infected intravenous drug user." Why do you think Beck included this? What or who is the target of that comment? Also, why does she use the term "anal-receptive sex"? When does the need to be precise conflict with the reader's ability to understand technical information?

6) Columnists enjoy a freedom—to editorialize, stake a position, give their personal views—that is usually denied reporters. Consider how Beck uses this freedom, especially in paragraphs 11 through 15, as she discusses the messages of premarital abstinence and marital fidelity. Do you have any doubt where she stands on these issues? Should a columnist let readers make up their own minds on an issue?

7) Beck concludes this column with three paragraphs that share the same opening phrase: "We do need..."
Read these passages aloud. What is the effect of such repetition? Discuss the importance of rhythm in writing. Does it remind you of any other forms?

## Assignment Desk

1) Act-Up is an AIDS activist group that has held many demonstrations, trying to bring attention to what it considers the failure of the U.S. government to adequately combat the AIDS epidemic. Research the group. Write an editorial criticizing its approach. Write an editorial that supports it.

2) Be on the lookout in your reading for analogies. Include some in your own stories.

3) Write a column that encourages people to take AIDS prevention seriously. You can focus on the dangers of sharing needles, or unsafe sex, or both. Target a specific audience: drug users, teenagers, homosexuals.

# Facing the void of a life
# and a love lost in a moment

JULY 22, 1993

At 12:30, my husband and I were having a pleasant lunch in a restaurant. At 1:30, we were back home, sitting at the kitchen counter planning a trip to Vienna and Budapest in September with cherished friends. At 2:30, I was walking out of the hospital emergency room in shock, a widow, my life changed forever, beyond comprehension.

All the fears of all the years of loving and living with a smoker came true in less than an hour: Acute myocardial infarction—a heart attack. 911. Attempts at CPR rehearsed so often in the mind now tried for keeps and in desperation. More skillful attempts at resuscitation by paramedics, in the ambulance, in the emergency room. "There was never a flicker of heart beat," they said.

"It was so fast he wouldn't have known what was happening," his doctor told me. "CPR rarely works," said the nursing supervisor in the emergency room. "It's not like you see on TV."

How can a failing heart wipe out an incredibly intelligent brain and destroy an artist's marvelous creativity so quickly? How can the beloved essence of a man be gone so fast just because his heart has stopped?

How do you call your grown-up children and say the dreadful, unrelenting words? How do you ever get over the shock and numbness when your own heart has been amputated and you feel so bruised and empty inside?

How do you shift the tenses and pronouns of your life? How do you reset your mind from "we" and "us" to the singular and change the verbs about the man you love—loved—for so long from present to past?

How can you make yourself start to delete him from your life, to cancel his credit cards, to cut up his cash station card, to change the name on his bank account? How do you force yourself to erase the familiar voice in the message on the phone machine, knowing that hearing him again unexpectedly upset so many callers?

How do you go on living, when the love and the support you have taken for granted for decades is suddenly gone? There wasn't even time to thank him for all he has meant to me, done for me, shared with me, cared about me. There was no chance to thank him for fathering two of the most wonderful children ever, for creating a home and a family together, for always being there when I needed him, for letting me take that "being there" for granted, for having the broadest shoulders to lean on and the warmest hands to hold.

I met him years ago, when we were freshmen in the same class at Northwestern, he 19 and I, 18. That spring, just before the freshman formal, there was an epidemic of rubella on campus. His date got sick and so did mine. His roommate and mine decided he should take me to the dance.

But he had gone off to the Indiana dunes on a geology field trip and had come back late, tired, dirty, all of his formal clothes, including his shoes, having been borrowed by fraternity brothers. He was angry about having to take me to the dance, to scrounge up a tux, to give me the corsage his roommate had bought. The first words he ever said to me were, "Here's some gardenias. I hate gardenias."

Neither of us ever dated anyone else after that night. We were married three years later, when we had only $400 and both of us had graduate school ahead. I have been greatly blessed with the love of this man ever since—and with the blessing of loving him.

How do you sum up a life in an obituary? The facts were easy. Date of birth. College. Graduate school. Military service. The medical textbooks he had illustrated. The atlas of anatomy he created. The medical teaching posters and three-dimensional artwork he designed. The medical journals of which he was editor. The lifetime achievement award from his professional association. His two grandchildren. Date of death. Ernest W. Beck, 1923-1993.

But where can you say how much he was loved? How enthusiastic and supportive he was with his children? How incredibly beautiful his artwork? How enormous his talents? How many friends he had everywhere? How much I need and miss him? How empty I am without his touch and hugs?

What do I do now? I have learned, in reluctance and necessity, to pump my own gas, to open the lock box in the bank, to plan a memorial service, to see that the grass gets cut and the bills paid. But the pain is unrelenting, the shock fresh and raw a hundred times a day, the impulse to talk to him about the trivia and transactions of our life still as natural as breathing. The realization that I no longer can is as panicking as drowning.

Build an independent, new life, I am told. Find new interests, make new friends, write more, read more, travel on your own. And I must try, of course. But for all of my adult life, his love gave me confidence and empowered me to achieve, and his support enabled me to do so. And now, how I miss his caring, the knowing that he was always there for me, the loving and being loved, the sharing of the details of our lives in hard times and happinesses, in hopes and anticipations.

Writing is supposed to be a catharsis for a writer. Perhaps. Thank you for at least letting me try it.

# Writers' Workshop

## Talking Points

1) In this column, Beck departs from her normal mode of dispassionate commentator. Consider the challenges and rewards of writing such a deeply personal and emotional piece.

2) Beck uses the clock to stunning effect in her lead. Study the three sentences that capture the event that transformed her life:

"At 12:30, my husband and I were having a pleasant lunch in a restaurant. At 1:30, we were back home, sitting at the kitchen counter planning a trip to Vienna and Budapest in September with cherished friends. At 2:30, I was walking out of the hospital emergency room in shock, a widow, my life changed forever, beyond comprehension."

How different would the lead have been had Beck begun her story this way: "In two hours on Saturday afternoon, my life changed forever."

3) To describe what happened to her husband, Beck used the scientific name and the lay term: "Acute myocardial infarction—a heart attack." Why do you think she used both? What is the value of using medical terminology?

4) Beck brings a staccato quality to her narrative in the second paragraph: "Acute myocardial infarction—a heart attack. 911." How would the pace differ if she had written. "Frantically, I dialed 911?" Discuss how much a single word can convey?

5) In paragraph three, voices follow each other, rapid-fire:

" 'It was so fast he wouldn't have known what was happening,' his doctor told me. 'CPR rarely works,' said the nursing supervisor in the emergency room. 'It's not like you see on TV.' "

Beck lets the professionals tell the story here. Notice her skillful use of attribution. In *Self-Editing For Fiction Writers,* veteran book editors Renni Browne and Dave King offer this advice: "When you're writing speaker attribution the right verb is nearly always 'said.' "

In the second sentence, Beck also displays another professional's technique: she places the speaker attribution at the first natural break in the first sentence. "This is an especially good idea when the paragraph is fairly long," Browne and King say. "The ear seems to require a break near the beginning."

6) Study the next four paragraphs, four through eight. They contain nine wrenching questions that strike at the very heart of life, love, family, existence. Why are they so effective at conveying the shock, pain, terror when a loved one dies?

These are rhetorical questions; no answers are expected, but they make a deeper impression on the reader than a direct statement would. Why is this device so powerful?

7) In the next two paragraphs, Beck zooms in to describe the moment 50 years earlier when she first met her husband. It's a wonderful anecdote that has the details and flavor of a cherished family tale. Examine how Beck compresses it into two paragraphs.

8) In the final paragraph, Beck concludes with a message most writers, and many readers, can identify with. "Writing is supposed to be a catharsis for a writer. Perhaps." "Catharsis," from a Greek word *kathairein,* means to clean or purify. Aristotle used it in his description of the effect of tragedy: the purging of emotion which brings relief of tension, anxiety, or grief. Does Beck's column provide this psychological cleansing? What is the value of writing about such a personal and painful subject? For the writer? For the reader?

9) How does Beck's voice differ in this column from her other pieces in this book?

## Assignment Desk

1) Write a column about a person close to you. Examine how the process differs from writing a news story.

2) Write a lead to a story using the element of time to convey an important development.

3) Focus on the quotes in one of your stories. Place the speaker attribution at the first natural break in the first sentence. Read both versions aloud and compare how they sound.

4) Rewrite paragraphs four through eight by changing the questions into direct statements. Which is more effective and why?

5) In two paragraphs, describe your first meeting with your roommate, spouse, editor, most important source. Be sure to include at least one line of dialogue.

6) Write an obituary of Ernest Beck, using his widow's column as your raw material.

# Clinton's health care plan: It's a matter of life and death

SEPTEMBER 9, 1993

It wasn't by choice that I have been checking out the health care system from the bottom up and the inside out these past several weeks.

What I am convinced of—after two surgeries, four hospital admissions, chemotherapy, a cadre of skilled physicians, a blessing of caring nurses, an emergency room visit, two blood transfusions and countless humiliating intrusions on personal privacy—is that we are not asking the right questions about the Clintons' health care plan.

The patient has been forgotten in the rush to reshape the system. And in the haste to save money by treating people like so many faceless digits, we are risking losing a quality of care we can never regain.

The health care system does need changing. Administration now eats up one health care dollar in four. An estimated 37 million people lack health insurance. Health benefits have become an increasingly burdensome expense to employers and a drag on job growth. Serious debate is heating up about when medical treatment should be withheld as futile or cost-ineffective. President Clinton is proposing to exclude the nation's more than 3 million illegal immigrants from coverage, despite warnings this could endanger public health.

Health care cost this nation $832 billion last year, 13.4 percent of the gross national product, a per-capita spending higher than in other industrialized countries. Medicaid is stretching state budgets out of shape. White House officials are considering proposals to chop $100 billion more out of Medicare spending over the next few years. Debate is intensifying over such cost-saving ideas as global budgeting, spending caps, rationing and expenditure targets.

But current efforts to solve these problems—including the long-awaited plan President Clinton is expected to announce in late September—generally concentrate on controlling access to health care for individuals and often curtail doctors' freedom to decide what is best for their patients as well.

Employers are increasingly pushing employees into HMOs and other variations of managed care plans. Typically such groups try to cut costs by assigning patients to a primary physician who acts as a gatekeeper restricting access to specialists and expensive technology. Many HMOs provide financial incentives to physicians to keep referrals to specialists and hospitalizations to a minimum.

More worrisome is the growth of for-profit HMOs, which try to squeeze enough savings out of patient care and administration to pay for advertising and marketing, dividends for stockholders and sometimes exorbitant salaries for executives.

Even when patients have health insurance that allows them to see a private physician, the doctor may have to get permission from the insurer—often an anonymous nurse on the other end of a phone line—for hospitalization or other major expenditure and risk being overruled by someone who has never seen the patient.

Some of these efforts, of course, are motivated by efforts to reduce exorbitant administrative costs. But it's far from clear that pushing all of us into managed care arrangements will result in much saving. Some studies show many HMO variations are not significantly less expensive than traditional fee-for-service arrangements. And the red tape likely to be required by new government regulations may make paperwork costs worse, not better.

(Billions of dollars might be saved simply by requiring patients to sign off on the accuracy of their bills before they are sent to an insurer. One of the horror stories of excessive charges and outrageous mistakes I've been collecting concerns a man whose bill for surgery and a two-day hospital stay exceeded $29,000. One item he discovered was a $21,000 charge for a $21 bag of IV solution. The insurer had paid the bill without a question.)

Despite their problems, managed care models are expected to play a key role in the health care plan President Clinton finally sends to Congress. The result will be a significant curtailment in patients' rights to choose their own doctors and in physicians' freedom to practice medicine according to their own best judgment.

Before the Clinton health care plan gets set in the concrete of law, we—patients, taxpayers, "consumers"—should insist it contain some basic protections for us. We are, after all, going to be paying for it through a still undecided mix of old and new taxes, forgone employee benefits, our share of insurance payments and higher prices on whatever we buy.

At a minimum, we should insist on being able to choose our own doctors. Being ill and needing medical care are worrisome enough. It helps to have an ongoing relationship with a trusted physician who knows us and is motivated by what is best for us—not by HMO rules or by the managed-care incentive to give us as little care as possible.

It's also important to remember that medicine is not yet an exact science and that treatment by formula may not be appropriate for every patient. We should insist that whatever system the Clinton administration and Congress put in place leaves room for good physicians to exercise their healing arts as well as their scientific judgment on our individual behalf.

Debate about the Clinton proposal will be intense and will likely focus on the plan's effects on jobs, on taxes and on the deficit, on the exclusion of benefits such as long-term care, and on whether illegal immigrants should be covered.

But all of us need to take a highly subjective, individual look at what will happen to us, specifically, if the Clinton plan or a congressional variation of it, is enacted. We don't have to sacrifice our right to freedom of choice in health care to solve the ills of the current system and we shouldn't believe those who are intent on "managing"—controlling—this intensely personal aspect of our lives.

Unless the Clinton plan preserves what is really a basic freedom, we should oppose it. What's at stake, after all, is our health and our very lives.

# Writers' Workshop

## Talking Points

1) Beck uses her own experiences as a cancer patient to introduce her assessment of the Clinton health care plan. Does that give her opinions greater authority?

2) Unlike Beck's moving column about her late husband, Beck mentions her personal experience only once. Do you think this piece would have been more effective if she had put herself into the story more?

3) The list is an effective device for presenting information, and Beck uses it in a particularly graceful way. In the second paragraph, Beck presents a litany of medical treatment: "two surgeries, four hospital admissions, chemotherapy, a cadre of skilled physicians, a blessing of caring nurses, an emergency room visit, two blood transfusions and countless humiliating intrusions on personal privacy." Notice how she mixes the specific ("two blood transfusions") with the poetic ("a blessing of caring nurses"). Why is this effective?

4) Writers searching for the focus of their story have found it useful to answer two questions: What's the news? What's the point? Answer those questions for this column.

5) In a single line, the first sentence of paragraph three, Beck captures the essence of the argument she advances in this column: "The patient has been forgotten in the rush to reshape the system." What evidence does she use to support this thesis?

## Assignment Desk

1) Columns can be fodder for story ideas for reporters. Plan a survey of hospital patients. Walk through a hospital ward interviewing patients, nurses, doctors. Hang out in a doctor's lounge or a ward lounge.

2) Use the litany in one of your next stories, whether it's a list of city council actions or the description of the bric-a-brac in a profile subject's office.

3) Before you write your next story, answer the two questions critical to finding a focus: What's the news? What's
the point?

# Joan Beck: Truth Teller
## Giving readers more than facts

**CHRISTOPHER SCANLAN: How would you describe your column?**

JOAN BECK: I am basically writing about social issues: changes in the social structure, changes in our cultural values, health, and education. I spent part of my pre-column writing years at the *Tribune* writing about children, and I got very interested in a lot of children's issues. So I tend to write about them. The whole great field of science has very little commentary, as far as the mass media are concerned; and there certainly is a lot going on in science that people ought to be aware of. What I try to do is look for issues that I know enough about or can learn enough about to have something useful to say and have a strong opinion. And I hope to change some viewpoints.

Once in a while, I just cannot stand to be serious, and I write very light things that I hope are funny. But I always feel uneasy about them. I have a little voice in my head saying, that's sophomoric, it belongs in a high school paper, it does not belong in the *Chicago Tribune*. But they are the ones I get the most comment about usually.

**Where do you get ideas for your columns?**

I read the *New England Journal of Medicine,* the *Journal of the American Medical Association, Pediatrics.* Publications like that often have very interesting, useful knowledge that rarely surfaces in the big newspapers or any newspapers. There is also a vast amount of good information in professional journals that never reaches the public.

- Joan Beck, op-ed columnist, *Chicago Tribune.*
- **Born:** September 5, 1923, in Clinton, Iowa.
- **Education:** Medill School of Journalism, Northwestern University, B.A. 1945, master's degree in 1947.
- **News Experience:** *Daily Northwestern,* 1941–45, editor 1944–45; *Chicago Tribune,* 1950 to present.
- **Awards:** Northwestern University Alumnae Award, 1977; Peter Lisagor Award for Editorial Writing, 1982, 1988, 1991. Inducted into Chicago Journalism Hall of Fame, 1994.

### So you are filling a gap?

Yes, I think so. These are things that people need to know. I have enough background in reporting on science issues that I can do it accurately, I think. I worry a lot about that. So much of what passes for science information in newspapers is based on things that are not really scientifically valid. When you get a university professor to quote, you assume you have a good story. But maybe he knows what he is talking about and maybe he does not. Maybe the scientific data do not back him up.

### What is your work schedule?

My columns are due Wednesday noon and Friday noon, for the Thursday and the Sunday paper. So I spend Monday worrying about ideas, and Tuesday and Wednesday mornings writing. And then Wednesday afternoon worrying about ideas, and Thursday and Friday morning writing.

### How do you produce your columns?

The hardest part for me is getting the right idea. As far as the *Tribune* is concerned, ostensibly, there are no restrictions on what I write about. On the other hand, it has to fit into about 850 words. It has to be timely. It runs in a large number of other newspapers, but not always on the same day. So it has to be an idea that is good for a week or two.

### Any other requirements?

I like to have a good news take. I like to have at least something that I can write about with some feeling of confidence—either something I know a lot about myself, or that I have kept files on over the years, or that I can get reliable information about in a reasonable amount of time.

Then I look for an interesting way to present it. I am very much aware that readers have a lot of other things to read. So I am very conscious of finding a way to hook the reader right away. I probably spend about a fourth of the time that it takes me to write a column on the first two or three paragraphs.

**Do you revise heavily?**

I rewrite paragraph by paragraph. I spend a long time rewriting that first paragraph, the second paragraph, and the third paragraph. After that, I probably rewrite each paragraph about four times.

But by the time I am done, I am done. I do not make an outline. I do not make drafts.

**Do you read your work aloud as you are writing it?**

No, not really. But there is something in my head that reads it.

**Are you conscious of voice?**

Not voice so much as cadence. The pace. I always read a couple of chapters in the Bible every morning, whether I am working or not. I always have, ever since I was a child. I think those cadences get imprinted in your brain; when you write you tend to write in those kinds of patterns and rhythms. The cadences—only in the King James Version—are so effective.

I think you get these cadences programmed into your head and you use them as sort of a touchstone.

**When you were inducted recently into the Chicago Journalism Hall of Fame, *Tribune* editor Howard Tyner quoted your daughter Melinda, a senior editor at *Newsweek*, as saying, "Column writing is really what she does for pleasure."**

She knows me better than that.

**Why? Is writing such hard work?**

Yes. It is hard for her and it is hard for me. I do not
know anybody who writes well who writes easily.
I think that is important for people to know. After
I had been through journalism school and graduate school and was working at the *Tribune,* I was
still surprised to see people whose bylines I had
admired for a long time still sitting there, head in
hand, trying to write. It was a great revelation to
me that it did not come easily to anybody that I
know.

**Why was that an important lesson?**

Because it was hard for *me.*

**How do you know your daughter knows you
better—has she seen you at work?**

Well, we talk almost every day. She will say, "My
story is not going well." It will be 9 o'clock on a
Friday night and she will be working on the cover
story. I will say, "You know, this is the process. It
is always like this." She will call me up and say,
"You sound discouraged." I say, "Well, I am halfway through a column; I do not like it." We know
each other.

**How do you talk each other down—or up, I
suppose—if you are in a pit of despair?**

We remind each other that this is the way the process works. I just remind her that it is always like
this, and she reminds me.

**What do you think are the central difficulties
faced by people who are trying to write well?
How do you overcome them?**

In my case I tend to mentally edit and criticize as
I am writing. There is a little voice in one ear that
says, "Are you sure that is right? Somebody out
there knows a lot more about this than you do.
And they are going to write Howard Tyner and tell
him you are dumb. So you have got to be sure you

know what you are talking about." These voices kind of get in the way when you are trying to write.

**How do you write past them?**

That is why I keep rewriting each paragraph until the cadence sounds right and the pace of the sentences sounds right. I can usually tell when that happens. Until I have checked the facts and checked the facts and checked the facts, and I am sure I have put a fair spin on them. I really try very hard to be fair. It is more fun to write a column when you have a hostile point of view or to really slam an idea home. But it bothers me to do that unless I am absolutely sure I am being fair.

**In your column about AIDS prevention, you end with three very emphatic paragraphs, each with the same opening phrase, "We do need..." As I read these paragraphs, I could almost see you striking a podium with your hand as if you were delivering a speech or a sermon. Was that structure deliberate?**

I was thinking more in terms of the people that were going to write me nasty letters, saying, "This is what we need, we do not need your moralizing." So, I was thinking yes to this group and yes to that group and yes to this other group.

**It strikes me that you have a running dialogue with your audience—mostly the people that you assume are your critics.**

Well, with the people that are going to write me letters or write letters to the editor.

**Are you glad of their presence there? Do they help you write your column?**

Oh, yes. They are part of the audience you are writing to. They are part of what is going on, part of the problem or the situation you are writing about.

Writing for a newspaper is not writing in a vacuum. You are writing to an audience. If you are not, you are not going to get very far.

**To you, what does the label commentary mean? What is the signal to the reader?**

That I am writing about something, but not as a reporter. That I am making a comment on something that has happened. It could be light, it could be serious, it could be amplifying. There are just all kinds of ways of commenting on something. But I am not doing the original reporting.

**Does the newspaper need the voices of commentary? Do you think what you do is an important part of your paper?**

Yes, for many reasons. I think a lot of times things happen and readers want more than just the facts. If something terrible happens, they want somebody to cry out and say, this is an outrage, this should not happen, this is really terrible.

They want somebody to say look, let's get rid of this guy, this should not have happened.

Or it could be something as simple as, hey, this is great. You know, let's for once be happy.

**Who is on your list of great commentary writers working today?**

Mike Royko, Steve Chapman, Clarence Page, Ellen Goodman, Anna Quindlen, A.M. Rosenthal, Russell Baker.

**What value do they have for you?**

I need to know what they are writing about so that if I am going to write on the same subject I will not take the same line. I would not want anybody to think they were influencing my thinking.

For example, Anna Quindlen had a column on Hillary Clinton and the problems of Whitewatergate. It was not anything that I would have written or the same approach, but it was the same subject. So I wrote one on Hillary and Bill Clinton. But I used a format from *The Ladies Home Journal,* "Can This Marriage Be Saved?" I wrote his side and her side, and then what a therapist would say to them.

**What a great idea!**

Yes, it was fun. This may be what my daughter was talking about. I get considerable pleasure out of manipulating words and phrases and making them work. Besides, straight expository writing gets boring for me after a while.

So I like to look for different kinds of formats and different ways of getting at ideas. I get great pleasure out of that.

I have written a Thanksgiving column every year now for about 20 years, and it is almost entirely made up of nouns mixed up with the titles of Protestant hymns, essentially lists of things to be thankful for. But there is a lot of alliteration, there are a lot of rhyme schemes, and a lot of just tossing up of all kinds of different ideas—phrases like licorice and libraries and lilacs and liberty. I get enormous response from that every year.

One year, Charlton Heston wrote me and said that he had read my column at his family's Thanksgiving. He sent me a tape of him reading it. Boy, when Moses reads your copy, it sounds great!

**How did you get your start at the *Tribune*?**

I was hired as a feature writer. They did not generally have women in the newsroom, other than a couple of sob sister types.

**What is a sob sister type?**

You would go interview the girlfriend of the guy who just got murdered and look for a teary quote.

**Was that the role for women in a newsroom at that time, in the late '40s?**

Yes. The feature section at that time consisted of beauty tips. They would tell you not to let your slip show and keep your stocking seams straight. That is how they wrote to women. Beauty tips, fashion tips, cooking tips, social events—who had tea with whom, weddings, engagements, that kind of stuff. That was all it was. I really pioneered the idea of writing stories about social issues.

**What subjects?**

Adoption, foster care, education issues, what do you do with children who—we did not know enough to call them abused at that point—but that phenomena. We were beginning to look at working women in two-career families.

**Was your position unusual for a woman?**

It was fairly ghettoized, because you worked for women's sections or feature sections. If your paper was very progressive, there was a features section *and* a women's section. The women in the newsroom were very few and very unusual.

**What was it like for a woman journalist in the 1950s?**

You were an aberration. Most of the women worked for the feature department if they were reporters or writers, most of them in fashion or beauty. We had a column called "The White Collar Girl," which was about secretaries. Lois Wille was a reporter at the *Chicago Daily News* with Georgie Ann Geyer, and both of them were trying to get off the women's pages and get into the newsroom.

Finally, the editor called them in and said, okay, I will put you both in the newsroom, but you have to promise me you will not cry. He said I am taking both of you, because I know that when girls go to the little girl's room, they like to have somebody to go with.

**Young women who aspire to a career in journalism worry about whether they can have children and a career. Your life, as a mother and successful journalist, suggests it can be done. What advice would you give a young woman with those concerns?**

My daughter is doing it. Part of it, I think, is demonstrating your value to your employer, so that he is willing to help you make changes in the way you work. After my son was born, I decided to work at home. I told my editor at the *Tribune*, you will get a good story every week. You will not have to worry about it. It will be there. It will be good. It will be on time. He knew me well enough to know that I would deliver.

**Can we talk now about the very moving column you wrote after your husband's death?**

That was a different kind of column. It was in my head and I could not get rid of it, so I wrote it.

I have had more response from that than anything I have ever written—just incredible—I am still getting it almost a year later. One woman at the *Tribune* said she sent it to her mother. Her mother said she had already received eight copies of it from other people.

**How does that response make you feel?**

Well, it makes me feel that I was not wrong to have written it. I have never had such warm responses.

**Did you have doubts?**

Yes. I almost did not send it in.

**Really? Why?**

Because it was so personal.

**Does it make you want to write more personal columns?**

No.

**Did the writing go quickly?**

Yes. It was about 11 o'clock at night. I thought, all right, this is in my head. It is not going to go away. I will sit down at the computer and get it out of my head. I wrote it in about two hours, very late at night. That is not the way I usually write columns.

**You said you normally write during the day.**

Yes. In a much longer process than that.

**Your use of rhetorical questions was very powerful. Were these questions you were asking yourself?**

Well, I guess they were things I was trying to deal with, that you ask yourself. But I did not do it deliberately; it just happened.

**Did it help to get them out of your head?**

Yes. It helped a lot.

**Writers are very fortunate that way, aren't they?**

I think it is the way we deal with things. It is for me. Writers tend to put things into words and deal with the words because that is what we are used to dealing with.

**Can you talk about the craft behind this column, the choices you made writing it? Why is it all questions and no answers?**

I could not possibly analyze it. I guess that was just the way I was feeling. But there certainly was nothing calculated or analytical about it. It just happened.

**Do you think, though, that a professional lifetime of writing made this possible?**

Oh, I am sure it did. I am sure there must have been some of that at the subconscious level, but it certainly was nothing that I was aware of. It was very strange. I do not think I have ever written a column in that way before—without consciously thinking about it, you know, planning it ahead of time and knowing what I wanted to say, where I wanted it to go, getting the facts together.

**Are there conditions that you need for your writing to go well?**

Deadlines. Without them, I do not think I would write. Basically, what I need is a factual basis to start with. But, other than that, the rest comes out of my head.

**Today, the emphasis in newsrooms is on reporting and writing that is ahead of the curve. Do you have any advice for people who want to stay ahead of the pack, who want to write about things that haven't been written about?**

Look at your own life. Look at your friends' lives. Just look at what is going on in the country, what bothers you, what you do not know enough about, what you want for the future—those kinds of things.

Newspapers, in a way, set the social agenda for this country and a political agenda. I think that is one of our functions. What we call attention to is what gets attention.

**What traps do you think reporters fall into when they are writing about scientific or medical subjects? What are ways that they can avoid them?**

I think that very few journalists—people who have come out of journalism schools anyway—have had any kind of background in science, and what the standards of proof are, what you look for, who are reliable people. There is so much that newspapers report on that needs this kind of scrutiny.

### What do journalism schools need to do?

I would require a course that would help reporters learn how to evaluate their sources; it would be broader than scientific news. I would let them at least know that every professor they call up at the local university is not necessarily dealing with facts, but is sometimes dealing with his own pre-conceived ideas.

I would have them learn enough statistics so that they could look at material and see whether it was scientifically significant or not. I would give them some idea that, for example, you do not nec-essarily learn universal truths by stuffing rats with saccharin. Because there are things that can pro-duce tumors in rats other than saccharin.

When my children were growing up, I had a neighbor who, when her child got a little cut or a scrape or a bruise, would take a silver knife and lay it on the cut. I said, why are you doing that? She said, well, it always gets well. Cause and effect.

You have to teach them that it is not that simple.

**Your column on scare science struck me as a reasoned, low-key approach to a very contro-versial topic. You seemed to be ultimately criti-cal of junk science, but I did not sense that you really let the reader in on your opinion until the last paragraph. It struck me as a cool and very useful approach to a real hot-button subject. Did you have a goal for that column?**

To warn people to be skeptical about what they read. If some guy goes on a talk show and says, "A cellular phone gave my wife brain cancer," you should say, "Whoa! Has brain cancer gone way up now that everybody has a cellular phone? What is the mechanism here?" Yet, a lot of people took that seriously.

**You also focused on drugs for nausea and pregnancy.**

Those drugs are not available now because there were just so many lawsuits. And based on the way

I read the research, it looks to me as if the cases the pharmaceutical company won were judged correctly, because there really was no evidence. When you have a drug that is taken by 3 million or 4 million pregnant women, some of them are going to have children with birth defects whether or not they take the drug.

It is very easy when something bad happens to you to start looking for the cause and say, "Oh, I took that drug. And now my baby has a problem. It must have been the drug. Let's sue."

But the long-range consequences are that women now do not have a drug for nausea in pregnancy. Maybe all these lawsuit costs have pushed up the cost of other pharmaceuticals that the company makes. It does not help to blame it on something that is not the real cause. We have to keep looking until we find the real cause.

I know it sounds corny, but I also care about truth.

**If you had to pick a metaphor that expressed your view of yourself, what would it be?**

Truth teller, or someone who provided knowledge. That is how I see myself.

**You've been doing this work for nearly 50 years. Yet it does not sound like you have ever come close to burning out.**

No. Because there are always new ideas. There are always new things happening. If you look at any other job, where do you get more variety, more chance to be exposed to ideas? I cannot think of anything I would rather do.

# Donna Britt

## Commentary/Column Writing

In a city where politics and power brokers dominate the news, columnist Donna Britt covers a different beat. She is an investigative reporter whose assignment is the emotional landscape of modern life. "It is Donna Britt's great strength," says *Washington Post* executive editor Leonard Downie, "that she pays such careful attention to the background music of our lives. Britt hears the themes that accompany common events, and through uncommonly skillful writing entices readers to listen, too."

Britt joined the *Post* in 1989 and quickly established herself as a writer of special vision and voice with a gripping memoir about her brother, who was killed by two policemen in her hometown of Gary, Ind.

She writes her twice-weekly syndicated column from the comfortable, African art-filled home in suburban Maryland that she shares with her young

sons, Hamani and Darrell, and her husband, Kevin
Merida, a *Washington Post* reporter. She usually
types her columns on a laptop in a second-floor
study where she can watch squirrels play in the
trees outside. Her thinking goes on everywhere.
"I really do believe," Britt says, "that if you
present any idea with enough grace and thought
and sensitivity and chutzpah, that it will get
printed."

# A life of grace and strength offers one last precious gift

MAY 7, 1993

It's strange, remembering the drool when I have so many lovely mementos:

A lacy black cocktail glove. A pastel-tinted photo of a couple in 1930s dress. A gold watch with chains as delicate as blades of new grass.

But there's something obscene about me having my grandmother's things. They belong in Pennsylvania, on the mantelpiece of Mom-Mommy's stone-columned home, hidden beneath a drawerful of decades-old finery.

They don't belong in Maryland with me.

So last week, I started avoiding my keepsakes. But slipping off the watch didn't stop the memories I'd just as soon forget.

The late-night call came three weeks ago, on my birthday. "Honey," my mother said gently, "Mom-Mommy's in the hospital again. They think she had a stroke."

I wasn't really shocked. My 88-year-old grandmother had been hospitalized several times for high blood pressure. Tamping down my doubts, I promised to drive the next day to Media, Mom-Mommy's lifelong home.

By the time I pulled onto Interstate 95, my uneasiness had blossomed into a mantra: "Let her be alive when I get there. Let her be alive. Let her be alive."

She was—but not as she was in her previous hospital stay. That time, I found Mom-Mommy sitting up, her soft hair a mess, her face merry as she chuckled with nurses.

This time her eyes were closed. Her hair, still fresh from being styled just hours before the stroke, lay flat, smoothed away from her face.

But what really shook me was the moisture, pooled in a corner of Mom-Mommy's mouth. If I could find this independent, once-glamorous woman so helpless, the whole world must be askew.

"Has there been any change?" I asked a nurse, dabbing a tissue at Mom-Mommy's face. "Not really," she said kindly, and left.

I sat down. In the dozens of hours alone with Mom-Mommy that followed, between prayers, promises and pleas, I thought.

About how as a teenager more than 70 years ago, Theodosia "Dote" Houston King told a white bus driver during a school visit to segregated Washington, D.C., that no, the only colored girl on the trip was *not* getting off the school bus. Many of her white classmates supported her.

About how she regretted having missed an opportunity to have singing lessons from Marian Anderson, the local Philadelphia diva who went on to do pretty well. How as a high school track star, award-winning insurance saleswoman and beloved pillar of her church and entire community, she defied stereotypes without ever losing her grace.

And I kept thinking about how this woman who never did anything without purpose had had a stroke on my birthday. What, I wondered, could be the gift in that?

Perhaps it was the opportunity of sitting within whispering distance as she healed. Maybe it was learning that even wiping up spit could feel like a blessing. Or was it being able to tell her, over and over, how much I loved her?

Because despite my fear of losing her, I'd never given myself over so completely to love.

I had been offered, as they say in the working world, a window. A sliver of time between taking-for-granted and loss, a moment when an affection I'd thought pure was distilled into an unimaginable clarity.

Before the vigil in Room 410, I never realized how dangerous love seemed, how tautly I'd constricted its expression. I felt that telling *any* adult, even Mom-Mommy, how much you love them might spark something akin to repulsion.

Freed by fear, I told her, "I love you so much—come back. Let us care for you as you've cared for us. Come back—there's so much love here."

The more I talked, the more I read passages marked in her own, worn Bible, the more she responded—stirring, shifting, tightening her grip on my hand.

"Look at how she responds to you," a nurse marveled. "I really think she's going to wake up."

I hoped so, but, I had changed too. At some point, the love had overwhelmed the fear, filling the room. In its midst, I knew Mom-Mommy would be fine.

Six days after the stroke, she died, still holding my hand. Left alone with her by hospital staffers, I stroked Mom-Mommy's hair as her breathing slowed, as the tender throbbing in her neck went still. Whispering goodbye for my mother and my children, for my brothers, my fiancé and for me, I told her—meaning it—that it was all right to go.

And I knew what her gift was to me.

Since April 13, that perfect peace has sometimes ebbed. "Did I love her well enough?" I've asked myself. "If my prayers had been more perfect, would she have stayed?" After the endless visitors and arrangements, after a spirit-filled funeral, I waited until everyone had left her house.

Then, pacing from room to room, I sobbed. What's the use of living and loving, I asked the house, if it just comes to goodbye?

I sounded exactly like my 7-year-old son when he wailed after her death: "It isn't good, it isn't fair and it isn't true....I must not be good, Mommy, because I prayed and she still died."

I remembered the words that had come to me then.

"You are good, but it was time for her to leave," I'd told him. "The only way never to have felt this would have been for us not to have had Mom-Mommy. Not to have had her loving us for so long."

That was more than three weeks ago. As unnatural as it seems, on Sunday—Mother's Day—I'll have Mom-Mommy's stuff here with me. Perhaps I'll refasten her watch on my wrist. Or maybe I'll balk from the flood it could trigger.

Either way, I'll find a room where I can sit alone, remembering her many gifts to me.

# Writers' Workshop

## Talking Points

1) Britt opens this moving column with a startling image: drool on her beloved grandmother's face. It stands in sharp contrast to the delicate and dignified collection of her Mom-Mommy's keepsakes. Why is this juxtaposition so effective?

2) Consider the ethics of presenting her grandmother in her final, vulnerable moments of life. Janet Malcolm in a controversial essay in *The New Yorker* maintained that writers are always betraying their subjects. In "The Journalist and the Murderer" she writes, "Every journalist who is not too stupid or too full of himself to notice what is going on knows that what he does is morally indefensible. He is a kind of confidence man, preying on people's vanity, ignorance or loneliness, gaining their trust and betraying them without remorse."
Was it fair for Britt to describe her grandmother's condition so graphically? Would the piece have been as effective without these details?

3) Notice how Britt summarizes her grandmother's life in just three paragraphs, in a way that captures not only her life but the times in which she lived.

4) Britt's columns are usually constructed around epiphanies, a literary term for a sudden, intuitive insight into the reality and basic meaning of an event. Try to identify the epiphanies in her other columns.

## Assignment Desk

1) Compose a list of mementos you would leave behind.

2) Write several paragraphs about the lesson you learned from an elderly relative.

3) Write a few concise but dramatic paragraphs summarizing a relative or friend's life that places him or her in the historical context of the time in which he or she lived.

4) Write an entire column about a specific emotional episode involving you and another person—a friend, coworker, relative—that taught you an important lesson about life.

# The need: A child's gift of joy, pain

AUGUST 6, 1993

When a mother's bond with her child is new—and her memory of their shared, pre-birth connection of blood, food and fluid is fresh—it's impossible to forget the need.

She's reminded each time she dashes for a bottle or rattle; when she can't get her nursing bra undone fast enough to provide a clamored-for feeding; by wails all day and deep into the night.

But when your kids get bigger, and the world has magically expanded beyond diapers and bottle liners to downstairs dunk contests and friends staying over, you can forget the need.

Almost.

Most recently, I was reminded by the appearance of The Face. My 7-year-old son Darrell's grim, "I-know-you're-the-grown-up-so-I-can't-win-but-I-won't-budge-either" face is unmistakable and has changed little since it first appeared when he was 2.

A month ago, The Face glared at me from the back seat of my fiance's car as we all drove toward National Airport. Suddenly, it spoke.

"I'm not going," The Face said.

"Yes, you are, honey," I replied, firmly, uselessly. "You know you visit your father every year, and that you go swimming and get new shoes and have a great time."

"But I'm not going."

I explained to Darrell how important it is that their dad in St. Louis spend a month with him and his big brother each summer. How the divorce settlement *requires* it. How even moms who love their little boys more than vanilla Häagen-Dazs need short breaks.

How much we'll appreciate each other when we see each other again.

Said The Face: Not going.

The tears began sliding out as we pulled into short-term parking, flowing faster as we made our way toward the TWA departure gates. A stop at a magazine rack stocked with *Jurassic Park* periodicals provided the wisp of a distraction—until a sympathetic female salesclerk cooed, "He doesn't look too happy."

Bursting into tears, Darrell flung his arms around my waist and wailed, "She's *teasing* me!"

A panic grips parents at times like these, a frantic rush of feeling that strangles you, cuts off any effective response. Shock, anger, embarrassment, guilt and the realization of how effectively I had repressed my dread of this moment—strapping my kids onto a plane and having them whisked out of my sight.

In the midst of it all was the sharp, sudden, remembrance of need. Of how important I am— despite all my flaws, lacks and inconsistencies —to this sobbing little boy. For a second, we clung to each other.

Then my other son—the sophisticated 11-year-old Boy About Town who understands that St. Louis means major-league spoiling by grandparents—hissed, "I'm *so* embarrassed....Next year, I'm going to a different airport."

We got Darrell to the waiting area. As I checked the boys in, he stood apart, next to a wall of glass, glaring. Coaxing, pulling, chattering constantly, I got him onto the plane and buckled into his seat. A steward named Eric, God bless him, asked the boys if they'd seen *Jurassic Park* and how they felt about the Chicago Bulls' three-peat.

Once seated, Darrell—still sobbing—made only one attempt to unbuckle his seat belt and leave with me. When I finally made it off the plane—with Eric's reassurances ringing in my ears—I sat stiffly in a waiting room chair for 10 minutes, fully expecting Darrell to emerge, wailing, from the entranceway.

He stayed on.

For 28 days, rooms in my house stayed neat when I cleaned them. I had not a single conversation about whether Shawn Kemp or Tim Hardaway will win this year's NBA dunk contest. I did laundry less than once a week.

Silence became a palpable presence, filling the house. I gulped it in.

And I thought about how scary it is, how awful and cumbersome, being so needed.

Certain close friends depend on me. My fiance has learned to take pleasure in my company, in keeping the beat of our personal dance.

But not one of them needs me like Darrell does. None ever depended on me for breath and sustenance, for their first lessons on the meaning of love. Rather, I stepped into the spaces created years ago by them and their mothers and fathers, and found them welcoming.

Me and my baby—yes, even at 7, that's what he is—are still building our space. So we're wary about leaving it.

Now that he and his brother have just returned home, I'm so hungry for them that my eyes track their movements like spotlights trained on a pair of performers. In less than a month, the edge to my need has been honed so sharp that part of me shrinks from it, terrified it will cut me.

Of course, someday it will.

One of these summers, Darrell will be more like his brother. He'll see St. Louis as a chance for new clothes, privileges and adventures.

Perhaps he'll move quickly onto the plane, mortified by my kisses and my "Be good!" admonishments.

And in the silence he leaves, I'll remember how wonderful it once was, being so needed.

# Writers' Workshop

## Talking Points

1) Some of the best stories hold up a mirror, letting readers find themselves in the newspaper. How does this column fill that role? Discuss the likely audiences for this column.

2) Britt has a unique ability to take small dramas of domestic life and, by exploring their meaning, discover ways to help her readers better understand and cope with the strains of life in the '90s. Consider why the heart-wrenching scene in the airport might resonate with readers of *The Washington Post*?

3) Britt begins with a general observation about the intense bond between mother and child and then shifts to the specific—a close up of her truculent 7-year-old son. Could she have reversed the order? What would be the advantages/ disadvantages?

4) Britt often uses short sentences, some just one-word long. "Almost." "Said The Face: Not Going." Discuss how such brevity affects the pace of a piece of writing.

5) Consider how Britt varies sentence length in the following passage:
   "Once seated, Darrell—still sobbing—made only one attempt to unbuckle his seat belt and leave with me. When I finally made it off the plane—with Eric's reassurances ringing in my ears—I sat stiffly in a waiting room chair for 10 minutes, fully expecting Darrell to emerge, wailing, from the entranceway.
   "He stayed on."
   What effect does Britt create?

6) In the lead, Britt describes a newborn's need for its mother. Notice how, in the final paragraph, she returns to that theme, but now it has been transformed into a reflection on the mutual need between mother and child. How has the month her sons spent away changed Britt? Do you think a reader would be changed by the experience of reading about it?

7) Britt brings parenting to life in this column through her use of details drawn from the day she put her son on the

plane. What is the effect of such specifics as "short-term parking," "vanilla Häagen Dazs," "*Jurassic Park* periodicals," and the "Chicago Bulls three-peat."

8) For the columnist, who generally must write to a preordained space, compression is a vital tool. All newspaper writers can benefit from the craft they practice. Notice the details Britt uses to describe the changes wrought during the month her two sons were visiting their father in another state:

"For 28 days, rooms in my house stayed neat when I cleaned them. I had not a single conversation about whether Shawn Kemp or Tim Hardaway will win this year's NBA dunk contest. I did laundry less than a once a week.

"Silence became a palpable presence, filling the house. I gulped it in."

What do these details communicate about Britt and her children?

9) Study how in these two paragraphs, Britt moves from the concrete—"I did laundry less than once a week"—to the metaphorical—"Silence became a palpable presence. I gulped it in." Compare the effects of the two styles. What are the differences between the two approaches?

## Assignment Desk

1) Recall and write about a traumatic leave-taking in your past.

2) Write a single paragraph that captures the essence of that experience.

3) Study the paragraph that describes the 28 days Britt's sons were away from home. How different might these details be if she were the mother of daughters? If she were describing an elderly parent who lived with her? Rewrite the paragraph as if it were describing those and other domestic arrangements.

4) In just a few paragraphs, describe how someone's presence or absence changes a environment: a coworker on vacation, a roommate. Vary the descriptive styles.

# Learning how to see our love

NOVEMBER 16, 1993

The image, which took up two pages in a recent
*Life* magazine, was as gentle as anything so brutal
could be.

In the photo, Jenson, a 10-year-old in Bogotá,
Colombia, holds a flute to his lips. He would be
staring into the camera, except that he has no eyes.

Even so, few would describe photographer
Alain Keler's photo as graphic. Shadows obscure
the nothingness framed by thick, black lashes; we
can't peer too deeply into what isn't there.

Jenson's mother says that her son was 10
months old and sick with diarrhea when she took
him to a hospital near their village. The next day,
she found the baby's eyes bandaged and bloody.
Later, a doctor at the Bogotá hospital to which she
had rushed Jenson explained, "They've stolen his
eyes."

Even the deepest cynic might have trouble believing that money could inspire someone to remove a baby's eyes from his head. But Amnesty
International has for years received reports of cor-
neas stolen in Argentina and Colombia to be sold
to the wealthy. Most reports can't be proved because the witnesses are dead.

But Jenson is alive, and playing a flute in a
charitable institution.

Recently, I stumbled upon the boy's photograph. I had first heard about it weeks ago on the
plane bound for my honeymoon in Greece. Looking at the spaces where Jenson's eyes should be,
and at the surpassing peacefulness of the boy's
face, I thought again, "Some things are too terrible to be believed."

Then I added, "And some things are too
wonderful."

It's odd that such horror could remind me of
beauty, and of the suspicion with which we regard
it. But anyone searching for balance must face the

fact that most people question the good in the
world far more vociferously than they question
the awful. Which do you find easier to believe: the
nasty criticism or glowing compliment?

And while we embrace love when it comes in
measured doses, or when its flow is tripped by the
unthreatening—a beautiful child or ballad, the
feel-good movie—most of us are frightened by
our tenderness. We fear other people's unfettered
love as much as any ugliness spawned by greed or
hate.

Recently, a columnist pal who's known for
his bite wrote a piece suggesting that only love,
not more bullets or police, can solve inner-city
problems.

Discussing it at lunch, the columnist seemed
uneasy. When a passing friend teased that the column showed his "softness," the writer almost
squirmed.

"See, they never say those things when I write
the hard stuff," he said. "We make love seem like
foolishness."

I don't know why seeing Jenson's photo again
stirred up all of this. When my husband first tried
to show me the boy's picture two days after our
wedding, I refused to look. "Not now," I said,
turning away. "It would just make me sad."

It was more than a week later that I felt able to
contemplate, in Jenson's mutilated face, the spiritual void in whoever had blinded him.

I saved the magazine.

Maybe I hoped the photo's awfulness would
help me to appreciate the love that I'm sometimes
tempted to disregard, or to escape. Maybe I kept it
to help me recall how much easier it is to criticize
or blame than to commit, as Jenson apparently
has, to creating beauty no matter what.

But mostly, I saved it to remind me of my honeymoon. And of how you can be as weirded out
by the good stuff as the bad.

It's tough to explain how disorienting it was,
being steeped in so much affection. Not just from
my new husband—that much I'd expected—but
from absolute strangers. Seemingly everyone we

met touring the Greek Isles in late September had just been married, or was acting like it.

Giddy from our weddings and freed from the boundaries imposed by caution, custom and skin color in the United States, couples from New York, Los Angeles, Atlanta and other cities converged in Greece—to dine and explore together, borrow from and confide in each other.

At home, we might never have spoken.

There was the stylish, cigarette-wielding couple I'd dismissed as pretentious, who during lunch and an impromptu island tour revealed great wit and warmth. A couple of seeming squares from San Diego were independent thinkers who'd been engaged 14 years—because *she* was reluctant.

The chilly looking pair seated near us at a restaurant were hilarious psychologists impassioned about their work with troubled families.

Time and again, people surprised me—the Greek pair whose open-air wedding invited tourists to share in their joy; strangers at ruins who smilingly offered to snap our pictures.

And I began to understand, more clearly than ever before, that I had been missing out. I knew that despite all of my assumptions, all of the stories as horrendous as Jenson's, there is more love in the world than I had dreamed. Love that might have been available to me if I'd been open to it.

And I realized what truly was tragic: that with a perfectly good set of eyes, I could still have been so blind.

# Writers' Workshop

## Talking Points

1) From the opening paragraphs that describe the gentle qualities of a brutal image, this column is built on a series of ironies. Find the others.

2) This column is organized around a single disturbing image and an eye-opening experience. How does Britt meld these disparate elements?

3) In paragraph 18, Britt uses the uncommon colloquialism "weirded out" to convey her reaction. What synonyms could have expressed the same thought? Why do you think she used this expression? What, if anything, does this word choice imply about her view of her audience?

4) Identify the thematic elements that Britt uses to stitch the narrative together.

5) Transitions allow writers to move from point to point, to move the narrative in time or from place to place. Consider how Britt moves from discussion of the blinded child's photo to her own honeymoon.

6) "Know thyself or seek to know thyself," Charlotte Di-Gregorio advises would-be columnists in *You Can Be a Columnist: Writing and Selling Your Way to Prestige.* Columnists must mine the everyday world and their responses to it for nuggets they can collect to pay the deadline piper. Notice how Britt selects from her own life and then skillfully draws lessons from them.

7) In *Writing for Your Readers,* Don Murray says "clichés of language are significant misdemeanors, but clichés of vision are felonies...In journalism we too often leave the city room knowing what we'll find, and then, of course, we find it. The cliché is compounded by editors who tell reporters what to find and give them a hard time when they don't fill in the blanks of the editor's stereotype." Examine how Britt's initial stereotypical impressions of her fellow honeymooners were dispelled and how that contributes to her central theme.

8) Britt waits until her final paragraph to deliver her epiphany: "And I realized what truly was tragic: that with a perfectly good set of eyes, I could still have been so blind." Could that moment of self-discovery come earlier? Is it an effective ending?

## Assignment Desk

1) The inspiration for this column comes from a photograph. Look through a magazine or photographic anthology (the *Day in the Life* series offers a bounty of arresting images) until you find one that strikes a deep emotional chord. Write a column exploring those feelings and relate it to the photograph.

2) Have you ever met anyone you couldn't stand at first but who later became a great friend, spouse, coworker? Write, in as specific detail as possible, about the factors that changed your opinion.

3) Write about an experience that challenged assumptions you held. Convey the sense of discovery. Relate it to some larger issue.

4) Britt uses the sense of sight to explore her own blindness. There's a valuable lesson for all writers: Question all assumptions. Could you write a similar column exploring the way people hear but don't listen?

5) Don Murray lists some stereotypes of vision: the victim is always innocent; it's lonely at the top; it's boring in the suburbs; bureaucrats are lazy. Come up with a list of your own. Write a story that dispels one of these clichés of vision.

# A one-word assault on women

NOVEMBER 30, 1993

A few years ago, I saw a black teenage girl with a delicate necklace clasped around her throat. I've forgotten her features but remember what sparkled in rhinestones around her neck:

"BITCH BITCH BITCH."

My immediate reaction was to weigh how offensive it would be to approach this child with one obvious question:

"Why are you wearing that?"

I never asked. But the necklace proved something I'd doubted: There really are women who want to be identified as female dogs by all who encounter them—which is good news for the rappers, rockers and regular guys who call all women by the epithet.

Frankly, some women refer to each other that way. On a recent *60 Minutes,* a female lawyer mouthed the word to describe a female judge she disliked.

Still, most women hate being called that. One widely publicized proof: the reaction of female journalists last summer to rapper Bushwick Bill's defense of his use of the B-word at a national African American journalists' convention.

Maybe you read about it. One of several hip-hoppers on a music panel, Bill—a dwarf who supposedly lost his eye in a gunfight with a girl-friend—was asked by a woman why he and other rappers routinely call women "bitches" and "ho's" (whores) in their music.

Not all women qualify, Bill said. He'd never describe his mother that way, he continued, because he isn't having sex with her. But, he told the woman, "if I was [having sex with] you, you'd be a ho."

Hmmmmmmmmm.

I see why dozens of incensed women stalked out, why several columnists deplored Bill's comments. Yet months later—in the midst of a national debate over the violent words and images characteristic of a small segment of rap music known as "gangsta" rap—the whole thing still makes me sad. Why? Because it makes too much sense.

It makes sense that a less-than-handsome young man who lost half his sight tussling with a woman—and who now, if he's like other rich male celebrities, combs groupies out of his hair—would be contemptuous of *all* women.

It's also undeniable that almost every name-calling rap or rock video is decorated with the bodies of hip-grinding young women. Even the faintest promise of fame remains as much an incentive for girls to strip for the camera as it was 40 years ago, when young starlet Marilyn Monroe posed nude.

Years later, Monroe said she posed only for the money, because "I was hungry."

But what is it that the name-calling male performers are hungering for? While contempt for women isn't new, entertainers' constant, public use of "bitch," aired on radio and TV, is.

Perhaps it's a genuine expression of increased male resentment, or of certain singers' willingness to disrespect women in hopes of stirring controversy—and increasing record sales.

Are young performers reflecting a harsh world's reality? Or is real life—as in innocent kids parroting epithet-laden songs—reflecting the performers' influence?

Some rappers say they're just being honest. They say nice women—those who are neither sluts nor skeezers (women who use men for money)—should take no offense to names that don't apply to them. They're just dissing the women who deserve it.

Cool. So that means these same brothers would make allowances for a white politician who was revealed to routinely call black folks "niggers" if he only explained, "I use that term only in reference to black people who kill others, you know, criminals. The rest of you—take no offense."

The worst thing about the B-word—and the N-word and every denigrating term—is what it assumes. It assumes that everybody—all women, all black men, all members of any group—are alike. The brother who disses all women because of the actions of some is as unenlightened as the racist who denies all black people's humanity because some blacks act inhumanely.

But I keep going back to Bill—who later apologized to the group for "being myself."

It's no accident that the most negative feelings the rapper revealed weren't directed at women, but at *himself.* Only a man with a twisted self-concept would assume that any woman who'd have sex with him should require payment.

But maybe, like so much else, it all boils down to money. The fellas who make millions singing their contempt for women—and who at the same time pride themselves for slamming racism in their music—are actually in the business of selling racism's most destructive lies. Singers who wave their Glocks, grab their crotches and dis their women—while thousands of us pay to watch and listen—do more than make themselves and record producers rich.

Too often they tell the world—and the young whites who reportedly are gangsta rap's biggest consumers—what morgues overflowing with the bodies of black men suggest: how deeply some African Americans have internalized the racism they deplore.

The messages many are selling to—and about—blacks:

You don't deserve to live. Your women are sluts and animals. You kill without remorse, and copulate without love or responsibility.

Sure that's all a lie. But slap a beat on it, apply a coat of glamour and someone, somewhere will dance to it.

Or clasp it in rhinestones around her neck.

# Writers' Workshop

## Talking Points

1) Britt skillfully engages her readers in a direct but casual conversation. Notice how she introduces background on derogatory comments about women made during an infamous appearance at a National Association of Black Journalists convention by rapper Bushwick Bill: "Maybe you read about it." Discuss how rules of style differ for columnists. How does Britt's approach differ from the way such information would be introduced in a news story? What effects, positive or negative, are created when a newspaper writer addresses the reader as "you"?

2) Consider Britt's description of rapper Bushwick Bill in that same paragraph: "a dwarf who supposedly lost his eye in a gunfight with a girlfriend." Her use of "supposedly" suggests skepticism. Is she trying to flag the reader to be wary?

3) The *Los Angeles Times* drew a torrent of mostly skeptical attention in 1993 when it started revising its 14-year-old style book and drew up a long list of words and terms it would prefer not to see in its pages. On the list: birth defect (use "congenital disability"); "welsh," as on a bet; and "inner city," "barrio," and "ghetto." A staff memo said the effort did not reflect a desire to be "politically correct. It is important for us to communicate with our readers fairly and accurately." Dwarfism refers to a specific medical condition. In this context, discuss the relevance of Britt's use of the word "dwarf." Is it necessary to describe his stature at all?

4) The 10th paragraph consists of one long "Hmmmm-mmmm." What's the effect of this one-word paragraph? Does it work? Is it necessary?

5) "Less than handsome." Britt appears to bend over backwards to be sensitive. Why not just come out and say "plug ugly." Is her sensitivity warranted?

6) Consider how Britt uses a series of questions to marshal her attack on "gangsta" rap.

"But what is it that the name-calling male performers are hungering for?

"Are young performers reflecting a harsh world's reality?

Or is real life—as in innocent kids parroting epithet-laden songs—reflecting the performers' influence?"

Rhetorical questions such as these invite the reader to ponder the issue. Is it an effective approach?

7) Britt effectively demolishes the rapper's defense of their anti-women lyrics. Could her column appear as an editorial? What changes would have to be made to tailor it to that forum? What is the difference between a column and an editorial?

8) In paragraph 23, Britt describes "Singers who wave their Glocks, grab their crotches and dis their women..." What's a "Glock" and why do you think Britt assumed the readers familiarity with it? What do you think of that decision? Is it possible she was indulging in a little wordplay?

9) In that same paragraph, Britt uses the youth slang expression, "dis." *The Oxford Dictionary of New Words,* 1991 edition, defines the word (also spelled "diss") as a verb that means "to show disrespect for a person by insulting language or dismissive behavior." While the concept of "dissing" has moved beyond its origins in American Black English through its use in rap music, it is still predominantly a slang expression favored by young people. Does the writer who employs slang run the risk of losing readers unfamiliar with it? Why is Britt's use of the word so integral to the topic and theme of this column?

## Assignment Desk

1) Do a thorough analysis of the lyrics to several gangsta rap songs. Examine their attitudes towards women, whites, racial discrimination, violence against blacks, the police.

2) Interview men and women about women who appear in sexually graphic music videos. How do they feel about treatment of women? Why do the women do it? Write a column based on their attitudes. Incorporate your own attitude.

3) Write a column that, like Britt, strikes at the heart of exploitative or abusive behavior.

4) Using Britt's final six paragraphs as your model, write a pointed criticism of such attitudes.

# It's time to play the blame game

DECEMBER 31, 1993

*Click!*

"Good morning! Don't touch that remote because it's time to play 'Who's to Blame?' the zany new quiz show that's got America talking—and blaming!

"My name is Jay-Jay Smythe—guess I'll blame Mom for that! For the next half-hour, I'll be your host on a whirlwind ride through the wacky world of blame!

"Contestants have one objective: to avoid taking responsibility for anything that's ever happened to them! Our judges and a studio audience decide which players are best at shifting blame from themselves to, well, *anyone else!*

"No wonder it's America's favorite game!

"Players on each show are screened to make sure their problems are similar—that way, judges can better determine who's most creative at avoiding blame. Today's contestants are all underemployed, overweight and here to help us learn—whooooo's to blame! Let's meet them!

"First up is Mortymer Z. Eckther III, an Omaha fry cook whose goal of becoming a CEO at a Fortune 500 company seems mysteriously stalled! Hi, Mort. What's your beef?"

"Well, Jay, through no fault of my own, I'm a white guy! And I'm sick of being blamed for every damn thing that comes down the pike!"

"Me too! So, whooooo's to blame?"

"Women! And blacks, Hispanics, Indians—oops, Native Americans—though it's not *my* fault Christopher Columbus made a wrong turn! There was a time when just being a white guy meant something. But nowadays, every third corporation actually has a woman or Latino or black person—all with doubtful qualifications—in management! I mean, I have my GED!"

"But Mort, white men *everywhere* feel put upon! Where's your creativity?"

"Know who I *really* blame? Other white men!"

"Now that *is* different!"

"Maybe our forebears should never have taken blacks out of Africa, or even have left Europe—a clean, safe place where nobody ever heard of diversity! Was religious freedom worth having to put up with Al Sharpton? With rap 'music'? And whoever first published Betty Friedan—I say break his legs!"

"You've gotten us off to a flying start, Mort! Our judges score: a hefty 95 out of a possible 100 points! Great blaming!

"Our next contestant: ex-forklift operator Samuel Hosstenson from Youngstown, Ohio. Hi, Sam! So how did a gorgeous redheaded lady like yourself end up with a name like Samuel?"

"Excuse me, Jay, but I need a moment to recover from the trauma caused by your demeaning 'compliment.' If you must know, I legally changed Samantha to Samuel when I realized braying, sexist mules like you would never seriously consider my résumé with a feminine name on it! You should have seen the mill foreman's face when I sauntered in for the forklift interview!"

"And you got the job! Which testosterone-addled coworker made you lose it?"

"It was a *woman,* for Goddess's sake! The mill medical tech! The bit-—I mean, my sister in estrogen—refused to let me sign up as a company sperm donor! A woman can do *any* job as well as a man! I wasn't even allowed to try. I had to quit!"

"Sure you did—this is supposed to be America! Our judges have your score and—yes, another big 95!

"On to our last contestant: Shaka Willie Jamalla-Johnson, Yale Ph.D. and freelance incense salesman based in Chicago. How's it going, dude?"

"I beg your pardon, white devil."

"How's it going, Dr. Jamalla-Johnson, *Sir!*"

"Better. First off, Jay, I have noticed—as have millions of your astute African American viewers—that typically, the *brother* came last in your racist game show lineup, after the white man and his woman!"

"And I thought it was an alphabetical thing! I see you've had trouble marketing your new product, sir. Whooooooooo's to blame?"

"Who *else* could be to blame for my not being able to market a perfectly good mango-flavored melanin supplement?"

"The white man?"

"No—the black woman! Do you realize how rare true African queens are? How few 'sisters' are willing to ditch their jobs slaving for the white system to help a brother-entrepreneur brew a much-craved melanin potion? A potion that you, as an ice-person, sorely need?"

"Who knew? Sir, our judges have awarded you a whopping 95 points! You're *all* world-class blamers!"

"As you know, a tie is broken by a randomly selected studio audience member! Today that's Marcus S. Taylor, age 12. Young man, it's all up to you—whooooo's to win?"

"My feeling, Mr. Smythe, is that while your contestants may represent groups with real gripes, these three people are to blame for their own problems. So they complain, while people like them—but with real concerns—get ignored. All of this blaming just tears us further apart!"

"My, Marcus, aren't *we* the sanctimonious little snot! If we bought that, we wouldn't have a top-rated show! Without people blaming each other for everything, where would America be today? Where's your patriotism?

"Our judges agree—we'll ignore this twerp and award grand prizes to all our fine contestants! Congrats!

"That's it for today, folks! Join us tomorrow for the next 'Who's to Blame?' Meanwhile, remember our motto: The buck stops *anywhere* but here!"

*Click!*

# Writers' Workshop

## Talking Points

1) Britt parodies the patter of a game show format to convey her message about affirmative action, diversity, and discrimination. Parody is designed to ridicule in nonsensical fashion or to criticize by clever duplication, according to the *Concise Dictionary of Literary Terms*. What other forms of popular culture could a writer use as models for parody?

2) Britt is an equal opportunity basher: her targets include blacks, whites, feminists. Notice how her points are barbed, yet funny, as in this line from paragraph 10: "I mean, I have my GED!" What's behind this joke?

3) The first and last lines in this column are identical: *"Click!"* What effect is Britt striving for? Is it necessary?

4) Columnists enjoy more freedom than other writers on most newspapers. Discuss whether a news story could be written as a parody.

5) Discuss the point Britt is trying to make. In what other ways could she have made her argument?

6) Britt's attitudes come into sharp focus at the end of the column when she introduces Marcus S. Taylor, age 12.
   " 'My feeling, Mr. Smythe, is that while your contestants may represent groups with real gripes, these three people are to blame for their own problems. So they complain, while people like them—but with real concerns—get ignored. All of this blaming just tears us further apart.' "
   Consider why Britt uses the game show parody to make her points? How effective would her column have been if she adhered to the traditional column format and style?

## Assignment Desk

1) Taking "It's Time to Play the Blame Game" as your model, write a column on a controversial topic using the game show format.

2) Write a column on the same topic, or one of your own choosing, and parody another pop culture format: Infomer-

cial, Sunday news talk show, Dave Letterman's Top Ten List.

3) Write a focus paragraph—"nut graph" in newsroom jargon—that summarizes what you think about the issues of diversity and discrimination in our society.

4) Rewrite Britt's column and, this time, play it straight; no parody, just a clear, compelling expression of the views found in her piece.

# Donna Britt: Alchemist
# Transforming the ordinary

**CHRISTOPHER SCANLAN: In an interview with your paper after the ASNE awards were announced, you said that when you were growing up the possibility of column writing seemed so far out of reach it was not a concrete goal. Why was that?**

DONNA BRITT: It's funny how much what you want is shaped by what you see, and what you can conceive as being possible for you. When I was growing up in Gary, Indiana, in the '60s and '70s, newspapers described lives that had no discernible connection to my own. I didn't see columnizing as a concrete goal, because I didn't know that was something I could do. And because the newspaper felt like such a foreign entity, I didn't identify with it. So to be in the newspaper talking about my concerns, and my life, and how I envisioned things, was out of the realm of possibility.

**What was it about the paper that made it seem so foreign?**

The sections that I was most interested in —the women's pages, the comics, then on to news and sports—had almost no black people in them. The only time I ever saw anything about us was on crime pages or maybe in politics, because at that point, black people were becoming very powerful politically in Gary. But there was no reflection of our real, everyday lives. It was almost as if real life happened to white people, but problems happened to black people and Hispanic people and Asian people. One of the things that so impressed me about *USA*

■ Donna Britt, columnist, *The Washington Post.*

■ **Born:** April 7, 1954, in Gary, Indiana.

■ **Education:** Hampton University, B.A. in Mass Media Arts, 1976; University of Michigan, master's degree in journalism, 1979.

■ **News Experience:** *Detroit Free Press,* 1979–86; *USA Today,* 1986–88; *The Washington Post,* 1989 to present.

■ **Awards:** American Association of Sunday and Feature Editors award for commentary, 1991.

*Today,* my former employer, was that it made a concerted and conscious effort to be inclusive. If they ran a story about a toy fair, there was a good chance there was going to be a black kid interviewed. Or if there was a story about something that had no color, like TV show preferences, they were just as likely to show an Asian or a black person.

**How do you describe what you do?**

I'm a columnist at *The Washington Post,* but it's a column unlike any that you've probably read. It veers in all kinds of strange and unpredictable directions, and it's very reflective of my life and of me. I use my life and my kids and my husband and my friendships, my fears and likes and wants as being representative of those of many, many people.

**Your column in today's *Post* is about black hairdos. In a column like that one, are you conscious of redressing an imbalance in coverage about the ordinary lives of black people?**

I guess what I do is humanize black people. And I get lots and lots of letters from black people who appreciate seeing their plain, ordinary, everyday lives explored in much the way that white people's lives have been explored forever.

**What are the wellsprings of your columns?**

At some point along the way, I decided that the things that vitally interest me must vitally interest other people. Because I used to read the paper and not see anybody talking about the stuff that my friends were talking about, or that I was obsessing about. I guess it wasn't really until I got to the *Post* that I decided, "Well, I'd better start saying these things."

I will write about stuff that nobody writes about, and I don't think it's because I have any great vision, it's just those are the things that are the most interesting to me.

Maybe there really are people who care more about NAFTA than how their husband is looking at them on a certain day, or that their kid is turning 12. I'm just not one of those people. I'm much more interested in the human connections. And so I write about those things. And I'm one of the only columnists that I know about who will write regularly and frankly about God, because I was always sort of stunned that people can talk much more openly about their sex lives than about their spiritual lives. Lots of columns come from life. Not necessarily my life, but they come from feeling.

**Why focus so much on feeling?**

Feeling is at the basis of everything. When I was asked to consider becoming a full-time columnist, part of my hesitation was that I knew I could not pretend to be this dispassionate, all-knowing, authoritarian voice on high. I couldn't do that. That would be a lie.

And it is a lie, even for the people who adopt that voice—and we know who they are. Their name is Legion. For me, it's like *The Godfather.* Everything is personal.

**How do you report your column?**

It depends. I have a column coming up on a piece that ran in the paper that talked about black kids' self-esteem. This guy wrote it based on discussions he had in his classroom. I interviewed a kid that was in the class. I interviewed teachers who taught with him. I interviewed him. So a column like that is going to be very much like any column in which you do the leg work.

If I did a column on beauty, and women feeling entrapped by the whole notion of that, I would probably talk to women I know, because it doesn't matter. You know, I don't have to call Naomi Wolfe, who wrote *The Beauty Trap.*

It's more interesting to stop some woman at my kid's day care, or someone at a mall, and just have them talk about their feelings than to go to, quote, *experts*. And then there are columns on which I'm relying on me. Those are the ones where you're interviewing yourself. And I am trying to be as frank and as candid and as open as I can be. And it's a pretty scary act.

**Your columns are rich in detail and they're clearly the product of great reflection and deep investigation of your feelings. Do you carry a notebook?**

I need to do it all the time, but I don't. When I see something that I want to remember, I will repeat it to myself. My husband was trying to get me to do something the other day and he said, "Oh, come on, honey." And my 8-year-old looked at me and said, "You know, honey is 'please' in love language." And I said, I must remember that. In Gabriel Garcia Marquez's book, *One Hundred Years of Solitude,* he said that things were so new that they had not yet been given names. As a writer, part of the adventure is trying to see things as new, with that sort of childlike vision.

**If you had to pick a metaphor that expressed your view of yourself, what metaphor would you use?**

Alchemist. Because I try to take the small, the overlooked, the ordinary—be that an emotion, a person, an idea—and transform it.

**What is the alchemist's role?**

I guess I picked that because I'm just fascinated by the notion of transformation. Alchemists take a certain type of matter and transform it into something else. And you couldn't do that if the properties weren't already there.

Otherwise, you are a magician. So my hope is to let people see, through my craft, what's already there that they may not have noticed.

**You were saying before that it's difficult to talk about how you produce your column. Why is that?**

Because there doesn't seem to be any rhyme or reason to it. Sometimes it's like having a child. You know, you have all these assumptions. It's going to be this or that. And it comes out and it's your Uncle Harold. I don't know what it's like for other people, but I almost never write a column that turns out exactly the way I would have predicted.

**Well, what if a camera were trained on you while you're writing your column? What would it show?**

It would show me writing really fast, getting stuff down, and stopping and looking at it, and thinking, Can I say this better? Can I be more direct? Can I make this tighter? Can I clarify this point? Is this insensitive? Is this funny? What can I do to make it jump off the page? What's going to make somebody go with it to the end? You know, ride with me the whole way.

So it's lots of activity and then lots of silence in which I question everything. I will call the desk at midnight to change a word. It's crazy. Maybe you have to be nuts.

**Why do you work so hard at it?**

I really want it to be wonderful, so I work really hard at the craft of it. I work not to do the obvious, or to choose the easy word. I work to look at things the way my kids look at things, and to see things with a fresh eye, so that I can make people feel the image. Making yourself do that twice a week is no small task.

Writing is the constant challenge of making people see. It's the details. And what I hate about it is that I feel like I don't do it as well as I would like to. Sometimes there's just not enough time. Sometimes I'm too distracted. Sometimes the words don't come as fluidly as I would like them to come.

Most of the time sitting down to that challenge is not fun, because there's a big possibility that you're not going to live up to your own ideal.

**What constitutes a lead in a Donna Britt column? Is it the first paragraph? Is it the first several paragraphs?**

It's the first several paragraphs. At the very least, it's three paragraphs. It's usually three-quarters of a screen on my laptop, if you wanted to be that specific.

It's always hard to figure out where to start. You never know what you're going to land on. You never know if it's going to work. You know how you'll just say, "Oh, well, I'll just start out this way"? That always ends up being your lead. It always ends up being what you go with.

**In your column, "A Life of Grace and Strength Offers One Last Precious Gift," you open with the startling image of the drool pooled on your grandmother's face. Why?**

When I walked in that room, the thing that was most wrong was that this very stylish and manicured and consciously lovely woman had drool in the corner of her mouth. How could this be? So to take an ugly image and to bring people around to the beauty in it, as I was brought around to the beauty in it, seemed like something worth trying.

**Did you set a goal for yourself when you decided to write that?**

My goal for that piece was to write something that would help me remember the amazing thing that happened in that room. I never wanted to forget, and I knew if I didn't write it for the column, it would never get written. So that one was for me. But I think we live in a culture that doesn't want to acknowledge the lasting import of a death.

**In your column about Mom-Mommy and many
of your other columns, you display a special gift
for capturing the universal in the specific.**

It's never about Mom-Mommy. It's about all our
grandmothers who meant so much in ways they
could not possibly know.

**Your column is so personal, intimate even. Do
you ever worry, "Who cares about another column starring my kids?"**

That's why it has to be good. I try not to use them
unless I really have something to say.

And there really are people who aren't going to
appreciate it, and who are going to feel like it's a
"me, me, me," kind of thing—and certainly, in a
way, it is.

But I feel like there's always a point. When I
talk about my engagement ring and my wedding,
I'm validating the romance that lives in every
woman that I know. And I get calls from them
saying, "You give me hope," or "I'm so glad that
you wrote that." Or when I write about my little
macho 7-year-old throwing a fit because he's getting on a plane to go visit his father, if I do that
column right, everybody who's a mother will feel
it. And I think all that small stuff needs to be explored and celebrated. I really do.

It's the most pointedly beautiful part of life, the
everyday wonderful stuff, that we notice. And
that stuff has to be validated. So much ugliness is
validated.

**Do newspapers need more personal writing
like yours?**

Certainly the popularity of my column would suggest that. I think newspapers are much better at
giving people the real now than they were when I
was coming up. They're much more likely to deal
with close-to-the-bone issues. I still think we have
a long way to go when it comes to honesty, and
acceptance of other people's honesty. Your hope is

that people will appreciate what they see. And that doesn't always happen. A lot of people don't want to do that and I understand that. But if you want to connect to people, it takes risk.

**How did you get into journalism?**

Because I could write.

**What was your first writing?**

The first story I remember was called "White Milk, Chocolate Milk," and it was about discrimination among dairy products. And that's the truth. I think I was in the third grade. Civil rights was very much in the forefront of what was happening on television and in *Life* magazine. I was actually seeing people who looked like me, and it was pretty disturbing that they were getting hoses turned on them, and dogs sicced on them. And this piece was sort of about the madness of that. I don't remember the details. I just remember there were these two bottles of milk. And back then, people would bring you your milk and, you know, put it on your stoop. And I guess the white milk didn't think he should be subjected to being next to the chocolate milk. That's all I remember. But I always remember being told that I could write.

**Who told you?**

Teachers. I was never without a book. I just loved to read and hear other people's stories. And so many of the books that I read were books that my mother had read. I had these old lovely, beautifully bound copies of Louisa May Alcott books, and things like *The Little Princess,* and very romantic, fanciful, moral books—the books that my mother had read when she was a little girl. And getting into pulpy novels and all. I must have read *Gone With the Wind* 14 times.

**Teachers were important to your development as a writer. What role does your editor play now that you're a professional?**

She's not like me, so I like that. She's basically not as emotional. And she's white. Having someone who does have some differences in those surface kind of ways is good, because I want everyone to understand it.

Then my copy editor is a black woman whose background doesn't seem to have been all that different from mine, and that's good, because any column I write, I'm going to have a huge readership of white people and a huge readership of black people. And having the two people who first respond to it be representative of smart and caring people of both those groups is ideal for me. I trust their vision.

**How much of an impact do they have?**

Marcia Davis, my copy editor, is very specific. "Well, maybe if we moved this word here, that will be a bit smoother." Or, "I didn't quite understand what you meant here." I try to write conversationally, so I will break grammatical rules, and sometimes she'll challenge that, but lots of times she'll just let it go. She knows it's how I am. With Jo-Ann Armao, my editor, it's more of a visceral thing. Trying to hear how much she likes it and to get her to talk about what she does or doesn't like about it, or what's missing. So it's more specific with Marcia. With Jo-Ann, it's more the big picture.

**I knew a columnist once and everything to him was a column. Conversations were studded with moments where his eyebrow would lift and you'd realize he was thinking, "This could be a column." Is that a columnist's natural reflex?**

Oh, yeah, because it's always there. George Bernard Shaw described it as living underneath a windmill, and every time you put your head up, you know, your head gets smacked.

**I'm told that a regular topic at the National Association of Black Journalists Convention is**

**the complaint, "I can't tell my story." You've overcome whatever obstacle it is that is keeping other people from telling their stories. Can black journalists not tell their stories and why not?**

Most people get their ideas from editors. Editors usually draw on their own experience and what's already been done when they give assignments. In a mostly white press, most editors are going to conceive of and assign stories that they know about. Our stories are often stories that a white person may not even know about. So it becomes a black journalist's special sort of duty to introduce his editors to areas that he or she may not know exist. And some people aren't comfortable with that. I mean there are reporters who like to get assignments, good assignments, and just do the work.

In telling your story, you have to introduce the idea of the story and convince an editor, who may not have any sense of it and no visceral sort of connection to it, that it's valid, which isn't always an easy thing. And if you do that once, twice, a dozen times, and there's very little interest or follow up, it can be really frustrating.

At the same time, I know of black reporters who have told themselves, "I can't do my story and I won't even try." So they won't even introduce the idea of a story.

Or sometimes you can suggest a story, and it will get twisted into something completely different because of the very different sort of vision that your editors might have.

I think it's a valid complaint. I think that it's one you have to push against a lot, and some people are uncomfortable pushing.

**Do newspapers need a chorus of different voices?**

They really do. And they don't even know how much they do.

It was always short-sighted and a little mean to be limited in your voices. Now, it's just plain stupid. Because you need every single subscription you can get.

**You're enormously open about your feelings, your flaws, and yet many reporters find personal writing difficult. Why do you do it?**

And there's not that much respect for it, either. When I first started doing it, I got the sense that people dismissed it and thought it was pure ego, and that it was too easy. But I felt driven to write that way, without really knowing why. I knew that what I wanted to do in the paper, more than anything, was to illuminate different, often unheard, people's humanity, and that I could often use myself, my experiences, my insecurities, my strengths, all that stuff, to let people know about people like me.

**What do you wish you had known when you started out?**

One of the hardest things to learn to do is to trust that your story, your vision, your focus, is valid. And to risk it by putting it out there. I think it's a very scary thing, and the inclination is to let someone else do it, to wait for someone else to say it. What I've learned is that once you do it, once you do step out on faith and explore whatever that is, there are people who will not get it, who will not feel it, who will not see it, who will not understand it. But there will be enough that do all those things that it will be worth the trip. I wish I had known that earlier, to trust that inner voice that said, "This is important. This matters. That's wrong. That should be challenged." I think I let a lot of stuff go by because I didn't trust myself to be the person to challenge it.

**Where do you get your ideas?**

Everywhere. Conversations. Newspaper stories. Crocuses in my front yard.

**How does an image, an idea, translate into a column?**

It's like your mind is this field of daisies, and every daisy is a little bit different. And it's column time, and you sort of walk through the field and you decide which daisy to pick. So there's just this field of daisies, and you saunter through and pick whichever one nods at you.

**When it's column time?**

Twice a week, without fail.

# Betty DeRamus

## Finalist, Commentary

Betty DeRamus was born in Tuscaloosa, Ala., but grew up in Detroit, where she still lives and works. She has been a reporter and editorial writer and is now a columnist for *The Detroit News.* She has received a number of major writing awards, including the Overseas Press Club's 1981 award for a series on African hunger; a first place Best of Gannett award for commentary in 1991; and a second place Best of Gannett award for commentary in 1990. In 1993, she was a finalist for a Pulitzer Prize in commentary.

Robert Giles, her editor and publisher, says, "In a tough city where we sometimes become hardened to the problems of our neighbors, Betty DeRamus writes with a passion and clarity that keeps us focused, that moves us with the daily struggles of life in Detroit." Newspaper columnists are the voices that reveal the humanity behind the news. They deliver the smiles, the tears, the fury, and in the case of Betty DeRamus, the glimmer of hope.

# Amid the violence, some voices cry out against the fury

NOVEMBER 23, 1993

He was riding his bicycle when some kids with chains surrounded him and demanded the bike. Some spark of strength, some streak of stubbornness, made the young man look straight into their eyes and say no.

The boys beat him bloody with their chains and left him stretched out on the sidewalk near a nursing home. He stayed there for an hour before someone carried him away. It took 40 stitches to close up his head.

His sister felt as though she'd been slapped when she saw his battered head and wide, confused eyes. She said she couldn't understand how anyone could walk or drive past him without stopping.

I understood—sort of.

People probably told themselves he was just a derelict or a drunk, sleeping off his high. People probably feared it wasn't safe to step into somebody else's life, to leave their own tight little circles. That doesn't mean there weren't any good people out there that day. It means we sometimes let evil take the day by looking the other way.

The truth is this is a city of sunshine and a city of shadows. A place where the beautiful and the ugly, the caring and the cold, often sit side by side, fighting for our souls.

It's a city where a young armed thug tried to force a middle school student to skip school with him this September. The 14-year-old student stood his ground and refused to follow the other youngster.

The uplifting and the depressing. The shocking and the sweet. You'll see it all if you roam these streets.

I met a man once who was driving a smashed taxicab. He said he was waiting his turn at a self-service gas station when the driver of another car suddenly aimed for him and ran into the side of his cab. He had never seen the man before and believes he mistook him for someone else.

Yet I also met a minister who spent much of his time walking through neighborhoods, trying to talk teen-agers out of selling drugs and ducking bullets. He was so successful he received a death threat from a drug lord who accused him of luring away his best dealers.

This is a city where old men poke in piles of garbage for scraps of hamburger.

It's also a city where Mother Waddles is hoping to receive enough canned goods and turkeys to feed hundreds of the hungry this Thanksgiving.

I still remember the day I walked into a restaurant and had to drop to the floor as shots exploded behind me. Outside the restaurant, a man being arrested had somehow gotten the drop on a policeman, shot the officer and then drove off in his police car.

But just a week later, I saw three men in another restaurant surround a man waving a gun and talk him into putting it away and leaving. When I asked one of the men why he'd risked his life trying to subdue a gunman, he replied: "It beats dying from a stray bullet."

So it does. And all around us, people are struggling to sweep up the bullets, bandage the wounds, mop up blood. They're rebuilding houses, reopening restaurants, organizing street patrols.

The Von Steuben Community Council—along with the Southern Christian Leadership Conference and other community organizations—will hold a march against violence at 10 a.m. Saturday, Dec. 4, beginning at Seven Mile and Gratiot.

Following the march, participants will hold a town hall meeting at the Rosa Parks School, 8030 E. Outer Drive, to discuss ways to stop the killings.

The good people do sometimes raise their voices, blow their horns and pound their drums. That is worth remembering when blood stains our streets, and the storms seem to go on forever.

# Lessons Learned

BY BETTY DERAMUS

The readers who responded to this column about urban violence appreciated the fact that I offered them some hope, some prospects for change, at the end. My readers were relieved that I didn't simply tell them that a boy had been beaten and left to bleed on the sidewalk. I put the incident in perspective; I gave it a backdrop.

The lesson I learned, or re-learned, is that people are tired of columns that merely describe problems. They want something that helps revive their flagging spirits, something that points them toward at least the start of a solution.

# Paul Gigot

## Finalist, Commentary

Paul Gigot is a member of the editorial board and writes the Potomac Watch column for *The Wall Street Journal.* He also appears regularly as part of *MacNeil/Lehrer NewsHour*'s political analysis team.

He joined the *Journal* in 1980 as a reporter in the Chicago bureau, and in 1982 moved to Hong Kong as the roving Asia correspondent. In 1984, he was named the first editorial page editor of *The Asian Wall Street Journal,* contributing editorials and commentary to the U.S. and Asian editions of the *Journal.* In 1986, he took a year's leave of absence to serve as a White House Fellow at the White House and Treasury Department. He was raised in Green Bay, Wis., and is a graduate of Dartmouth College, where he was chairman of the daily student newspaper. He has worked for two magazines, the *Far Eastern Economic Review* in Hong Kong and *National Review.* In 1984, Gigot won an Overseas Press Club award for his reporting on the Philippines.

Every Friday, readers of *The Wall Street Journal* are treated to Paul Gigot's biting wit and incisive commentary from the nation's capital. His style is intelligent but accessible, the arguments sharp and unrelenting as in "John & Bill, Anita & Gennifer, Sex & Standards," a column that skewers liberal politicians and journalists for holding political foes to different moral standards than their friends.

# John & Bill, Anita & Gennifer, Sex & Standards

DECEMBER 31, 1993

*"The committee found examples of indiscreet conduct toward women...which call into question his judgment and his ability to set an appropriate example."*
—Sam Nunn, attacking John Tower, 1989

*"How do you defend something like this? How do you prove something like this didn't happen?"*
—Sen. Nunn, defending Bill Clinton, 1993

The reports of President Clinton's philandering have faded into the holiday mood of forgiveness. But before they're forgotten, something should be said about ethics and double standards. For Sen. Nunn isn't the only one struck by sudden pangs of conscience.

There is Liz Smith, who writes a gossip column but somehow finds the Arkansas trooper charges too gossipy. *The New Yorker's* Sidney Blumenthal, who wasn't above assaulting George Bush's war record, is now appalled by "political" journalism. A rajah from *The New York Times* avers that he doesn't work for a "supermarket tabloid." This is the same *Times* that celebrated Kitty Kelley's insinuations about Nancy Reagan and Frank Sinatra on page one.

The point here isn't merely hypocrisy, however redolent. It concerns what the standard for political ethics has become, and ought to be. The Clintons are hardly the first politicians to have their personal lives publicly vetted. If this is so far beyond the pale now, what are we to make of what happened to John Tower, Chuck Robb, Clarence Thomas, or, in the latest example, Oregon Republican Bob Packwood? Who set this standard, anyway?

In this regard, it's illuminating to compare these past cases with the arguments now being used to disqualify the trooper stories. The standards have suddenly shifted. For example, although the *Los Angeles Times* and *American Spectator* quote two troopers on the record and another two off, their claims are said to lack "corroboration." But this is more on-the-record proof than was ever mustered against John Tower; he was guilty only of "appearances" and "perceptions."

It is said that the troopers have suspect motives, because they are represented by Clinton enemy Cliff Jackson. A fair point, but at least Mr. Jackson is on the record. The Senate staffers who coaxed and leaked Anita Hill into testifying were silent conspirators, known to but unreported by the mainstream media. The troopers are also doubted for wanting to pursue a book contract, but Ms. Hill has just signed to write two books herself. Her celebrity has made her a hit on the lucrative lecture circuit as well as a political hero who was hailed, at an American Bar Association meeting last year, by none other than Hillary Rodham Clinton.

Our born-again moralists also assert that not one woman has come forward. But of course Gennifer Flowers did. As Douglas Frantz of the *Los Angeles Times* said on CNN's *Reliable Sources,* "All four troopers with whom we spoke extensively corroborated Gennifer Flowers' allegations." Ms. Flowers now has more corroboration than Anita Hill ever did.

The president's defenders do have a point that Americans may not care about any of this now, at least not the adultery. But it's notable that the abuse of office alleged by the troopers (state resources for personal use) is what Kay Bailey Hutchison has been indicted for in Texas. And remember how Mr. Packwood was assailed for investigating the backgrounds of his accusers? Clinton operative Betsey Wright has gone further, once again contacting private eye Jack Palladino to deal with what she once called "bimbo eruptions."

Part of the double standard at work here is cultural. The elites in the press and politics will believe a law professor who attended their schools. But they are skeptical of redneck troopers or a cabaret blonde. Liberals also think adultery is less heinous than sexual harassment. To put it another way, if you make a pass and succeed, you get a morality bye. But if you're an oaf and a boor like Bob Packwood, even if you stop when the women resist, you deserve to be driven out of the Senate.

The deepest motive is political, the use of personal ethics as a weapon. Liberals, shut out of the presidency for 25 years (Carter wasn't really theirs), established this standard as a way to attack conservatives who worked for popular presidents. The press, unleashed by Watergate, was a willing collaborator. It's true that a few Democrats have been sacrificed along the way (Gary Hart), but the most frequent victims have been Republicans, especially conservatives. Yet now that one of their own is in the White House, liberals profess to be shocked, shocked that the same standards might apply to them.

If liberals want to put their ethics genie back in the bottle, there are certainly ways they can show a New Year's resolution. They can forgive Bob Packwood his boorishness from an era that had different sexual standards. Then they can dismiss the charges against Sen. Hutchison. *The New Yorker,* which has become the *American Spectator* of the left, can stop harassing Clarence Thomas. Otherwise, all of this high-mindedness about Bill Clinton's private life is so much political spin.

# Lessons Learned

If my mail is any guide, many *Wall Street Journal* readers
don't think I've learned nearly enough. They are probably
right. But one thing I have learned is that a columnist tor-
tured by self-doubt, or afflicted with modesty, will soon
write a boring column. So betraying no doubt and feigning
no modesty, here are other lessons I've absorbed in six years
of punditry.

Name names. A wise writer once told me that a column
without personalities will soon have no personality. This is
especially true of a political column, which becomes mere
policy wonkery without people attached. Politicians have
motives that are typically as interesting, and revealing, as
their arguments over substance. Blend motive with personality and substance and you have a good column. Readers
also like columns that hold politicians accountable by name.
Politicians hate such columns but will still read them.

A corollary to this rule is to pick on people your own
size. A newspaper column is a big cannon best used on big
targets. Spare the small fry or the politically easy target,
however irksome. Making fun of Dan Quayle took no great
wit during the Bush presidency; the columns that defended
him were better reading. Focus on the people with real
power, especially those who receive less scrutiny than their
power warrants. I like to mix it up with politicians who tor-
ment others but use their clout to deter coverage of themselves: John Dingell and Henry Waxman, to name two
undercovered Congressional names.

Look for the hole in the doughnut. My former *Wall Street
Journal* colleague William Blundell has used the phrase to
encourage reporters to look for the counter trend. This is
even better advice for a columnist. If everyone else wants
the president impeached, try playing devil's advocate. If
your views are largely conservative, find a liberal to praise.
This will keep some readers coming back for the element of
surprise.

Keep in mind the persuasive power of facts. Columns
that are all opinion can dazzle for a while but aren't built to
last. Columns built on facts let readers reach their own con-
clusions along with you; readers will appreciate your respect
for their intelligence. Even people who disagree with your
world view may turn to your column if they think they may

garner something they didn't know before—an anecdote, an argument, an array of facts. But even your intellectual allies will abandon you over time if they're just going to get the catechism.

For similar reasons, the stiletto in the ribs pays more than the punch in the jaw. Stylistically, this means that adjectives and adverbs aren't all they are cracked up to be. Verbs and nouns can carry more persuasive clout when harnessed to facts. So can simple declarative sentences or clauses juxtaposed in the right way. It is tempting to declare that so-and-so is a hypocrite, for example. But it works better simply to contrast what so-and-so wrote before with what he is writing now. I also try to avoid using "should" and "ought to." A column can be powerful without hectoring.

Perhaps the best lesson I've learned is that the best columns are the ones I feel most intensely about. Passion shows through prose as much as boredom does. Every columnist worth reading will be wrong sometimes. But a columnist who doesn't risk being wrong probably isn't worth reading.

# Michael Gartner
## Editorial Writing

Two years ago, Michael Gartner occupied an office at Rockefeller Center in the heart of Manhattan. As president of NBC News, he presided over a staff of 1,200 people, including some of the best-known faces on television. Gartner left that job in 1993, the most visible casualty of the controversy over rigged tests in an NBC *Dateline* story on the safety of General Motors pickups. Today, Gartner works at a battered desk facing the slanted tables where the Ames *Daily Tribune* is pasted up six days a week. The son and grandson of Iowa newspapermen, he is co-owner and one-man editorial page of the *Tribune,* a 10,000 circulation daily 38 miles from his hometown of Des Moines. His annual newsroom budget is less than the cost of putting on a single hour of prime time television news. But Gartner insists he is "the luckiest man in America," doing what he likes best, writing editorials in a town he loves. He won the ASNE award, the first given to a past president of the American Society of Newspaper Editors, for editorials written in his first months on the job.

At the *Tribune,* he's also fulfilling an editor's most important role, teaching his small staff of twenty-somethings vital lessons drawn from nearly 40 years in the news business. While he peppers his "kids" with instructive memos, public praise, and private criticism, they probably learn most from watching him working the phones, chasing the facts that are the lifeblood of his editorials.

# Tattoos and freedom

OCTOBER 7, 1993

Let's talk about tattoos.

We haven't seen the arms of Jackson Warren, the food-service worker at Iowa State University, but they do sound repulsive. A swastika on one, KKK on the other.

Ugh.

That's obnoxious.

The administrators at the university think so, too, so in response to a student's complaint they've "temporarily reassigned" Warren to a job where he won't be in contact with the general public.

Ugh.

That's outrageous.

What in the world is Iowa State thinking of? Where are those campus champions of liberty and robust debate? Where are the folks who teach about the founding of this country, about freedoms and rights, about the First Amendment? Hasn't anybody there read the Constitution?

In this country, you tolerate speech you despise.

In this country, you tolerate views you abhor.

In this country, you tolerate opinions you loathe.

That's what you're supposed to learn in college. You're supposed to learn that dissent is part of democracy, that the First Amendment is there to protect the outraged and the outrageous, the abhorred and the abhorrent, the despised and the despicable.

Remember the flag burners in Texas? The Nazi marchers in Skokie? The war protesters everywhere? Protected citizens, one and all. Obnoxious, sometimes. Outrageous, sometimes. Despicable, sometimes.

But never unspeakable.

All were exercising their rights of free speech, our courts ruled. Under the First Amendment, Justice Oliver Wendell Holmes wrote long ago, there is freedom not only "for those who agree with us, but freedom for the thought we hate."

That's what someone should tell Chantel Thibodeaux, an Iowa State graduate student who raised the issue about Jackson Warren's tattoos. "He shouldn't have any contact with students," she said. "I'm all for free speech, but when your speech crosses the line, then that's a problem."

She went on: "People are upset. You have to realize that you have developing students on campus. What message are you giving to them when the first person they see is a man with a KKK tattoo?"

The message you're giving is clear:

This is a school that believes in free speech.

This is a school that protects dissent.

This is a school that cherishes America.

That's what Iowa State officials should be saying.

For Jackson Warren, bedecked in symbols of hate, should himself be a symbol of freedom.

### REPRISE

"If the government is allowed to violate even one right of one person, then no right of any person is safe."

It seems like only yesterday that we were quoting that from a speech Nadine Strossen, the president of the American Civil Liberties Union, gave Tuesday night at Simpson College.

Put that on your refrigerator door, we said.

Maybe someone should buy a refrigerator—or at least a refrigerator door—for the folks at Iowa State.

# Writers' Workshop

## Talking Points

1) *The Wall Street Journal* has described Michael Gartner as "absolutist" on the First Amendment right to free speech. Discuss how this editorial supports that label.

2) You won't find a more concise description of the First Amendment's protection of free expression than that found in this editorial. Isolate Gartner's summary of its tenets. In this case, the editorial writer is functioning as a teacher. Is that the editorial writer's most important role?

3) Consider how Gartner sets up the conflict behind this editorial and his response to it.

"We haven't seen the arms of Jackson Warren, the food-service worker at Iowa State University, but they do sound repulsive. A swastika on one, KKK on the other.

"Ugh.

"That's obnoxious.

"The administrators at the university think so, too, so in response to a student's complaint they've 'temporarily re-assigned' Warren to a job where he won't be in contact with the general public.

"Ugh.

"That's outrageous."

What's the effect of this parallel structure?

4) Notice Gartner's use of one- and two-word sentences. What effect is he striving for? How does the rhythm of these paragraphs compare with most editorials you've read.

5) Gartner frequently uses repetition in his editorials. Watch how he begins three sentences with the same phrase: "In this country...."

Find another example of repetition in this editorial. What's the effect?

6) This editorial opens with an invitation: "Let's talk about tattoos." Gartner's editorials deliberately cultivate the qualities of conversation. Study how Gartner draws the reader into his editorials.

7) This editorial has two endings. Consider why Gartner added the section he calls "Reprise." What is a reprise? Did

Gartner need to add the subhead? For that matter, do you think he needed to repeat the quote that had run on the editorial page just a few days before?

## Assignment Desk

1) Rewrite this editorial by telling the story through the eyes of the student who objected to Jackson Warren's tattoos.

2) Write an editorial using the techniques of repetition and short, punchy sentences to convey your opinions.

3) Collect several news stories on the subject of free expression (Gartner alludes to three other celebrated examples). Write an editorial defending the behavior under attack.

4) With a colleague, role play an interview with Jackson Warren. During one interview, have "Warren" spout off inflammatory racism. In another, let him express regret about his tattoos; he says they are the product of an earlier time in his life that he now rejects, but he can't afford to have them removed. Write an editorial or column based on these two "interviews."

# A subtle message

OCTOBER 19, 1993

Give some money to WOI radio.

We don't often shill for things on these pages, but when we do we're blunt about it and go all out.

Give some money to WOI radio.

WOI-AM and WOI-FM are two great assets of Ames and Mid-Iowa, and they make this a nice place to live if you have a radio, and who doesn't?

Give some money to WOI radio.

They get about $720,000 a year from Iowa State University, about $300,000 from the government in Washington and another $275,000 or so from friends and listeners, but their costs are going up and the money from Iowa State has leveled off, which, things being as they are in this state, shouldn't surprise you.

Give some money to WOI radio.

Last May, they had their first on-air fund raising, and that brought in about $50,000, so now, starting Saturday, they're having another, and they hope to raise $100,000 in a week because they think that they'll be a lot slicker at it the second time around and that you won't be able to resist them.

Give some money to WOI radio.

The stations are terrific sources of news and information and music, with *Morning Edition* and *All Things Considered* and *Weekend Edition* and *Car Talk* and *Whatd'ya Know* and *Fresh Air* and *A Prairie Home Companion* and programs like that and no Rush Limbaugh. And that's just WOI-AM.

Give some money to WOI radio.

And the *Book Club* and the *Music Shop* and *Music Through the Night* and the symphonies and the jazz and the blues and all that other wonderful stuff and, of course, Marian McPartland on Saturday evenings. And that's just WOI-FM, and there's no Rush Limbaugh there, either.

Give some money to WOI radio.

And did we mention Doug Brown yet? There's nobody like him, anywhere, and he's reason alone to support the stations, and if you give enough you can get a tape of him reading a book, which if you listen to it in the car will make your next trip anywhere seven-and-a-half times as enjoyable as it would otherwise be and also will keep the kids quiet but you might miss a turn or two when you get too engrossed. But you won't care.

Give some money to WOI radio.

Including Doug Brown, who they only count as one person, there are only 16 employees at WOI-AM and WOI-FM, which means that nobody is shirking or just sitting around so don't think that the money you give will be squandered, because the guy who runs it, who is a good guy named Rick Lewis, won't let that happen.

Give some money to WOI radio.

We should probably mention, because it might be reassuring to you and might cause you to take this message seriously, that WOI radio has no real connection to WOI television, which does run Rush Limbaugh at night (delaying *Nightline,* for Pete's sake), which makes it all the nicer that WOI-AM now is on at night, too, running, among other things, the BBC news.

Give some money to WOI radio.

And that's our message for today.

You probably thought you could guess the last line of this editorial. But if you didn't get the message by now, one more pitch won't make a difference. So instead of saying give some money to WOI radio, we'll just say:

Thanks for listening.

# Writers' Workshop

## Talking Points

1) This editorial is, in effect, a fund-raising pitch for public radio. Debate the ethics of such boosting, even for a worthy cause. How would you react if the editorial were encouraging readers to tune into a commercial radio station?

2) Count how many times Gartner repeats the phrase, "Give some money to WOI radio." What is this device mimicking? Is it effective or does he run the risk of turning off his readers? How do writers know when enough is enough?

3) Clearly, Gartner is having fun here. Richard Aregood of the *Philadelphia Daily News* and three-time ASNE editorial writing award winner, says that "a function of any page in a newspaper is entertainment and that includes the editorial page." Do you agree? What do you think is the function of the editorial page? Does it have more than one role?

4) In this editorial, Gartner gets in several digs at arch-conservative TV-radio talk show host Rush Limbaugh. What signal does that give about Gartner's political leanings? Study all his editorials and decide how you would describe his political philosophy. What do you base that on?

5) The headline for this editorial—"A Subtle Message"— is an object lesson in irony. Why?

6) Gartner's editorials are noteworthy for the brevity of their sentences. Find examples of one- and two-word paragraphs in other editorials. Contrast them with the following paragraph:
"And did we mention Doug Brown yet? There's nobody like him, anywhere, and he's reason alone to support the stations, and if you give enough you can get a tape of him reading a book, which if you listen to it in the car will make your next trip anywhere seven-and-a-half-times as enjoyable as it would otherwise be and also keep the kids quiet but you might miss a turn or two when you get too engrossed. But you won't care."
What do you think about this departure from his normal style? What do you suppose Gartner's intent was? Are these run-on sentences effective?

## Assignment Desk

1) Rewrite this editorial by tailoring the lengthy sentences in this editorial to resemble more closely the short, punchy sentences that are Gartner's hallmark.

2) Write an editorial promoting a local public radio station or some other community activity that plays off an aspect that is integral to its identity.

3) Try rewriting this editorial without using the line, "Give some money to WOI radio." Can you come up with a different transition and a punchy focus?

# Will we let others tell us what's best?

NOVEMBER 8, 1993

Linda Dasher. Eric Gabrielson. Mark Jones. Leo Milleman. Carol Patterson. Jeff Stevenson. Bill Tufford.

These are the people who met in secret the other day.

They represent Mary Greeley Medical Center of Ames and the Story County Hospital of Nevada, two publicly-owned institutions whose trustees must meet in the open.

But they did not break the letter of the law. They invited to the meeting just enough people from both boards to fall short of a quorum.

How slick.

Great change is coming in health care here, and emotions are running high, Carol Patterson, a Mary Greeley trustee, said. And she added: "I think it's easier to discuss these feelings when you don't feel that every word is going to be printed in the newspaper."

How patronizing.

The very idea behind the Iowa open-meetings law is to keep people informed about the institutions that they own. And it is not the routine, the ordinary, and the matter-of-fact that they need to be informed about. It is, rather, the controversial, the extraordinary and the emotional.

But a handful of people are telling the rest of us—including, incredibly, their fellow trustees—that they know what's best. Perhaps the next meeting will be open, they said, though they have set no date and made no promises. Meantime, they say, trust us. We can deal with emotions. We are wise and mature.

How quaint.

The people of Ames and Story County have invested millions of dollars in these two hospitals. Now the crunch is coming. The economics of medicine, the science of medicine, the technology of medicine and the politics of medicine are forcing dramatic changes.

These changes will affect us as patients and as taxpayers. They will affect our towns, and they will affect our futures. If ever there was a time when we all needed to be informed, when we all needed to be advised, when we all needed to be consulted, it is now.

This little band of trustees, doctors and administrators clearly wants our money as taxpayers, our support as patients and our backing as neighbors. Yet it doesn't want to tell us what is going on.

How come?

# Writers' Workshop

## Talking Points

1) Gartner begins this editorial with a list of names. Discuss why he chose this approach.

2) Gartner is a lawyer as well as a journalist. In many ways, his editorials resemble a closing argument at a trial. Study his editorials to see how he lays out his arguments, bolsters them with evidence, and then concludes.

3) "How slick." "How patronizing." "How quaint." "How come?" Gartner organizes the entire column around these two-word commentaries on the actions of the hospital trustees. Many writers describe the process of writing as a voyage of discovery. "I write to find out what I'm thinking about," says playwright Edward Albee. Do you think Gartner settled on the "How..." device before he wrote or did he stumble upon it during the writing? (You'll find his answer in the interview that follows.)

4) Like many writers, Gartner is a believer in the value of things in threes. Look at the next-to-last paragraph: "This little band of trustees, doctors and administrators clearly wants our money as taxpayers, our support as patients and our backing as neighbors." Look for other examples in his work and elsewhere. What is the attraction of this device?

## Assignment Desk

1) Rewrite the editorial without naming the people attending the meeting. How does it affect the editorial?

2) Write a paragraph explaining the value of open meetings.

3) Research your state's open-meetings law. Summarize it in a paragraph or two as Gartner does.

# New dialysis deal doesn't add up

DECEMBER 16, 1993

Well, we hope the new dialysis deal works.

We hope it's in the best interests of those 40 or so people who go there for treatment for several hours three times a week.

We hope it's in the best interests of the city and the taxpayers.

We hope it does everything its backers promise.

But we're skeptical.

Mary Greeley Medical Center has joined with Satellite Dialysis Inc., a nonprofit organization in Redwood City, Calif., to set up a joint venture to handle dialysis services at the city-owned hospital. At the moment, the hospital handles this itself.

Backers say they're doing this because the hospital is losing money in its dialysis operations. They say the California company brings an experience and expertise that they can't match. They say it's another round in the health-care revolution.

The hospital says it has been losing $400,000 or so a year on its dialysis center, one of about a dozen in Iowa. It says the new venture will make money from day one.

But we're puzzled.

The new venture will be using the same doctors, the same equipment, the same space in the hospital and most of the same employees as it provides service to the same patients. And those patients will be paying the same fees, which total around $1 million a year, Jeff Stevenson, the hospital's president, says.

So if revenue stays roughly the same, and there's a $500,000 swing in profits, that means costs must come down $500,000—and that's a 33 percent cut, by our calculations. How do you do that when you're using the same doctors, the same equipment, the same space, the same employees? What other significant costs are there?

"Savings will come through technology, through using the right size of staff, through training, and through some (new) administrative and operating systems," says Stevenson.

But we're curious.

If that's the case, why couldn't the hospital itself bring these changes without having to make this alliance? Why couldn't the hospital do this and keep all these new profits for itself, instead of sharing 50-50 with Satellite Dialysis Inc.?

After all, the man who runs the dialysis department, Dr. James Robertson of the McFarland Clinic, formerly was the medical director at a Satellite Dialysis operation in California. Surely he knows their methods and systems.

"His expertise is the medical treatment of patients," Stevenson says. What the company brings is different—"non-doctor types of experiences" that will lead to efficiencies, he says.

But we're uncertain.

One thing does seem certain: The public hospital, which has shown an increasing reluctance to meet in public, now has sheltered its dialysis operations from taxpayer scrutiny. The new joint venture will have a four-person board, and Stevenson says its meetings will be closed.

We aren't surprised.

\* \* \*

Timing is everything.

And the timing of this deal was a real break for the hospital. The new hospital board approved it, 3 to 2, and then Tuesday the City Council approved, 4 to 2. But if the vote had been next month, the Council wouldn't have OK'd it.

Ted Tedesco, who replaces Joyce Hertz on the council in January, says he would have joined council members Pat Brown and Sharon Wirth in opposing the contract, which is virtually unbreakable. "The prudent thing to do is to table this until we answer the primary question of whether we're going to privatize the whole hospital," he says. "They've taken part of this asset and given it away forever."

We're discouraged.

# Writers' Workshop

## Talking Points

1) Gartner again uses the device of repetition to good effect in this editorial.

Notice how he uses the phrase, "We hope..." to establish a rhythm for his editorial and as a graceful means to introduce factual information and set up the first of his lines of argument:

"Well, we hope the new dialysis deal works.

"We hope it's in the best interests of those 40 or so people who go there for treatment for several hours three times a week.

"We hope it's in the best interests of the city and the taxpayers.

"We hope it does everything its backers promise.

"But we're skeptical."

What are the benefits of beginning his editorial this way? How different would it be if he had started with paragraph six?

2) Bill Blundell, author of *The Art and Craft of Feature Writing,* says he always tried "not to let two paragraphs with numbers bump against each other—ever. Because I think numbers are absolutely deadly." Look at paragraphs 10 and 11:

"And those patients will be paying the same fees, which total around $1 million a year, Jeff Stevenson, the hospital's president, says.

"So if revenue stays roughly the same, and there's a $500,000 swing in profits, that means costs must come down $500,000—and that's a 33 percent cut, by our calculations."

Is this number overkill? Could Gartner have handled the figures differently?

3) Gartner uses a refrain throughout this editorial to convey his comments about the dialysis deal:

"But we're skeptical."

"But we're puzzled."

"But we're curious."

"But we're uncertain."

"We aren't surprised."

"We're discouraged."

What is the impact of these sentences on the reader? If you took them out of the story, could this run as an article on the news pages? What is the difference between an editorial and a news story?

4) Gartner frequently does his own reporting for editorials rather than relying on the information found in news stories. *The Wall Street Journal* editorial page also produces what its editor, Robert Bartley, calls "reported editorials." Discuss what reporting Gartner may have conducted for this editorial.

5) This editorial focuses on two elements: Gartner's skepticism about the arrangements for a dialysis system at a local hospital, and the decision by hospital authorities to hold closed meetings to discuss the setup. Does this twin focus dilute the strength of the editorial? Could Gartner have written two separate editorials?

## Assignment Desk

1) Write two distinct editorials on this subject. In one, focus on the financial arrangement of the dialysis system. Make the need for open meetings the focus of the second. Based on the information in the editorial, write two news stories with these two elements as the focus.

2) Remove all of Gartner's refrains that begin "But we're..." and rewrite the editorial.

3) Cut the first five paragraphs of the editorial and rewrite the rest.

# Coach Johnny Orr puts his foot in his mouth

DECEMBER 21, 1993

This is a true story, but we'll tell you the moral right away. It's this: If you want to know right from wrong, don't ask Johnny Orr.

Now, the story.

Chapter one: Hurl Beechum, an Iowa State basketball player, goes into Tazzles, a Campustown bar. So do the police. And that's a bad break for Hurl Beechum. Beechum is 20 years old, which is a year short of what you should be if you're in a saloon in Ames. So the police charge him with a misdemeanor.

Chapter two: *The Daily Tribune,* which keeps track of things like that, prints the fact of the arrest. It's a three-paragraph story. No big deal. In all, three youths are arrested that night. All three citations are listed in the newspaper's police report.

Chapter three: Orr, the Iowa State basketball coach, suspends Beechum for a game. But get this: The coach doesn't suspend the player because he is picked up for being in a bar. He suspends him because his name is in the newspaper.

Really. This is a true story. It happened last week.

"Let me tell you something about that," Orr told reporters Saturday. "I think they picked up 20 guys, they were going in and carding them or something like that that night, and only one kid's name did I see in the paper, and that was my basketball player. And he's a hell of a kid...

"We had to suspend him for this game...I told him we just couldn't let it go by and not do anything. Had it not been in the paper, I wouldn't have done anything about it at all because he didn't do anything. But we had to do something."

That's what he said. *"Had it not been in the paper, I wouldn't have done anything about it at all because he didn't do anything."*

This is—have we mentioned?—a true story.

So this appears to be the Orr morality: It's OK to break the law, but don't get caught. Actually, it's even OK to get caught, but don't let your name get in the newspaper.

We're not sure that's a really terrific message for a big-time basketball coach to be spreading to young people throughout the state. Sure, it was a minor infraction (Beechum pleaded guilty and paid a $50 fine yesterday), and it may or may not be reason for suspension. That's Coach Orr's call, but it's a call that should be made on the behavior, not on the publicity.

Still, if there's a new Orr philosophy, we'd like a little elaboration:

• Just exactly which laws is it OK for a basketball player to break as long as most of us don't know about it? We know, now, it's OK to wrongly be in a bar if you can keep your name out of the newspaper. What about to be drinking in the bar? Is that OK? What about to drink too much and then drive home? Is that OK? What about to drink and become a little rowdy? In other words, where does Coach Orr draw the line about acceptable but illegal behavior?

• Just exactly whose names shouldn't we print in this newspaper? Was it OK that we printed the names of those other two (not 20, as the coach said) youths arrested that night? They weren't basketball players, so does that make it OK? Would it be all right to print the name of, say, a cheerleader who is arrested? Or a cross-country runner? Or an assistant coach? Or, heaven forfend, Coach Orr himself?

The charitable view of all this would be to say that the coach was pretty happy with his 119-to-55 victory over Texas-Arlington and didn't really mean what he was saying about Beechum. But Coach Orr has a record of meaning what he says —and saying what he means.

Which brings us to one other thing he said:

"It's just a shame the way that we've gotten in the world today."

It is indeed. We're not sure what he was talking about there, but we know what we're talking about when we quote him.

As we said, this is a true story.

Unfortunately.

# Writers' Workshop

## Talking Points

1) You don't wait around for the point from Gartner. Consider his lead:

"This is a true story, but we'll tell you the moral right away. It's this: If you want to know right from wrong, don't ask Johnny Orr."

Consider why Gartner decided to start this way. Is it effective? How different would this editorial be if this paragraph had been last?

2) The reader doesn't learn until paragraph five that Johnny Orr is Iowa State University's basketball coach. Why didn't Gartner identify him until then? Since Ames is the home of Iowa State, is it fair to assume that most readers will know Orr? How much should writers be guided by the needs of their audience?

3) In paragraphs three to five, Gartner cleverly borrows from a book format, breaking down the story of Hurl Beechum's arrest into "Chapter" one, two, and three. Notice how the device makes it easier to absorb the background necessary to understand the editorial.

4) Why does Gartner keep coming back to the refrain, "This is a true story"? Does he run the danger of overdoing it?

5) The questions Gartner poses to Coach Orr in paragraphs 14 and 15 drip with sarcasm. Why does he keep repeating, "Is that OK?" At this point, the editorial resembles a cross-examination. Is that fair? Is it effective? If it's effective, does it matter if it's fair? What do you think is Gartner's goal for this editorial?

6) Notice how, in paragraph nine, Gartner repeats Coach Orr's statement: *"Had it not been in the paper, I wouldn't have done anything about it at all because he didn't do anything."* Was it necessary to do that or is Gartner guilty of overkill? Is this editorial too long? What, if any, elements, could be cut without harming it?

7) Consider the final sentence in paragraph 15: "Or, heaven forfend, Coach Orr himself?" According to the *Random*

*House Unabridged Dictionary,* "forfend" is an archaic form of "forbid," dating back to the year 1350. Can you decipher its meaning from the content of the sentence? Why would Gartner use an outmoded word? Make an argument for and against its use.

## Assignment Desk

1) Rewrite this editorial. In your version, make the lead the end. How does this change the editorial?

2) Write a new version of this editorial as if you were writing for a newspaper in upstate New York. How does this affect how and when you identify Coach Orr and Hurl Beechum?

3) Try to cut this editorial by a third. What would you leave out? What elements have to stay? Cut it by removing entire sections instead of cutting out words here and there.

4) Rewrite paragraphs three, four, and five, without using the device of the book chapters. How does that affect the pacing of the editorial?

# Michael Gartner: Musician Composing editorials

**CHRISTOPHER SCANLAN: A.J. Liebling** once said, **"Freedom of the press is guaranteed only to those who own one."** Is that the single best reason for owning a paper?

MICHAEL GARTNER: I can't think of anything better than owning your own newspaper in a great little town and writing the editorials. After I had been going to Ames for about three months, I told my wife, "I might not be the happiest person in America, but I'm certainly in the top five."

I write what I want to write in a newspaper that I own, in a state that I love, in a community that I love. And I'm surrounded by these 23- and 24-year-old kids who are smart and irreverent and hard-working, and I have a lot of fun with them. What more could you ask for?

**You write only local editorials. Why?**

If I don't write about what's going on at the hospital or the city council in Ames, nobody else is going to.

If I'd write about Whitewater or the Mideast, that means there's something in Ames I'm not writing about. And I haven't run out of things that the people in Ames ought to know about.

Unless you're *The New York Times* or *The Washington Post* or *The Boston Globe, The Wall Street Journal, USA Today, L.A. Times,* maybe *The Miami Herald,* almost all of your editorials should be local. Certainly if you're a small newspaper, all of them should be. But even if you're the *Des Moines Register* or the *Louisville Courier*

■ Michael Gartner, editor and co-owner, Ames, Iowa, *Daily Tribune.*

■ **Born:** October 23, 1938, in Des Moines.

■ **Education:** Carleton College, B.A., 1960; New York University, J.D. degree, 1969.

■ **News Experience:** *Des Moines Register,* 1953–60, 1974–85; *The Wall Street Journal,* 1960–74; Gannett Co., 1985–86, Louisville *Courier-Journal* and Louisville *Times,* 1986–87; Gannett Co. and Ames *Daily Tribune,* 1987–88; NBC News, 1988–93; Ames *Daily Tribune,* 1993 to present.

■ **Awards:** President, American Society of Newspaper Editors, 1986–87; Honorary degrees from Simpson College, Grand View College, and James Madison University; Pulitzer Prize board 1982–92, chairman, 1992.

*Journal* or the *Charlotte Observer,* I think 80 percent of your editorials should be state or local, because if you don't do it, nobody else will. It's your duty to your reader.

## How do you find subjects?

All of my editorials are sort of, "We think you ought to know about this, here's something going on in town," or, "These people are meeting in secret and that's really crappy, and here's why they shouldn't be doing it."

## Your editorials read like stories.

That's what an editorial in my paper is. It's not an "I'm so mad, I'm going to beat you over the head." It's just kind of a little story with a little ending. Endings are very, very important, in newspaper articles, in editorials, in anything.

The editorials that I like best are stories with lots and lots of facts and a viewpoint that builds, either through repetition or alliteration or word play, and then culminates with an ending that's not a whack over the head with a 2 by 4, but a kind of mild consternation. Rarely do I get so outraged I call somebody a jerk.

## What's the most important element of an editorial?

Facts. A lot of editorial writers try to get by on their writing or their outrage, and not on their reporting. That just doesn't work. You've got to have facts. In an article, you use them to inform. In an editorial, you use facts to persuade as well as inform.

## You commute about 40 miles to Ames from your home in Des Moines. Do you write on the way?

You're always writing in your head, looking for a better lead, a better ending, trying to make sure that you talk to the right people. You're always watching, you're always listening. If you're an editor, you're always wondering: Am I going to put this in my paper? Am I going to write about this? I wonder if the kids know about this up at Ames? You're always at it.

**You've been the president of NBC News, you were the Page One editor of *The Wall Street Journal*, the editor of the *Des Moines Register*. And yet, when you described yourself you said, "I'm a copy editor."**

I'm a copy editor who happens to understand business and so I kept getting other jobs that involved management. But I could be perfectly happy working on a copy desk somewhere.

**I can't imagine too many kids growing up and saying, "Gosh, I want to be a copy editor." I can imagine them saying, "Gee, I'd like to be Tom Brokaw," or, "I'd like to be the editor of the paper," or, "I'd like to be a foreign correspondent." Why do you consider copy editing such a noble calling?**

There's a special place in heaven for copy editors because they get no credit on earth. Rarely does a reporter come over and say, "Geez, thanks, you took that paragraph from the fourth take and made it the third paragraph and, suddenly, it made sense."

**How important is curiosity to your writing?**

Oh, it's everything. If you're not always wondering, "How did that happen?" "Why is that?" you should go into insurance.

**This morning you interviewed a woman for your editorial about closed meetings of the hospital board. Tell me about that.**

I wanted to tell her I'm writing an editorial today that she's not going to agree with. I think that you owe it to people to tell them in advance so they're not surprised when they pick up the paper. It also tends to diminish the anger and irritation they have. You have to deal with these people every day; we're all in the same town. You don't want to pull your punches so what you do is write what you think, but tell them in advance: "You're not going to like this." I find that that works, by and large.

**Where did you get that approach?**

I learned it from Danny Dorfman at *The Wall Street Journal.* He used to write the "Heard on the Street" column. Every morning, he'd have this column and it could cost somebody millions of dollars, it could wipe them out. And the first thing he'd do when he'd come in in the morning is pick up the phone and call them up before they'd have a chance to jump out the window. He'd say, "Hi ya, this is Danny Dorfman. Are you still mad at me?" and it would just defuse the whole thing. I said, "Why do you take all that abuse?" And he says, "I'm going to have to call that guy tomorrow on something else. I want him to take my calls."

So I call people up and I let them yell and scream at me for two minutes and then it's over.

**What's the function of your editorial page?**

To write fact-filled essays that have my view in them so that people can make informed opinions themselves.

Now sometimes you'll just write an essay about spring or the weather. You're not trying to persuade anybody, you're just trying to kind of brighten their day and also educate them. Every once in a while, you've got to do an editorial that is uplifting. One time it was a beautiful winter day and I called up the County Conservation Commission and the city parks and said, "What are all the things you can do in the winter in this county and this town? Give me exact details, where these trails are, what it costs to rent ice skates, what hours the hockey rink is open." I wrote this very long editorial about all the things you could do, so long that we had to print it in smaller type. One of the great things about mechanics now is you can change the size of type and you don't have to cut your editorials. And if you own the paper, you *don't* cut the editorial, you make the type smaller.

**Are your editorials the product of extensive revision, or do they appear full-blown on the page?**

Sort of in between. Sometimes you can just sit down and write it and you don't do much scrubbing. Other times, you can be three-quarters of the way through it and you'll write a paragraph and you'll say to yourself, "Oh, shit, this is the lead."

I'm constantly going back and reading as I write: "It's taking me too long to get into this," I'll say to myself, or, "You're going down the wrong road," or, "Jesus, make your point." I'll talk to myself the way I talk to these kids, but a little more harshly to myself. Often I'll read it out loud at home at night to see how it sounds. And if I'm not reading it out loud, I'm pretending I'm reading it out loud, to my ear anyway.

**Why so much effort?**

My favorite thing I ever learned in newspapering I learned, fortunately, when I was 21 years old. I was sitting at the copy desk at *The Wall Street Journal* one night rewriting a story. I had been there about three weeks. Barney Kilgore, the guy who ran *The Wall Street Journal,* walked by. He was a walking-around editor, which is what I like to be. He introduced himself and said, "What are you doing?" I said, "I'm rewriting a story," and he said, "Well, just remember one thing. The easiest thing for the reader to do is to quit reading." And he walked away. And I thought, I may never hear anything as important as that. And so I'm constantly saying to myself, "Is the reader still here?"

**You have a reader in mind, it seems.**

Oh, yeah, I've always written for my father.

**Why?**

Because he's smart, he enjoys language and words, and he'll stop reading if he doesn't like it.

**Tell me about him.**

His name is Carl Gartner, and he's 92. He always calls me "Little Boy." I'm 55 years old, but I'm still his little boy. He was a copy editor at the *Des Moines Register* and a writer and reviewer and rotogravure editor; and he started their Sunday magazine, which is what he was doing when he retired in 1972. He still is a voracious reader and just a wonderful writer. So I always have him in mind: Will he read this and learn anything from it, and will he kind of smile when he sees something?

**Do you fact check?**

I don't take anybody's word for a fact. I learned early on, never trust a secondary source when the primary source is available. I always live in fear I'm going to have a fact wrong. When you have a fact wrong, it diminishes the credibility of everything else.

**You're a lawyer who writes editorials as tightly reasoned as an appellate brief. How does being a lawyer help you in your work as a journalist?**

Law school teaches you that there's a zillion sides to everything and that you should calmly explore them and never take anything for granted. The great lesson from law school for reporting and editing is that, often, there's no right and no wrong, but all kinds of facts.

**In one of your winning editorials about dialysis, you quote Jeff Stevenson, the hospital's president. Did you interview him?**

Of course. I would never quote anybody I hadn't interviewed.

**You wouldn't lift a quote from a news story?**

No.

**Don't you think that's done, though?**

I've been written about so much in the last few years and so much of it just wasn't true, so little of it was ever checked out with me. I asked the NBC librarian last spring, "Send me the pieces that were written about me, go into NEXIS." She calls me up and says, "Well, I'm at 600 so far." First of all, talk about a waste of reporters' time. But second of all, only five reporters ever called me. Nobody else ever, ever called. I had a listed number in the Manhattan phone book. I had a listed number in Des Moines. I was easily reachable through NBC. They didn't call. And I was astounded. I read some of the stuff. I mean even my name would be wrong. But everybody wanted to get in on the story, every TV critic and every little newspaper around the country. And so they would go into NEXIS or pick something up from the AP and they'd put their own little spin on it and most of it was just bullshit. And so that's why I always call.

If it's in my own paper, and I can't get hold of the person, I go over to the writer and say, "Let me see your notes on this quote."

**Should there be a way to sensitize reporters to that kind of sloppiness?**

Make them all news-makers for a month.

**So why do you write for newspapers?**

A quick, honest answer: Because I have to have instant gratification.

**In the editorial, "Tattoos and Freedom," you
repeat the same phrase in three consecutive
sentences:**
**"In this country, you tolerate speech you
despise.**
**"In this country, you tolerate views you
abhor.**
**"In this country, you tolerate opinions you
loathe."**
**What's behind this use of repetition?**

It's the refrain. I use that a device a lot,...the rhythmic refrain with a different tag on it each time. It's
almost a musical device. I love Broadway musi-
cals and have always thought I could write a musical. Couldn't write the music, but I could write
the lyrics because I like word play and rhymes,
rhythms, and beats, and cadences. Sometimes I
think these editorials are the lyrics to a song that
has never been written.

Think about it. "In this country..., In this country...," you could put that to music.

**If you had to pick a metaphor to describe your-
self as a writer, what would it be, a musician?**

Yeah, that's really what it is.

**You once said in a speech "The very nicest
thing you can say about an editor is what H.L.
Mencken wrote in 1927 about John Haslup
Adams, a *Baltimore Sun* editor who died that
year: 'The thing he esteemed most in this world
was simply fair play.'" What's the nicest thing
someone could say about you as an editor?**

That I'm fair. Fairness is everything. Fairness is
your credibility and what makes you sleep
soundly at night. If you take a cheap shot at somebody, you know you're not being fair. Even if they
don't know it, you know it. I've seen enough of it
and I've done enough of it and I've been a victim
of enough of it. I always tell these kids, "Be fair,

be clear, be thorough, be accurate. And if you can add on top of that, 'Write with grace,' you'll be a great success."

Another way you can say it is, when you write the story, ask yourself, "What if this were about me? What if this were about my father? What if this were about my publisher? Would I make one more phone call, would I ask one more question?"

**Are there conditions that must be met for you to write well?**

No, I can write in solitude or in clamor. I write out here in the midst of daily chaos. At home, I have a little office where the kids are always coming in and going out.

**I don't mean just environmental conditions.**

You have to have the material if you're writing an editorial. You have to have the facts or you have to do the reporting. I could probably fool the reader, but I can't fool myself. So you don't want to write an editorial that you haven't reported well.

**Do you rehearse in your mind?**

Yes, I'm constantly talking to myself. In fact, I'm surprised sometimes that it's not coming out of my mouth. You're planning the lead, chiseling it, doing all these things to pick just the right word and the next paragraph. You're constantly writing stories in your imagination that you have to write in fact the day after tomorrow. So when you sit down to write it, you've gone through the first 20 drafts, but they were all in your head.

**In the editorial on Coach Johnny Orr, you have a line, "heaven forfend." Why use a word that may have been old-fashioned in the 15th century?**

It has a nicer ring to it. "Forbid" doesn't quite work; "forfend," it's got the double F, heaven forfend, and the V in heaven, heaven forfend. It's got a better rhythm. You can't use it every day, but you can use it once every six months.

**Do you assume that people will understand it from the context?**

Some of them. I don't believe in writing down. They understand it by context, and if they're more interested, then they can go look it up and learn a new word.

**Do you see a future for the newspaper?**

Oh, a great and glorious future.

**Do your kids read the newspapers?**

No. But they will.

I have this theory about newspapers that you become a reader as soon as you need to know what the school lunch menu is. I have this other theory: Newspaper circulation would go up dramatically if they took everything printed in agate [small, bold typeface generally used for statistics] and printed it in 9 point type, and everything in 9 point and printed it in agate. The most interesting information in newspapers is in agate, whether it's drunken driving arrests or house transactions or births or deaths or stock quotes or baseball batting averages. That's the stuff people are interested in. Go to somebody's house and that's what's on their refrigerator door.

**What's the best advice you ever got about editorial writing?**

It was something Vermont Royster, a former editor of *The Wall Street Journal,* told me in 1974 when I left the *Journal* to be the editor in Des Moines.

He said the main thing to remember about writing an editorial is give the other side the space and give your side the thought.

**In the fund-raising editorial for public radio, you're a booster. In the editorials about tattoos and freedom and Coach Orr, you're a harsh critic. What other hats does the editorial writer wear?**

An explainer and an informer and sometimes just kind of an uncle. I thought Gerald Ford was a shitty president, but I always thought he'd be a great guy to have over for Thanksgiving dinner. He'd sit around and he could carry on a discussion with you and your kids and, afterwards, go out and toss the ball around in the back yard.

And that's sort of what the editorial writer is sometimes, the dinner guest talking about a subject and afterwards, he's going to go out and throw the ball around in the back yard. He's going to go home when it's over, but you're going to have a good time with him and there's not going to be any big fights or arguments and everybody's going to enjoy themselves and leave with a good feeling. And that's sort of the way some editorials are. I mean you can't get pissed off about something every single day, no matter where you are. That doesn't mean you can't have firm, strong views.

**In your editorial about the dialysis operation, you provide a simple explanation of a complicated arrangement. How do achieve that compression and clarity?**

That's what I did for a living as a rewrite man for *The Wall Street Journal:* Write in a way that people could understand intricate doings at the International Monetary Fund. What you try to do is throw out all the junk, get down to the essential facts, and then organize them, usually in a time sequence, so you can see what flows from what.

You do it the way you talk to somebody. You know, if you say, "What happened," you say, "Ah, back in 1966...," such and such. "Then three years later, the city council passed...," such and such. "Then two years later, there was an amendment on...," such and such. "And so yesterday...," such and such.

**How do you encourage that kind of conversational voice in writers?**

I always say, "Write it the way you just told it."

**How do you find the right voice, and how do you tune it?**

If you don't have it by the time you're 55 years old, you're never going to have it. It's sort of like being an entertainer. Jack Benny pauses, Henny Youngman uses rapid fire, George Burns has a cigar and an eyebrow and never finishes a song lyric. Everybody develops his own style.

**And Michael Gartner...?**

I tend to chat. And I try to be full of information in a low-key way. I try to start low. I never come out with bang right at the top, "This is the single dumbest thing I've ever seen in my life." Rarely do I ever start with a long sentence. I usually start with a short sentence and then just build on it until I think I've made my case.

**Your leads are often an invitation: "Let's talk about tattoos."**

It's like I'm at your breakfast table with you while you're reading this, "Let's talk about this. Here's what I think." And I almost pause to listen to your response. And then I say, "But here's what I think. What about...such and such." It's almost a conversation.

**What's your advice to a new editorial writer?**

Brush up your reporting skills. If you want to write good editorials, you've got to be a terrific reporter, and more so than if you're writing a news story because your range has to be greater. You can't write editorials without reporting.

**Is it true you have 300 books on writing or words?**

I've got about 500.

**Which ones would you suggest for an aspiring writer's bookbag?**

The first thing I'd get is the little book by Strunk and White, *Elements of Style*. And *The Writer's Art* by James Kilpatrick. The essays of E.B. White and the letters of E.B. White. The essays of Red Smith, Lewis Thomas, Vermont Royster. I'd read Reynolds Price and John Cheever, Fitzgerald and Calvin Trillin. And then I would just read, read, read and then I'd write, write, write, write, write. I mean that's the only way you can do it. You know, you can't sit down and play the piano if you don't practice. And writing is sort of like playing the piano—it's pure keys.

**One of your former reporters, Peggy Engel, said that words are your ammunition against confusion and obfuscation in the war for truth.**

Oh, that's nice. Save that, carve it on my tombstone.

# Daniel P. Henninger

## Finalist, Editorial Writing

Daniel Henninger is a familiar figure in the pages of *Best Newspaper Writing*. The deputy editor of *The Wall Street Journal* was also a finalist in the ASNE editorial writing competition in 1985 and 1986. A native of Cleveland, he graduated from Georgetown University in 1968 with a bachelor's degree from the School of Foreign Service. After graduation, he worked for *New Republic* magazine until 1971 when he joined Dow Jones as a staff writer for *The National Observer.* Henninger joined *The Wall Street Journal* in 1977 as an editorial page writer.

In the years since, he has served as the paper's arts editor, editorial features editor, assistant editor of the editorial page, and chief editorial writer and senior assistant editor with daily responsibility for the Review and Outlook columns. Henninger won the Gerald Loeb award for commentary in 1985.

In a culture assailed by conflicting views, the editorial writer must make sense of the clamor and challenge readers to think for themselves. Henninger's editorial "No Guardrails," his blunt and controversial assessment of the decline of self-restraint, more than meets those exacting standards. Agree or not, readers are compelled to measure their own beliefs against his passionately held and vigorously presented opinions.

# No guardrails

MARCH 18, 1993

The gunning down of abortion doctor David Gunn
in Florida last week shows us how small the bar-
rier has become that separates civilized from un-
civilized behavior in American life. In our time,
the United States suffers every day of the week
because there are now so many marginalized
people among us who don't understand the rules,
who don't think that rules of personal or civil conduct apply to them, who have no notion of self-
control. We are the country that has a TV
commercial on all the time that says: "Just do it."
Michael Frederick Griffin just did it.

An anti-abortion protester of intense emotions,
he walked around behind the Pensacola Women's
Medical Services Clinic and pumped three bullets
into the back of Dr. Gunn. Emptied himself,
Michael Griffin then waited for the police to take
him away. A remark by his father-in-law caught
our eye: "Now we've got to take care of two
grandchildren."

As the saying goes, there was a time. And indeed there really was a time in the United States
when life seemed more settled, when emotions,
both private and public, didn't seem to run so con-
tinuously at breakneck speed, splattering one un-
godly tragedy after another across the evening
news. How did this happen to the United States?
How, in T.S. Eliot's phrase, did so many become
undone?

\* \* \*

We think it is possible to identify the date when
the U.S., or more precisely when many people
within it, began to tip off the emotional tracks. A
lot of people won't like this date, because it makes
their political culture culpable for what has happened. The date is August 1968, when the Democratic National Convention found itself sharing

Chicago with the street fighters of the anti-Vietnam War movement.

The real blame here does not lie with the mobs who fought bloody battles with the hysterical Chicago police. The larger responsibility falls on the intellectuals—university professors, politicians and journalistic commentators—who said then that the *acts* committed by the protesters were justified or explainable. That was the beginning. After Chicago, the justifications never really stopped. America had a new culture, for political action and personal living.

With great rhetorical firepower, books, magazines, opinion columns and editorials defended each succeeding act of defiance—against the war, against university presidents, against corporate practices, against behavior codes, against dress codes, against virtually all agents of established authority.

\* \* \*

What in the past had been simply illegal became "civil disobedience." If you could claim, and it was never too hard to claim, that your group was engaged in an act of civil disobedience— taking over a building, preventing a government official from speaking, bursting onto the grounds of a nuclear cooling station, destroying animal research, desecrating Communion hosts—the shapers of opinion would blow right past the broken rules to seek an understanding of the "dissidents" (in the '60s and '70s) and "activists" (in the '80s and now).

Concurrently, the personal virtue known as self-restraint was devalued. In the process, certain rules that for a long time had governed behavior also became devalued. Whatever else was going on here, we were repeatedly lowering the barriers of acceptable political and personal conduct.

You can argue, as many did and still do, that all this was necessary because the established order wouldn't respond or change. But then you still need to account for the nation's simultaneous dive into extensive social and personal dysfunction. You need to account for what is happening to those people within U.S. society who seem least able to navigate the political and personal torrents that they become part of, like Michael Griffin.

Those torrents began with the anti-war movement in the 1960s. Those endless demonstrations, though, were merely one part of a much deeper shift in American culture—away from community and family rules of conduct and toward more autonomy, more personal independence. As to limits, you set your own.

\* \* \*

The people who provided the theoretical underpinnings for this shift—the intellectuals and political leaders who led the movement—did very well, or at least survived. They are born with large reservoirs of intelligence and psychological strength. The fame and celebrity help, too.

But for a lot of other people it hasn't been such an easy life to sustain. Not exceedingly sophisticated, neither thinkers nor leaders, never interviewed for their views, they're held together by faith, friends, fun and, at the margins, by fanaticism. The big political crackups make the news —a Michael Griffin or the woman on trial in Connecticut for the attempted bombing of the CEO of a surgical-device company or the '70s radicals who accidentally blew themselves up in a New York brownstone. But the personal crackups just float like flotsam through the country's hospitals and streets. You can also see some of them on daytime TV, America's medical museum of personal autonomy.

\* \* \*

It may be true that most of the people in Hollywood who did cocaine survived it, but many of the weaker members of the community hit the wall. And most of the teenage girls in the Midwest who learn about the nuances of sex from magazines published by thirtysomething women in New York will more or less survive, but some continue to end up as prostitutes on Eighth Avenue. Everyone today seems to know someone who couldn't handle the turns and went over the side of the mountain.

These weaker or more vulnerable people, who in different ways must try to live along life's margins, are among the reasons that a society erects rules. They're guardrails. It's also true that we need to distinguish good rules from bad rules and periodically re-examine old rules. But the broad movement that gained force during the anti-war years consciously and systematically took down the guardrails. Incredibly, even judges pitched in. All of them did so to transform the country's institutions and its codes of personal behavior (abortion, for instance).

In a sense, it has been a remarkable political and social achievement for them. But let's get something straight about the consequences. If as a society we want to live under conditions of constant challenge to institutions and limits on personal life, if we are going to march and fight and litigate over every conceivable grievance, then we should stop crying over all the individual casualties, because there are going to be a lot of them.

Michael Griffin and Dr. David Gunn are merely two names on a long list of confrontations and personal catastrophe going back 25 years. That today is the status quo. The alternative is to start rethinking it.

# Lessons Learned

## BY DANIEL P. HENNINGER

Sometimes, editorial writing is like prospecting for gold. Editorial writers like to think they go to work every day in a field rich with ideas and issues. But we're never quite certain that anything we write is going to strike to the heart of readers' concerns, much less the readers' emotions. "No Guardrails" was a big strike for me, and an instructive one.

The nominal news peg was the fatal shooting of abortion clinic doctor David Gunn in Florida. This murder, the work of an unhinged pro-life advocate, came during one of those periodic, rising cycles of awful violence. The normal editorial instinct would have been to deplore the violence and depending on one's politics, prescribe the liberal or conservative policy fixes that the politicians had so far failed to adopt etc., etc.

On this occasion, though, I decided not to say what had been said before about violence. Instead, I went down to the deep end of the pool and dived in to ask "Why?" What could be the origin of all this apparently relentless craziness around us? "No Guardrails" was my answer.

The response we got was huge. I thought it was a pretty good editorial when we went to press, but this response was way out of scale to a "pretty good" effort. Long and thoughtful letters poured in, invariably pegged to the editorial's belief that our current pathologies could be traced to the wildness in the streets of the 1968 Democratic Convention in Chicago. No, that's wrong, the writers said, our craziness began with JFK's assassination; no, it was Watergate; it began with Vietnam, with the school prayer decision, with Ollie North, with Mike Milken, with the courts—and on and on. Amid that readerly tumult, however, one saw virtual consensus on one point—morally, the U.S. had somehow run *off the rails.*

What I learned: There are heavy currents of public opinion that run strong beneath the surface of the news, usually unnoticed. The abortion clinic killing was really incidental to what "No Guardrails" set off. It was one of those "Thank-God-someone-has-finally-said-this" reactions from the *Journal*'s readership. Editorialists should be alert when an opinion wave this strong unexpectedly washes back over them. Deeply held opinion always feeds back into politics; it affects political outcomes.

This is an experience the editorialist can put in the bank. Its real value is that it allows an editorialist to write with a lot of confidence the next time. Some subjects and moments are more important than others in an editorial writer's work; and on those occasions when something larger seems called for, I think readers want to sense that the writer is working with real conviction. In short, a big editorial can be a big deal, on both sides of the page.

I learned, or re-learned, that a phenomenon as occurred here with an editorial won't happen without good writing. Much of good writing is mainly about rhythm, including the metaphors. I don't think you get big reader response to an opinion unless they've been touched, perhaps unconsciously, by the writing itself. That takes extra effort, which is not all that easily sustainable over time in the daily editorial business. But we know that good writing can affect people deeply; so again, on those larger occasions, one should be able to draw on whatever skills of the craft achieve one's desired effects. I think that means keeping one's writing machinery oiled even on the off days.

Being allowed to think big about important subjects is one of the perks of this business. But being able to turn those thoughts into the exactly right words is where the pleasure lies.

# Rick Nichols

## Finalist, Editorial Writing

Rick Nichols is a native Philadelphian. He has a journalism degree from the University of North Carolina at Chapel Hill where he worked at the *Chapel Hill Weekly.* He wrote for the *Atlanta Journal and Constitution* Sunday magazine and was an editor, reporter, and columnist for the *Raleigh News & Observer* where he covered racial and labor upheaval. He was a Nieman Fellow at Harvard University in 1977, and later joined the editorial board at *The Philadelphia Inquirer.* He has traveled to Nicaragua and South Africa to witness social change, checked out the drug corners of North Philadelphia, written from the Earth Summit in Rio de Janeiro, and stalked TV violence in Hollywood. He has won the Inter-American Press Association prize for editorial writing in addition to many local and state writing prizes.

When a battle over free speech erupted at the University of Pennsylvania in the spring of 1993, Rick Nichols's editorials were a voice of reason and unqualified support for freedom of expression. As Jim Naughton, the *Inquirer*'s executive editor, put it, Nichols's "forceful, reasoned commentary" furnished a troubled community with something university officials failed to give: "an understandable moral compass." That he was able to do it with occasional touches of humor made his contribution even more valuable.

# Buffaloed: A great university becomes tongue-tied

MAY 16, 1993

You'd think that with all the brains at the University of Pennsylvania, the school would have to work overtime to look so foolish. We refer, of course, to the university's flailing about over an issue that shouldn't be so darn complicated—the freedom to speak one's mind.

The latest example regards one Eden Jacobowitz, an 18-year-old freshman, who has been hauled before a collegiate Star Chamber for allegedly hollering "water buffalo" at a noisy bunch of sorority sisters who happened to be black.

The charge? Violating Penn's suddenly overworked "hate-speech" code. (A few months ago, a conservative columnist for the Penn daily was accused of racial harassment under the code, charges that were wisely dismissed.)

The Jacobowitz saga, which began in January, took another turn Friday, when Penn marched him before a hearing, only to decide to delay the whole mess until fall. It then tried to forbid those involved from talking about it.

If this keeps up, the place is going to be a school for mimes.

President Sheldon Hackney could have taken a stand as things got out of hand. Instead, when the Penn daily was trashed by angry black students, he mused about "competing values." He could have called for some imagination—for vigorous protest, for rebuttal, for more speech, not less. But he did not.

Likewise, he kept a low-profile in the Jacobowitz affair, urging critics to allow "the process" to run its course. But the process itself has become a problem.

Mr. Hackney will be in the hot seat soon enough in upcoming hearings on his nomination to head the National Endowment for the Humanities. We hope he is asked why he didn't act promptly to protect the Penn daily, whether he still thinks "hate-speech" codes and tribunals are worth having, and whether letting a harried freshman twist in the wind for months on end is fair play—or likely, in the end, to enhance the prospects for racial harmony.

# Lessons Learned

## BY RICK NICHOLS

By the miserable end, Penn President Sheldon Hackney—
since departed—was referring to the university's "painful
spring." The year was 1993. And the pain was self-inflicted,
the result of rolling display of irresolution after a day's
worth of campus newspapers had been trashed, and a sopho-
more was charged with hate speech. He'd hollered, "water
buffalo."

I mention Hackney's evasion not to deny the pain: It was
real enough. But rather to point out the man's unending
problem with euphemism. By speaking with forked tongue,
in hooded reference, in honeyed phrase, and in artful am-
biguity, Hackney all but assured that different audiences
took away different messages. Thus, the crisis deepened.

The *Inquirer's* first job was clear: Strip away that
mumbo-jumbo and do some plain speaking. If clarity was at
bay in the Penn episode, the editorial page would bring it in.
Or try to.

To get my own mind straight, I started drawing on experience. As a student, I'd witnessed the damage done by
the Speaker Ban that legislators slapped on the University of
North Carolina, banning un-American types from whipping
up civil rights sentiment on campus. A few years later, I saw
Georgia Gov. Lester Maddox uproot *Atlanta Constitution*
honor boxes on the capitol square. Something we'd written
had gotten his back up.

The newspaper-dumping and speech-muzzling I'd been
exposed to had hardly advanced progressive agendas. It was
the tactic of bad guys. It left an impression.

I researched. I talked to campus lawyers, to an African-
American anthropologist, to Sheldon Hackney and his wife,
Lucy, herself a lawyer and closet opponent of speech codes.
I talked to students and ACLUers. And when I wrote, it was
with a certain measure of confidence.

In the piece reprinted in this book, I used what might be
called the "back door" approach, sidling up in the "aw,
shucks" manner of, say, a Sam Ervin or Will Rogers.
There's enough alarmist rhetoric roaring around editorial
pages. I'd wanted folks to think that what we had here was
a problem, not the gong of doom.

I used contrast: Brains versus foolishness. I used colloquialism: "So darn complicated." The idea was to invite the reader in for a chat.

You can bet, though, that the chat won't be memorable unless you spike it with humor or originality. What Penn established was an innocent-sounding "campus judicial review committee." I made it a "collegiate Star Chamber."

I could have gone into the details of the speech code. But the point was that it was "overworked."

It would have been easy (lazy?) to say that "Penn's prestigious Ivy League reputation will soon be endangered, blah, blah..." But who needs boring?

Why not give the reader a smile—and perhaps a line that will stick—warning of Penn's slide toward becoming "a school for mimes?" (In logic, I believe that little gimmick is called *reductio ad absurdum*.)

One can go overboard with that stuff. Indeed, the media piled on as Hackney prepared to head the National Endowment for the Humanities. *The Wall Street Journal* saw Western Civilization imperiled. Pat Buchanan ranted about "a virtucrat out of touch with Middle America." *Time* magazine gasped: "The Next Lani Guinier?"

That's not good writing. That's unloosing the power tools of the propagandist—sloganeering and disproportion. (Euphemists, on the other extreme, misinform as the courtier might—quietly, gently, obliquely).

A few other points I tried to keep in mind.

Don't get sidetracked. Racial conflict at Penn was real and provided context. But it wasn't the main event.

Provide alternatives. It was up to the *Inquirer* to offer a better course of action if it had one. We suggested more imaginative protest, rebuttal, and more speech, not surrender.

Don't declare. Appeal. Editorials are more effective if you make the readers do some thinking. "Buffaloed" asks them to consider whether fair play was well served—or whether racial harmony was enhanced.

Given the facts, I thought the conclusion was obvious. The trick was to let the readers reach it themselves.

# Ken Wells

## Headline Writing

As a boy growing up in south Louisiana's Cajun delta, Ken Wells earned spending money collecting greenback turtles to sell to medical research laboratories. Years later, he was working at the *Houma* (La.) *Daily Courier* when a *Wall Street Journal* reporter came to town and wrote a "sweet little feature" about the reptile trade. "That woke me up," he recalls. "I never even thought about *The Wall Street Journal* doing this kind of stuff. I sort of silently vowed then that one day, I'd do this."

Today, Wells is a senior writer for Page One of *The Wall Street Journal,* working as a story editor and occasional reporter for the *Journal*'s showcase page. He's a newcomer to the Page One desk—five of his winning headlines were written the month after his arrival from the paper's London bureau—but an 12-year reporting veteran at the paper. From San Francisco, he covered the oil industry and environmental issues, wrote features from such remote outposts as Barrow, Alaska, and helped lead the paper's coverage of the Exxon Valdez oil-tanker disaster. Wells went overseas in 1990, filing stories from the Middle East, Europe, and Africa. He brings a writer's eye and sensibilities and a goal of "ego-free editing" to the stories he shepherds to the front page. His headlines carry the unmistakable stamp of a writer who savors the joys of language.

# Urology was boring until Dr. Sehn met John Wayne Bobbitt

## The patient's loss, restored by deft, delicate surgery, is now the talk of the town

AUGUST 11, 1993

By Tony Horwitz

MANASSAS, Va.—Until recently, James Sehn was an anonymous practitioner of an unglamorous trade.

"I'm basically a plumber," he says of urology, a medical specialty devoted to keeping the bladder and related organs flushing smoothly. At parties, when he would tell strangers about his job, they would often respond, " 'Oh, such a pity for you,' " Dr. Sehn recalls. "Then the conversation would sort of trail off."

These days, the conversation never stops. Soon after his now-celebrated reattachment of a Virginia man's penis, Dr. Sehn arrived at a cocktail party—and was greeted by spontaneous applause. Flustered, he promptly tripped over a pot of tulips and fell flat on his face.

### A STRANGE CELEBRITY

Brushing himself off, Dr. Sehn was in for another shock. "The party polarized," he recalls, with wives in one corner wanting to hear "all the horrific details," and men in another with "their hands unconsciously covering their groins."

. Ever since, Dr. Sehn has been busy discussing the operation on national TV, on radio talk shows and in foreign magazines. As a result, he has become an unlikely and rather reluctant celebrity. Asked when he last received such public acclaim, the 48-year-old doctor puzzles over the question before admitting: "Gee whiz, I guess when I was vice president of the student council in high school."

A seminary high school, to be precise. The Detroit native studied for the priesthood before deciding to become a doctor. In medical school, he quickly opted for his low-profile specialty and wrote a post-doctoral thesis titled, "Neuromuscular Anatomy of the Bladder." And, though educated at Yale and Oxford, he has chosen to practice at a small hospital in Manassas, a distant Washington suburb known for little except its Civil War battlefield.

"I thought that being out here in the country would mean a quiet, obscure life," says the soft-spoken Dr. Sehn, an Oxford University tie and horn-rimmed glasses dressing up a white doctor's coat.

All that ended abruptly soon after dawn on June 23, when a phone call from the hospital jolted him awake. The message: John Wayne Bobbitt, 26 years old, had awakened a short time before to find his wife, Lorena, amputating his penis with a 12-inch kitchen knife. Mrs. Bobbitt, 24, was charged with malicious wounding. Mr. Bobbitt, accused by his wife of rape, has been charged with marital sexual assault. Both cases are pending before the courts.

Dr. Sehn, who happened to be on call that night, reached the emergency room to find an oddly calm patient, "and eight cops sitting around with their knees crossed," he says. Accustomed to more mundane problems, such as bladder infections and kidney stones, Dr. Sehn shared some of their queasiness. Looking at before-and-after slides of his patient, the doctor recalls: "I felt an out-of-body sensation watching myself go through the usual reflexes as a doctor, while on a gut level I felt sick."

Soon after, the knife-wielding wife called the police to say she had tossed the dismembered organ from a car window. A police search found it lying in some grass. Dr. Sehn and a plastic surgeon then spent more than nine hours reattaching it, using a microscope to reconnect minuscule nerves and blood vessels.

"It was the accomplishment of a lifetime for me," says Dr. Sehn. In fact, U.S. surgeons have employed the microscopic technique used in the surgery only a half-dozen times or so to date. "It's incredible," the doctor adds, "to see anatomy at that level."

The first media calls came in as he emerged from the operating room. After prodding from the hospital, which felt the case would offer helpful publicity, a reluctant Dr. Sehn agreed to talk. After all, he was proud of his surgical triumph, "and like most doctors I'm always anxious to teach," he says.

But during his first live interview, with a Las Vegas radio station, "everything I said provoked howls of laughter," he says. "It dawned on me that this whole subject was a minefield."

His fear was quickly confirmed when Fox News taped a long interview—then used only his brief comment about his prognosis for the patient's sexual function (which is expected to return). Then, on his first day back at his office, Dr. Sehn's secretary announced, "the *David Letterman Show* is on the phone." The doctor, who usually retires early, took the phone and said, "Who's David Letterman?"

When he found out, Dr. Sehn says, "I really panicked. I didn't see myself on a major talk show, and certainly not discussing penile anatomy." Dr. Sehn asked if he could vet questions first. The show never called back.

But other calls kept rolling in. From *Ms.* magazine. From Gay Talese, who is writing about the case for *The New Yorker.* From glossy Japanese and Italian magazines. From *The New York Times* science section.

Six weeks after the surgery, Dr. Sehn has resumed his daily ritual of connecting catheters and probing prostates—and correcting people who confuse his specialty with neurology, a medical field concerned with brains, not bladders. But incessant talk about the case still trails him each day to his office, on a bland suburban block, containing laboratory boxes filled with urine samples and venereal smears. One patient even blithely chats about the Bobbitts as Dr. Sehn gives him a vasectomy.

Eager to escape the fanfare. Dr. Sehn recently took his 10-year-old son on a West Virginia rafting trip. But as soon as they reached a campground, his son began running from tent to tent, announcing: "My dad's famous!" A crowd quickly formed and Dr. Sehn found himself, in the middle of the woods, "telling 300 strangers how you do a penile replantation."

Dr. Sehn has learned to accept such renown with polite bewilderment—and, gradually, with pride and a sense of humor as well. He now keeps copies of news clippings at the office and passes them out to curious patients.

One recent night, at his home in the rolling hills of rural Virginia, Dr. Sehn answers the phone at 10 p.m. to yet another radio show wanting all the details of his recent surgery. "Yes, it is possible to bleed to death from this sort of injury," the doctor says, as his wife, accustomed to such interruptions, keeps serving up fruit pie.

Other family members have also had to adjust. Not long ago, Dr. Sehn's sister in Oklahoma phoned a local radio station seeking a copy of a taped interview with her brother. She suddenly found herself on the air and fielding questions, among them: "And what do your little children call that part of the anatomy?"

The case, if it has meant fame, hasn't yet meant fortune for Dr. Sehn; he hasn't been paid for the surgery and, at best, the publicity has gained him a few new patients. Meanwhile, the Bobbitts have both hired entertainment lawyers to handle their stories. For Mr. Bobbitt, who is uninsured, a deal for book, TV or movie rights might help him meet medical bills that could total $50,000.

Dr. Sehn says he never expected the case to make him "the next Tom Cruise." But there is one sort of exposure he invites. "It would be exciting," he says, "to write about my patient's recovery in *The Journal of Urology.*"

# Writers' Workshop

## Talking Points

1) Wells plays this one—the highly-publicized penis-cutting in Manassas, Va.—seriously. Consider why *The Wall Street Journal* would favor this approach. How might headline writers for the other newspapers in New York City (the *New York Post* and *Daily News*, both freewheeling tabloids, and the staid *New York Times*) have handled this story?

2) Notice the artful way this headline drops two names, one a household word, the other an unknown. We don't know who Dr. Sehn is, but you'd have to have been unconscious in 1993 to be unaware of John Wayne Bobbitt. How is part of this headline's charm the mystery about the good doctor?

3) The best headlines display the rhythm of poetry. Read the second deck of this headline and imagine you're standing on stage in a smoke-filled coffeehouse:
> The Patient's Loss, Restored
> By Deft, Delicate Surgery
> Is Now the Talk of the Town

Is the headline writer the poet of the newsroom?

4) One word is missing, noticeably, from this headline, namely the organ that was the object of Lorena Bobbitt's ire. Wells reports that *The Wall Street Journal*'s taste mavens decreed that "penis" wasn't fit to print. Were they being unnecessarily prudish, especially for the '90s? If you were in charge, would you censor it, too?

5) Should a newspaper slavishly mirror society, or does it have a responsibility to uphold certain standards of taste? An alternative paper in Washington, D.C., published a courtroom photo of Mr. Bobbitt's severed penis. Was that appropriate? Would you run the same photo?

## Assignment Desk

1) In *The Editorial Eye,* Jane T. Harrigan, a journalism professor at the University of New Hampshire, offers four steps to headline writing:
   A. Read the story all the way through.

B. Summarize the story in one sentence, with a specific subject and an active verb.

C. Eliminate articles from the sentence and put the verbs in the present tense.

D. Now keep knocking out words, and substituting others, until the headline fits the space.

Write several other headlines for this story, following Harrigan's process.

2) Ken Wells must adhere to his publication's standards of taste. Compose headlines for this story as if you were writing for Page One of the *New York Post, Daily News, The New York Times,* or your own paper.

3) To meet space demands, Wells says, subheads sometimes end up being trimmed at the *Journal's* off-site printing plants. Write two to three additional subheads for this story. Compose them for New York City's three other dailies as well as for *The Wall Street Journal.*

# A river ran over it, and Missouri span is showing the strain

## But bridge inspectors, using grit and high technology, unlock its murky secrets

AUGUST 27, 1993

By Daniel Machalaba

GLASGOW, Mo.—The marauding Big Mo has left a big mess. Ed Hassinger and friends are trying to get to the bottom of it.

In a small boat bullied by the current, Mr. Hassinger, Jim Bowden and Chip Jones struggle up the Missouri River, looking for the ravages of recent record floods. The three are bridge inspectors for the Missouri Highway and Transportation Department; their target is the Glasgow Bridge, a massive steel and concrete span that takes state Route 240 across a 2,000-foot expanse of the swollen river.

The fear is that raging flood waters have scoured out tons of rock from the riverbed, undermining the bridge's supports. For now, the bridge is closed; how soon it opens again will depend on what the inspectors find.

### DEPTHS OF DESTRUCTION

"What other job lets you go swimming, diving and boating, and get paid for it?" asks Mr. Hassinger wryly. But later, when his motorized skiff spins out of control in treacherous currents and heads toward a bridge pier, one thing is clear: This isn't where the fun begins, but where it ends.

Bridges don't figure much on people's minds until rivers take them back. Now, with waters of the 1993 Midwest flood receding and cleanup under way, bridges are all some people are thinking about. As many as 40 appear to be damaged in

Missouri alone; scores of others have been undermined in six other states inundated by flood waters from both the Missouri and Mississippi rivers. Estimates to replace or repair them all, along with battered rail lines and roadways, run into the hundreds of millions of dollars.

That may be the smallest part of the cost. Without these bridges, farmers can't get to their fields, merchants can't rebuild their shops and whole towns find themselves cut off from the world. "It's like someone is putting a rope around your house and saying 'you can't go in it,'" laments Bill Meyer, a farmer frustrated by the state's decision to close the Glasgow Bridge last week.

His flood-damaged house sits on the flat lands west of the Missouri; Glasgow, population 1,295, and the supply line for his and other farms, is on the opposite side. A road that once provided access to towns west of his farm has been washed out. Mr. Meyer wants his bridge back—yesterday.

The 32-year-old Mr. Hassinger and company would like to oblige, but safety concerns are paramount. And, on one recent day, the river, still bloated with flood waters, is showing inspectors just what kind of challenges they face. The bridge's concrete piers have to be probed and plumbed with electronic tools brought along for the occasion. But an eight-knot current seizes the bow of their flat-bottomed skiff and slams it against one of the piers.

"Hang on," gasps Mr. Hassinger as Mr. Bowden, 45, wrenches the tiller of the outboard motor and steers the boat clear. He edges back toward the pier with Mr. Hassinger poised, like a whaler ready to strike, with a 20-foot fiberglass pole in his hand. At the pole's end is a sonar transducer, a gadget that uses sound waves to "see" through the swirling chocolate waters.

A dozen times Mr. Hassinger plunges the electronic harpoon into the river, Mr. Jones, 27, plots readouts on a depth-finder wired to the transducer, slowly building a profile of the river bottom. Calculating the findings later, Mr. Hassinger doesn't like what he sees. The riverbed appears to have dropped five to 10 feet since divers measured it three years ago. At that level, the bridge's piers are likely to be in trouble.

Mr. Hassinger previously had called his office in Jefferson City, Mo., hoping to locate plans that might show the piers run deeper than supposed. "Unless they find something that tells us otherwise, that pier is undermined," he says.

This scene is apt to be all-too-familiar as inspectors move along the multistate chain of devastation that includes hundreds of miles of washed out or waterlogged roads, railroad tracks and utility-transmission facilities.

The extent of damage is dumbfounding, even to veterans of other natural disasters. "It's unreal—like being on another planet," says Charles Kriegel, a Federal Railroad Administration track inspector for the past 15 years.

His recent inspections of several Missouri rail lines provide two graphic examples. The river at one point carved out a 2,000-foot gap, 73 feet deep, in a railroad embankment. At another spot, in a field near a Santa Fe Railway mainline track, two shapes that Mr. Kriegel originally mistook for fuel tanks were wooden coffins ripped by flood waters from a nearby cemetery.

Working in the wake of the flood thus poses unusual headaches and hazards for inspectors. Mr. Hassinger says he and his colleagues crashed their boat into a submerged highway "yield" sign while speeding above flooded roads and fields to inspect the Boonville, Mo., bridge. Other inspectors trying to reach the Interstate 70 bridge at Rocheport, Mo., found themselves in wet suits, and wading and swimming through rotting, chest-deep muck to reach the approach piers. At another nearby bridge, they found equally foul conditions. "Phew, dead fish," says Alan Trampe, recalling the day of slogging through stagnant waters in 90-degree-plus heat.

Despite the hardships, the Midwest floods represent a high-water mark for inspectors. "It's hot, the bugs are biting and the current buffets the boat," says Dan Cecchi of Collins Engineers Inc., a Chicago consulting concern. "But you get to be part of a historic event. It's like being in the World Series for bridge inspectors."

### 'ZERO VISIBILITY'

Back at the Route 240 bridge in Glasgow, commercial divers, more experienced in swift currents, are checking the pier where Mr. Hassinger suspects undermining. Working in "zero visibility," Kenneth Johansson, a diver for Oceaneering International Inc., feels his way down the concrete slab, searching for gaps between the bottom of the pier and the riverbed. "It's just total blackness, like being in a closet," he says. "I feel small sticks and rocks rolling by me."

Mr. Johansson reports some encouraging news: The main bridge piers appear to rest securely on the bottom. But on the downside, one of the bridge's approach piers is undermined, with a toppled section of a railroad bridge pressing against it.

Mr. Hassinger, after an agonizing telephone consultation with a superior, announces that the bridge will stay closed until repairs can be made. It may be a month before the bridge reopens. "We aren't always the bearer of good tidings" but safety requires that an unstable bridge not be opened prematurely, he says.

The decision is a blow to farmer Mr. Meyer, and to Carrie Henke, a third-grade teacher who depends on the bridge. "I feel like somebody kicked me in the stomach," she says. "It's enough to have a nervous breakdown."

# Writers' Workshop

## Talking Points

1) One delightful aspect of Ken Wells's headlines is the chance they offer to play a kind of parlor game: Find the Cultural Antecedents.

What is the novel—and movie with the same title—he's playing off with this headline? For extra points, name the author and director.

2) Wells is 45 and his headlines betray his baby-boomer roots. For example, what is the source for Wells's subhead "Depths of Destruction"? Hint: Barry McGuire. *The Wall Street Journal*'s audience includes many who belong to an older generation. Is Wells serving his readership with cultural referents that may go right over many readers' heads? Discuss how puns and other wordplay might differ for *Modern Maturity* or *Details*.

3) A thesaurus is one of the headline writer's most important tools. Consider why Wells used a synonym for "bridge" in the first deck. Was it just a matter of space, or were there other considerations at work?

## Assignment Desk

1) Write an alternative headline and subheads for this story.

2) Write a headline and subheads for a publication whose average reader is older than 65. Write one for publications whose average reader is younger than 20.

# Mr. Madini's nose knows the secrets of others' perfumes

## He'd rather blend his own, but modern Moroccans drive him to obsession

AUGUST 30, 1993

By Barry Newman

TANGIER, Morocco—Going for the face, then the throat, then the chest, Soulaiman Madini pumps six quick rounds from his atomizer gun at two sweaty men who have stepped into his shop from the souk's dark passageway. Sweet, lemony mists engulf them.

"This is my publicity," Mr. Madini says. "It's direct. Like a fax." One of the men grunts as if he has been maced. The other places an empty bottle on the counter and says, "Obsession."

Mr. Madini doesn't like what he has to do now. He'd rather reach up to the shelf behind him and fill the bottle from the spigot of a jar marked "tuberose" or "jasmine." But spray-on publicity for scents conjured up by his family for centuries can't overpower a scratch card from Calvin Klein.

The customers are obsessed.

### A CALVIN DECLINE

So Mr. Madini opens a cabinet and removes a decanter marked "Obsession Type." With a syringe, he draws out three tawny ounces and squirts them into the bottle, then digs out a plastic label that says, "Obsession," and sticks it on. Mr. Klein's price: $60, tax not included. Mr. Madini's price: $7, tax not mentioned.

Enveloped in a farewell blast from the atomizer, the men leave, and Mr. Madini's high-voltage smile dims a few watts. He says: "You cannot explain the choice. It's mysterious. They see a man in a magazine. So handsome, so nice. Publicity! It makes their minds up. The more publicity, the more they like it. Some people want good smells. Some people want only publicity. In two words, perfume is nice work, but it is mysterious work."

This isn't quite the meaning of "mysterious" that perfume makers have in mind when they hire a sculptor to design a two-ounce *flacon* of hand-polished crystal in the shape of a Mesopotamian ziggurat, or send a fashion model in a safari suit to stand in front of a DC-3 on a North African desert. That sort of mystery raises perfume prices to 20 times the cost of the stuff in it. At Mr. Madini's Parfumerie Oriental, the mystery comes free.

## COMMON SCENTS

Women in veils and men in hoods lead the cast of types pushing past his doorway deep in the souk's maze. Kids scream and shadowy shapes whisper, "You want hashish?" Blasting Berber tapes provide the sound effects. The smells come from two directions: mint, motorbikes, wood smoke, sheep and sweat outside the perfumery; musk, oak moss, sandalwood, Opium and Amarige inside.

The shop is no bigger than a *couturier's* closet. In a place of honor, to the left of the "fixed price" sign, rests a photo of Mr. Madini's late father, kneeling before Morocco's late king. Having mixed their own fragrances in Saudi Arabia for a few hundred years, the Madinis migrated to this spot in 1906.

"My father, my grandfather, his grandfather's grandfather—we make and sell, all of us," says Mr. Madini, who is 32. While his five-year-old son watches, he spends an hour pasting fancy names onto plain bottles: Eternity, Tresor, Shalimar. "We have perfume in our blood," he says. "We make and sell. Always."

Making and selling is surely a venerable enterprise, but the labels are a sticking point. The fancy names belong to others.

"He may be a delightful person, but he's no better than a criminal as far as I'm concerned,"

Louis Santucci says when told of Mr. Madini's shop. Mr. Santucci works for the Cosmetic, Toiletry and Fragrance Association in Washington. "This guy's probably got a hose out the back door where the tank trucks fill up," he says.

Could be. Though no pirate hunter has ever traced a shipment of knockoff perfume to Mr. Madini's back door, his lab is easy to find; it's just upstairs. Yet he recoils when asked for a peek. "It is secret," he says. "No one sees. Never." And apart from the spray gun, his best burst of publicity came in a book enticingly titled *The Rogue's Guide to Tangier.*

On the other hand, Mr. Madini has his own image of a rogue: the company that puts a fashion designer's name on an ampule containing a dram of odoriferous liquid, hypes it to the heavens and sells it for a scandalous price.

His only exports consist of Aquarian Age standards—patchouli, jasmine, musk—to a store called Talisman in Woodstock, N.Y., which also sells his family's immemorial (and inexpensive) mixtures. But here, his sales are mostly knockoffs. If Mr. Madini is a rogue in Tangier, blame Morocco's natives; the scratch card has gone to their heads.

"When I was small," Mr. Madini says, "people chose, they made their own blends. Special. Strong, sweet smells. Now, they are shown the way. If you make such mixtures, nobody will buy. Only the names count. Good name, good bottle, good package, good luck."

The publicity plague descended, by Mr. Madini's reckoning, when men began to let their wives go shopping. A woman would bring in a droplet of some airy Parisian essence, give him a whiff and ask him to copy it. So he did.

Big "smellalike" outfits (legal or illegal) do this by gas chromatography. Mr. Madini follows his nose.

One perfume can enfold 600 aromas, from rose to myrrh to civet. "I smell it and I know what's in it," says Mr. Madini, though Paco Rabanne for men took two years to sniff out. As he speaks, a woman in a head scarf enters with an empty flask of Dune. Mr. Madini passes it under his nose. He tells her to come back tomorrow; the Dune will be recreated.

By now, he has built a stockpile starting with Chanel No. 5 and working up to Eternity. DNA is on the way. Most are dead ringers for the originals. When a bejeweled women comes in to try Mr. Madini's off-the-shelf LouLou, she says, "Why buy the real one? This smells the same." Later, in blind tests of the genuine articles against Madini renditions of White Linen, Obsession, Beautiful and Anais Anais, five Western women can't smell the difference, either.

But for Mr. Madini, copying creates no scents of accomplishment. He would rather see his own name in lights above the counters at Saks Fifth Avenue, with Kenzo and Liz Taylor, even if it means tearing a page from the detested handbook of hype.

"Look, this is orange," he says, opening a jar of what looks like shoe polish. "Solid perfume. My creation. No one has it." He unboxes a jasmine-impregnated rock. "A new product. You can rub it on, put in drawers."

The smells are sweet and strong.

"It's easy to be famous," says Mr. Madini. "Remember Nescafe? Coffee from hot water. A miracle! It's easy to get publicity for new things. People try. They accept. This is the lesson of marketing."

Maybe the perfumed rock will stone them in Woodstock. In the souk, however, Mr. Madini has had to settle for another way of tuning his inventive urge to the redolent forces of high fashion.

A man he knows well walks in with an empty bottle. Moving along his row of spigots, Mr. Madini fills it with a little Paco Rabanne, a few squirts of Anais Anais, Opium and Aramis, and a shot of Poison.

"You smell it, you will like it," he says. "Good perfumes are always a mixture." Mr. Madini holds the bottle under the man's nose and reaches for the spray gun. The man sniffs, pays—and leaves in a lemony mist.

# Writers' Workshop

## Talking Points

1) The top headline relies on a homonym, one of two or more words that have the same sound and often the same spelling, but differ in meaning. Find the other example of this device in a subhead for this story. Headline writers have a variety of devices at their disposal: alliteration, rhyme, puns. Keep an eye out during your reading for examples.

2) Wells is especially adept at playing off the text. The deck contains a double-entendre, a phrase with a double-meaning. Usually, one of the two meanings is indelicate, risqué, or suggestive, according to the *Concise Dictionary of Literary Terms*. Discuss the double meanings of "obsession" in Wells's case.

3) It's parlor game time again. What's the real world inspiration of the subhead "Calvin Decline"?

4) A dissenting view of Mr. Madini can be found in paragraph 12. "This guy's probably got a hose out the back door where the tank trucks fill up," alleges a spokesman for the Cosmetic, Toiletry, and Fragrance Association in Washington. Could Wells have used this element? Why do you suppose he didn't?

## Assignment Desk

1) Compose an alternative headline using either alliteration, homonym, double-entendre, or if you're feeling especially ambitious, all three.

2) Write a headline for this story as it might appear in a trade newspaper published by the Cosmetic, Toiletry, and Fragrance Association.

# Ruff! Ruff! Ruffage! Here, Rover, have a nice bean sprout

## Turning pets into vegetarians is healthy, owners say; veterinarians are howling

OCTOBER 27, 1993

By Suein L. Hwang

Lions may be evolutionary predators, gorging on meat, blood and guts. But Teresa Gibbs finds these ancient carnivorous stirrings unacceptable for her own member of the feline family.

So Ms. Gibbs has turned Yoko, her black, long-hair cat, into a vegan—the strictest kind of vegetarian. Every day, Yoko feasts on garbanzo beans, lentils, split peas and broccoli—with a pinch of garlic. On special occasions, she nibbles asparagus spears.

"I don't think she misses meat in any way, shape or form," says Ms. Gibbs, herself a vegan. She takes a swipe at conventional cat food: "This is much better than...dead animal parts sitting around with flies on it all day long."

### OF MICE AND BEANS

Yoko is a pioneer—and critics would say a guinea pig—in a controversial new movement that unites vegetarianism and animal-rights activism: vegetarian pets. Thousands of American pet owners have joined the movement, tossing out the Purina and Alpo and introducing Fido and Fluffy to nutritional yeast and wheat-gluten flour.

The vegetarians purr about the benefits of a meatless pet diet, crediting it with curing all sorts of animal ailments from allergies to diabetes. Some even swear that cats on tofu and bean sprouts become so mellow that they stop chasing mice and birds.

"The health benefits are just incredible," insists Lorraine Sheppard, a Colorado massage therapist who converted her two dogs to vegetarianism five years ago. "They [pets] have more energy, more clarity of mind and a real peacefulness."

Such claims aside, some worry that the veg-pet people are barking up the wrong tree. "Dogs evolved on a high meat-based protein diet, and cats are truly carnivores," says Arleigh Reynolds, a clinician at Cornell University's College of Veterinary Medicine.

## CEREAL KILLERS?

Thus, to deprive canines of meat invites a host of medical problems. Dr. Reynolds says he has treated a number of vegetarian dogs suffering from poor coats, lost muscle mass and liver problems. And cats—which require taurine, a nutrient only found in animal flesh—are susceptible to reproductive, growth and heart problems on a meatless diet. Dr. Reynolds says that, while some vegetarian pets are fed supplements to make up for possible nutrient losses, he knows of at least one cat death related to vegetarian taurine deficiency.

As for the claim that a vegetarian diet purges cats of predatory instincts, Francis Kallfelz, another Cornell veterinarian and nutritionist, is skeptical, "I don't think it's possible for natural instincts to be changed by feeding procedures," he says.

None of these concerns make much of a dent on vegans, who hail animal vegetarianism as a final break from the flesh-eating world. "In a small way, I'm trying to make a difference," says Mary Currier, a vegan and leading advocate of vegetarian pet diets.

Ms. Currier is helping more than most. The onetime suburban housewife has turned pet vegetarianism into her life's work, providing sanctuary for 32 vegetarian cats and five vegetarian dogs.

In her remote, battered New Hampshire farmhouse, Ms. Currier has accomplished what most owners of finicky felines would consider the impossible. As four cats snooze peacefully on a crowded kitchen table, two others eagerly attack and eat half of a cantaloupe on a countertop. "Little Fancy Feast loves fake hot dogs, and I have to hide the potatoes from Beethoven," says Ms. Currier, peeling a cucumber and feeding pieces of it to Polar Bear, a white longhaired cat.

Buying chickpeas and olive oil—among many ingredients in her homemade vegetarian pet chow—for 32 cats requires some sacrifice. "It's really difficult," says Ms. Currier, who devotes $450 a month to her animals and hasn't gone to a restaurant since last Christmas. "But if you have a dream, you get by."

Not that coaxing genetic meat-eaters onto vegetarian diets is without problems. Ms. Currier's success aside, Ms. Gibbs says it took her two months of experimentation before she found a garbanzo bean, lentil and split pea stew that her three cats could swallow. Temptation is a constant worry. Ms. Sheppard says she is happy that her dogs nibble almonds and grapes but has no doubt that, offered a steak, "they would eat meat."

## PURE, GREENER DOG CHOW

Vegetarian pets also seem susceptible to stomach upsets, often requiring antigas remedies. Karen Porreca, a librarian for People for the Ethical Treatment of Animals and owner of four vegan dogs, regularly adds a few drops of Beano to their nightly rations that include brown rice and split peas. "One of them really needed it," she confides.

If the vegetarian pet movement is political to some, it represents opportunity for others. Wow-Bow Distributors Ltd. of Deer Park, N.Y., is among a half-dozen companies that have sprouted up to make commercial quantities of dog and cat health food. Wow-Bow's dog biscuit is baked from stone-ground whole wheat, yeast, fresh garlic, parsley and eggs (from free-range hens). Wow-Bow's logo: A Chinese Shar-Pei with a carrot dangling from its mouth.

No one knows how many pets—"companion animals" in animal-rights parlance—have gone vegetarian. But Nature's Recipe Pet Foods in Corona, Calif., says sales of its vegetarian dog chow jumped 24 percent to an estimated $2.4 million last year. That is enough of its soybean, rice, barley and carrot concoction to feed 19,000 canines. And the fourth edition of *Vegetarian Cats and Dogs,* published by a Montana maker of vitamin supplements for vegetarian pets, sold 2,000 copies in 1993—as many as in the previous six years combined.

## BEATING A DEAD HORSE?

For some, the vegetarian pet movement reflects a deep mistrust of commercial pet-food makers. Among a litany of accusations, one is that some meat in commercial pet food is unfit to eat; another is that some pet food is actually made from euthanized cats and dogs.

Both claims are untrue and the latter is "a rumor that goes around every 10 years or so," says Mark Finke, director of nutritional research for Alpo Pet Foods Inc., a unit of Grand Metropolitan PLC. "We try not to buy our materials preground, so you can tell what they truly are." He admits that most pet-food companies, including Alpo, use meat and entrails from animals (horses, cows and other farm stock) that have died of disease or old age. But Mr. Finke says that high-temperature processes used in making and canning pet food kill any pathogens. (Ralston-Ralston Purina Group and Nestle SA, also major pet-food makers, declined comment.)

Furthermore, pet-food makers say that, vegetarian revulsion aside, dogs and cats find animal parts paw-licking good. "Dogs happen to *love* lungs," says Alpo's Dr. Finke. Adds Cornell's Dr. Reynolds: "If you watch a lion when it goes out and kills, the first thing it eats are the guts."

Which is why even some vegetarians think the vegetarian pet movement is misguided. For Donald Garber, a vegetarian and veterinarian, his cat Vlackavar is a natural carnivore who shouldn't be deprived of his birthright by human notions of a "politically correct" diet.

"I don't have the right to impose my will on another creature," says Dr. Garber. "Vlackavar is a cat and cats eat meat."

# Writers' Workshop

## Talking Points

1) A sense of play pervades Wells's headlines, from the main headlines to the subheads. An amateur songwriter who plays jazz and blues guitar, Wells displays the same improvisational skills on a newsroom keyboard. How can newsrooms inject more fun into writing the news?

2) This story's subheads are the product of a punster gone wild:
   "Cereal killers?" "Of Mice and Beans." "Pure, Greener Dog Chow."
   What are the phrases that provided the raw material for Wells's punning?

3) Jane Harrigan in *The Editorial Eye* warns headline writers to "remember that no two editors agree on what's terrific and what's over the line; one person's 'Great!' is another person's groaner." But, Harrigan adds, "even groaning has its place." Get several reactions to the puns in these subheads and see how they break down between "Great!" and groans.

4) Nowhere can the word "ruffage" be found in the dictionary. The word is properly spelled "roughage." Consider why *The Wall Street Journal* editors would permit this departure. Could you mount a persuasive argument against printing the headline because of the deliberate misspelling?

5) In this headline, Wells immediately grabs the reader's attention without giving away the story. Then he gives a fuller, straightforward explanation in the deck, the second headline immediately below it. Explore the reasons why it's effective to pique a reader's curiosity and then immediately satisfy it.

6) Headlines must hew to the same standards of fairness and balance as news stories. Notice how Wells captures the essence of the two sides in the pet vegetarian debate in the second deck, yet manages to retain its lively flair.

7) There is a serious side to this story: the potential of health problems for animals deprived of meat. Do headline writers run the risk of trivializing or mocking issues that are of importance to many people?

## Assignment Desk

1) Write several headlines and subheads for this story.

2) Look for elements in this story that might lend themselves to different headlines, such as the reliance of some pet owners on Beano, an anti-gas remedy.

3) Play this one seriously. Write a headline that focuses on the threat vegetarianism may pose to pets.

# Cross Purposes

## The Catholic Church struggles with suits over sexual abuse

### While it pledges compassion, its lawyers play rough defending lapsed priests

### Suing parents for negligence

NOVEMBER 24, 1993

By Milo Geyelin

When Edward Morris sued the Philadelphia Catholic archdiocese alleging eight years of sexual abuse by his childhood priest, lawyers for the church had a swift answer. They countersued Mr. Morris's parents—blaming them for failing to discover their son's relationship with an alleged "child abuser."

When Timothy D. Martinez sued the archdiocese of Santa Fe over alleged abuse by a convicted pedophile priest there, church lawyers took a similar tack. They sent private investigators swarming through Mr. Martinez's past, asking former friends if he was homosexual.

And during a grueling deposition last year—with the ex-priest sitting silently across a conference table—church lawyers not only demanded details of Mr. Martinez's sex life but also asked: "When [the priest] touched you, did you enjoy it?"

Says the 30-year-old Mr. Martinez, "I felt they were trying to wear me down, like they were going to break me."

### PUBLIC POSTURE, PRIVATE DEEDS

For parishioners caught up in a web of sexual abuse by rogue priests, U.S. Catholic Church leaders have an unequivocal public posture: "It's long since time to get on our knees, to beat our breasts, to ask God's mercy...," Cardinal John O'Connor of New York said in an open letter last July. "Justice, compassion and charity comprise the foundation of our policy."

Yet many victims have found this pledge stops at the courthouse door. Worried about crippling damage awards and their effect on church programs, and concerned about false allegations, the church has adopted bruising, bare-knuckle tactics more common to corporate defenses in high-stakes personal-injury suits.

The church, of course, has every right to defend itself, and some would argue that hardball tactics are justified—or at least understandable—in cases of unproven sexual-abuse allegations. And many of the defendants, with lawyers working on a contingent-fee basis, are asking for tens of millions of dollars in damages, including punitive damages. But a close look at numerous suits brought by alleged victims shows scorched-earth defense tactics common even in cases where the priests have been criminally convicted.

"There's a difference between exercising legal rights and prerogatives in lawsuits and intentionally re-victimizing victims by repudiations, rebukes and attacks," says Jeffrey Anderson, a plaintiff's lawyer in St. Paul, Minn. He is handling more than 225 suits against priests accused of molesting children.

## BATTLES OF ATTRITION

The hardball attitude is clear in a number of cases in upstate New York involving Cardinal O'Connor's own archdiocese. In one, the Rev. Edward A. Pipala of Goshen was accused by New York state authorities of operating a secret club for 50 young boys and teenagers, identifying members by number and taking them for seaside excursions to New Jersey and Cape Cod to drink, watch X-rated movies and engage in sex. He pleaded guilty last summer in state and federal courts in New York to a variety of charges including sodomy and sexual abuse.

But the archdiocese—represented by a crack litigation team at Simpson, Thacher & Bartlett, one of New York's premier corporate-law firms—has denied all liability, rejected settlement discussions and inundated plaintiffs' lawyers with faxed demands for pretrial information. Among the requests: a precise description of what the children drank and where or with whom they were when they drank it.

The archdiocese is responding aggressively to allegations that the Rev. Daniel A. Calabrese of Poughkeepsie sodomized a teenage boy in a parish rectory last year after getting him drunk on beer and vodka. Father Calabrese pleaded guilty to criminal charges of sodomy in state court in Poughkeepsie. In response to a civil suit filed by the boy's family earlier this year in state court there, the archdiocese is blaming the youth, saying he "willingly consented."

## JUSTIFIABLE PAIN

The archdiocese says such tactics are painful but necessary to shield against huge damage awards that could force cutbacks in charitable and educational services. Cardinal O'Connor, in his role of bishop of his diocese, has a responsibility to defend it, "especially in lawsuits that might seek to teach the church a lesson or injure the church," says his spokesman, Joseph Zwilling.

Church officials nationwide share this view and are acting accordingly. On the one hand, they are expressing sympathy for victims, offering counseling and overhauling outdated procedures for investigating abuse. Recently, for example, the National Conference of Catholic Bishops sought Vatican permission to strengthen the church's hand in defrocking priests who have committed abuse. And earlier, the conference began work on a national action plan for investigating abuse allegations and removing offenders. Yet, church leaders say they can't turn the other cheek when it comes to damage suits.

"Just because a lawsuit is filed, it doesn't mean the church should open up a checkbook and say,

'Take what you want,'" says Mark Chopko, general counsel for the Catholic conference, the ecclesiastical body for the 188 independent U.S. dioceses. Though they keep no centralized records, church officials estimate damage awards and settlement payments so far have topped $60 million. Outsiders place the amount much higher.

The church argues, of course, that one justification of a vigorous defense is that accusations may be false. That's the position the Catholic conference took after Chicago's Cardinal Joseph Bernardin was named in a lawsuit two weeks ago accusing him of sexual abuse. "I believe him when he goes before his people and the whole country to say he is innocent," said Bishop John F. Kinney of North Dakota.

Cardinal Bernardin's archdiocese is taking the same position in two lawsuits accusing one of his priests, the Rev. Robert Lutz, of sexually abusing two young boys. Father Lutz is pastor of a parochial grade school in the affluent Chicago suburb of Northbrook, Ill. "This is a justice issue," says John O'Malley, general counsel to the Chicago archdiocese. "The tragedy here would be not to defend this man because the media and a lot of people have decided he did something wrong."

## INSURANCE WOES

Yet, increasingly, insurance issues also play a role in the church's attitude. The nation's Catholic dioceses all carry general liability policies, and numerous sexual-abuse payouts to date have come from insurers. More and more, however, insurance carriers are refusing to defend dioceses or provide coverage, contending sexual abuse is an intentional act and not insurable under general liability policies. That is especially true in cases where dioceses were aware of complaints of sexual abuse by priests but withheld such information from insurers.

"We take the position that you could have expected they were going to harm another child," says Richard F. Johnson, a lawyer for Lloyd's of London. It is one of the carriers for the Archdiocese of Santa Fe, which has been rocked by a slew

of sexual-abuse lawsuits. A dozen carriers there
have sued seeking to void their obligation to defend the archdiocese or pay damage claims in 31
sexual-abuse complaints involving 39 plaintiffs
now pending before New Mexico courts.

And even in cases where insurance companies
provide coverage, some have balked at settle-
ments—and resorted to countersuits and attacks
against plaintiffs as a way of defeating or discouraging claims. Church officials sometimes contend
they have little say in how insurance-company
lawyers conduct such litigation, and point to Mr.
Morris's case as an example.

## SUIT AND COUNTERSUIT

In his lawsuit, filed in 1989, Mr. Morris claims
that his family priest, the Rev. Terrance
Pinkowski, abused him over an eight-year span. A
Franciscan friar, Father Pinkowski was Mr. Morris's high-school religion teacher and spiritual
guide at a time when Mr. Morris was considering
becoming a priest. According to the suit, filed in
the Court of Common Pleas in Philadelphia, Father Pinkowski convinced Mr. Morris that sexual
relations were a form of therapy necessary for his
spiritual growth in preparation for ordination.

Mr. Morris, now 31 years old and the owner of
a Philadelphia import-export business, brought
the allegations long after the alleged abuse. The
catalyst was his 1988 marriage—and the family
priest's conspicuous absence from the guest list.
His parents "wanted to know why this man wasn't
coming to my wedding," Mr. Morris says.

After Mr. Morris sued, however, the church's
defense lawyer—hired by the insurance carrier—
quickly countersued Mr. Morris's parents, claiming negligence on their part. The tactic left Mr.
Morris in shock. "You go toward them and you
expect compassion and understanding and a degree of healing and you're treated like you're taking on a Fortune 500 company," he says.

While church officials say they protested the
strategy but had no control over it, the lawyer who
handled the case disputes that. The archdiocese,

as the policyholder, was the client "for professional and ethical purposes" and retained final say on strategy, says lawyer Bruce McCollough. "Nobody second guessed it."

Mr. Morris's suit dragged on for four years and was settled out of court last August under a confidentiality agreement barring disclosure of the terms. (Father Pinkowski died two years ago.)

## FAMILIAR TACTICS

Mr. Martinez found he got similar treatment in Santa Fe. The New Mexico archdiocese has become a magnet for sexual-abuse claims against clergy because one of the few treatment centers for pedophile priests—the Servants of the Peraclete—is located in nearby Jemez Springs. Though area parents were unaware of the practice, priests sent there for treatment were frequently reassigned to local parishes and allowed unsupervised contact with children.

Some alleged victims maintain that their complaints to former Santa Fe Archbishop Robert Sanchez went unheeded because he, himself, was engaging in sexual misconduct. Last March he abruptly resigned after three women accused him of having sexual relations with them when they were teenagers. Two weeks ago, the Servants of the Peraclete, which is independent of the archdiocese, agreed to pay about $8 million in damages to 25 victims of a priest it treated and released.

Now, facing a potentially huge, uninsured liability, the archdiocese is leaning on its lawyers to hold down damage awards while mounting a furious legal battle to force its insurers to pay legal costs and provide coverage.

Caught in the middle are plaintiffs like Mr. Martinez, an Albuquerque electronics technician for Martin Marietta Corp. and one of 12 people who contend they were abused as children and teenagers by Jason Sigler, a former priest. Mr. Sigler, according to state-court pleadings, had been reassigned to a small parish near Albuquerque after treatment for pedophilia at the Servants of the Peraclete.

There he befriended Mr. Martinez and his family—and, court records say, initiated an eight-year sexual relationship with Mr. Martinez, who was 13 at the time. "A lot of people have a hard time understanding what an authority figure a priest is," says Mr. Martinez, who claims the alleged abuse has left him depressed and with an abiding hatred for authority.

Mr. Sigler, no longer a priest, pleaded guilty in 1983 in a state court in Albuquerque to sexual molestation involving two minors; they also have sued him. Mr. Sigler has refused to testify in his own defense, citing his Fifth Amendment guarantee against self-incrimination; he now works as a paralegal for his lawyer.

The archdiocese nonetheless is preparing an all-out defense aimed squarely at discrediting Mr. Martinez. Private investigators have gone to great lengths to delve into his personal life, tracking down his college roommates, former girlfriends and even the janitor of the church he attended in Albuquerque as a youth. Archdiocese lawyers say they need such information to estimate liability and damages, noting the local church's treasury isn't bottomless.

"Everyone wants the diocese to roll over and play dead. We get hammered and get kicked in the teeth, and it's not going to be that way any more," says the Rev. Ron Wolf, chancellor of the archdiocese.

Church lawyers blame plaintiffs' lawyers for trying their cases in the press and making unreasonable settlement demands. On Monday, an offer by Mr. Martinez to settle for $1.25 million was rejected.

## CHURCH ON THE OFFENSIVE

Still, some can't get past the irony of the church's iron-fisted response to such lawsuits. Cardinal Bernardin's Chicago archdiocese is credited with developing the nation's strongest program for investigating abuse and removing problem priests and providing counseling to victims. This nonetheless hasn't stopped the archdiocese from waging legal war against those who have filed suit in Cook County Circuit Court against Father Lutz.

The church has financed a countersuit alleging invasion of privacy and defamation against the parents of one plaintiff; the parents took their case to the media after state prosecutors declined to press criminal charges against Father Lutz.

Private detectives hired by the Chicago law firm Sidley & Austin have sifted through the family's trash, staked out their home and telephoned neighbors in search of incriminating information. At least in this case, high-powered lawyering has raised some potentially valid defense points. According to depositions in the case, the accuser has a history of fabricating stories and recanted his accusations when questioned by a family psychologist.

Whatever their merits, counterattacks do often work. Consider the four-year battle waged by the Archdiocese of Altoona-Johnstown in Western Pennsylvania against a lawsuit brought by a former church member, now in his 20s. The plaintiff alleged that, beginning at age nine, he was sexually abused for seven years by the Rev. Francis E. Luddy, the family's priest and his godfather. Father Luddy has admitted to committing sexual acts with the plaintiff's older brother, according to records in a separate suit. (Those records are now under court seal, though they were briefly made public.) Since 1987, the priest has been under treatment at Servants of the Peraclete.

But in response to the suit, the Altoona-Johnstown diocese denied that any abuse had occurred and argued that if any did, the church wasn't legally at fault. Among the defenses: If sex did take place, the plaintiff consented to it and was thus contributorily negligent. In the interim, lawyers for the diocese fought a lengthy battle to keep court proceedings closed while stalling efforts by the plaintiffs to gain access to Father Luddy's personnel file. The issue was still pending in August 1992 when the plaintiff, whose name has never been publicized, gave up and dropped his claim.

The diocese declines comment, citing a gag order on the still-pending case against Father Luddy filed by the plaintiff's brother. Says the man's lawyer, Richard Serbin, of Altoona: "He was at a point where he had just had enough."

For the Rev. Andrew M. Greeley, a Catholic priest and popular Chicago novelist who has been in the forefront of victims'-rights efforts, such cases undermine the credibility of the church's reform efforts. If the church wins, he says, other victims will be discouraged from coming forward. "They'll beat you into the ground with their money," Father Greeley says. But "even if the church wins, it loses."

# Writers' Workshop

## Talking Points

1) When the subject is a serious one—like this front page leader about the Catholic Church's dubious defense of pedophile priests—Wells's tone is equally somber. Compare this headline with the ones for pet vegetarians and Mr. Madini's nose. What are the obvious differences? The subtle ones?

2) Wells's headlines echo the text rather than lifting directly from it. Examine this headline and others to see how he uses the story as inspiration rather than as raw material.

3) There are phrases in this story that a headline writer might understandably want to lift, such as "scorched-earth defense tactics." Consider why Wells didn't use it. Would you?

4) This story is one of *The Wall Street Journal*'s two front page "leaders" that appear in columns one and six. It requires a multi-part headline format that harkens back to the turn of the century. Jane Harrigan says, "Old newspapers often ran so many headlines, each one so long, that a modern reader perusing them wonders whether anything was left to say in the story."

Study the elements of this headline (a "flashline," a "top," a "deck," and a "barline") and discuss whether more newspapers should return to this old-fashioned style.

5) Wells's flashline, "Cross Purposes" is a play on words, albeit serious. Consider its literal meaning. Explore the reasons why it's effective.

6) Notice the use of "lapsed" in the headline. Is this an accurate, fair description of pedophile priests, or is the *Journal* playing it safe?

7) Notice Wells's subheads. Gone are the puns, the whimsy. What role do these subheads play in this type of story?

8) The barline, "Suing Parents for Negligence," echoes information in the lead. Don Fry, in *Best Newspaper Writing 1993*, argues that readers dislike reading essentially the

same words twice. Is this element in Wells's headline
flawed, or a point that merits repeating?

9) In *The Editorial Eye,* Jane Harrigan offers an editor's
checklist for headline writing. Among the items:
  Does the headline reflect what's most important about the
story?
  Does the headline fit the tone of the newspaper?
  Does the headline fit the tone of the story?
  Have you reread the headline to make sure it could not be
misinterpreted?

## Assignment Desk

1) Rewrite this headline, focusing on each one of the elements: flashline, top, deck, and barline.

2) Rewrite the subheads for the story.

3) Search the story for words, phrases, issues that you think
should be reflected in the story. List them and compose several headlines inspired by your list.

# Ken Wells: Hoopster
# Grabbing the reader's attention

**CHRISTOPHER SCANLAN: You've spent your entire career at *The Wall Street Journal* as a writer, first in San Francisco and then in London. How long have you been on the Page One desk?**

KEN WELLS: I'm new. I got here last July. It's interesting to be on this side of the word processors.

**What is the Page One desk responsible for?**

We're responsible for the first, fourth, and sixth columns of the front page. The news summaries in columns two and three, and the rotating columns—Labor Letter, Tax Report, etc.—are all done by others, though we give them a final read.

We'll often run a box on Page One referring to a story inside, but in the main we're sort of an island apart. Our sole responsibility is to Page One.

**How does the operation function?**

In the good old days, about 10 years ago, this was almost entirely a magazine-like operation. The *Journal* was not in the habit of breaking daily stories on Page One, and it took the stock market to crash or an act of war for us to act like a real newspaper and do a daily story. That changed radically when everybody in the '80s started getting into business reporting.

The clever minds here divined—correctly, I think—that we had to be tougher, smarter, faster, meaner in some ways, and especially more fleet of foot if we were expected to be

■ Ken Wells, senior writer, Page One, *The Wall Street Journal.*

■ **Born:** Aug. 9, 1948, in Houma, La.

■ **Education:** Nicholls State University, B.A. in English literature, 1972; University of Missouri, master's degree in journalism, 1977.

■ **News Experience:** *Houma* (La.) *Courier,* 1967–75; *The Miami Herald,* 1978–82; *The Wall Street Journal:* San Francisco Bureau, 1982–90; London Bureau, 1990–1993. Page One desk, July 1993 to present.

■ **Awards:** Pulitzer finalist, general reporting, 1982.

taken seriously as the paper that everyone had to read about business and finance.

So today we act much less like a magazine, although there's still a magazine feature element to working in this job. On any given day, depending on the news, you can be hitched to what's called a "crash leader," which is a story that springs up today and has to be edited and in the paper tomorrow morning. Column One is where you will often find a breaking story. The middle column, the A-head, is almost never that way.

**How would you describe an A-head?**

Well, the classic definition by Barney Kilgore (former managing editor of the *Journal*) is a story that floats off the page, and it's still as true as you can get. Literally, it refers to the size and style of the type. Originally, it was given over to a spot news story. Then Kilgore decided that we needed to give our poor, beleaguered, financially driven executives who read the paper a little relief from the trials of daily business life, and so came up with this idea of the A-head. It's what put the *Journal* on the map as a writer's newspaper. I came to the *Journal* having never written a business story, but I came because this column existed and I thought it was an incredible venue. I thought it was too good to be true.

**What's the job of a Page One editor for *The Wall Street Journal*?**

Our job is multi-layered, but principally what we do is rewrite. Most of our time is spent taking routine and perfectly decent *Wall Street Journal* stories and buffing them a bit, making them sharper and clearer, making sure that the nut graph is where it should be, maybe trying to polish the lead a bit, that sort of stuff.

**Ah, the famous *Wall Street Journal* "nut graph." How do you define that?**

It's a paragraph that says what this whole story is about and why you should read it. It's a flag to the reader, high up in the story: You can decide to proceed or not, but if you read no farther, you know what that story's about. The third or fourth paragraph is the usual position. I think the genius of our paper is that you can get a lot of interesting stuff in a story and not have to take time like it's *War and Peace* to read it. On any given day, I think that the front page delivers a great combination of news and stylish writing, and proves that you don't have to go on for 300 inches to tell a story.

## What do you do besides rewrite?

John Brecher, the Page One editor, is very receptive to editors coming up with ideas and working with reporters to get those ideas done. Most of the great ideas still come from the reporters who are our eyes and ears in the field. Now and then we come up with ideas as well. We also get hitched to breaking stories; either editing a story that's in decent shape but done in great haste, or taking 500 inches of memos from bureaus, which is what I've done on a number of occasions, and boiling them down into a 50-inch story for the next day's paper. It's a great adrenaline rush, assuming you survive it. I would say that only 5 percent of my time is really spent in that final kind of copy desk edit checking.

So much more of what we do is thinking about how stories are broken and how we can fix them; if they're not really terribly broken, how we can make them better, or coming up with story ideas.

## How do you begin editing a piece?

One of the rules I pretty much adhere to is that you should read everything three times before you put a mark on it. Glyn Mapes, a former Page One editor, had this axiom. Obviously this doesn't work on a deadline earthquake story, but if it's a feature, give yourself some time to get to know the story and give the reporter credit for writing it.

So I try to read it leisurely a couple of times and then I might take it on the train with me and read it again before I ever put the first mark on it.

One of my other theories of really good editing is that you're really ready to edit the story at a point when you know it so well you're completely sick of it.

**Isn't it difficult to go three readings without touching it?**

No. I took a vow of ego-free editing when I got here. Having been on the other side of edits where I believed, rightly or wrongly, that the editor was trying to impose his or her view of style and notions and construction on my story that I thought were unwarranted, I try when I can to let the writers write. To that extent I consider myself kind of a caretaker of stories.

You can't do that with every story, and sometimes it's harder to do than the opposite, which is just to take a story under your own wing and run it through your own typewriter. But I think it's also a cop-out to unnecessarily remake it in your own image. If there's something that really bugs me about a story, I'll call the writer and say, "I don't think this works. Is there a way that we can get around it? What would you do?"

**Why is this approach important to you?**

If I'm going to be a good editor, what I have to do is be smart enough to recognize good writing when I see it, and not to get in the way of the style and the prose of those who do it well. I think every editor who's in the kind of job I'm in should strive for that.

**What are you trying to do with the headlines you write?**

The main thing is to seduce the reader. I see writing headlines as the art of seduction. They're the invitation to read the rest of the story. If you can make an interesting play on words, turn a pun that's not a complete cliché, if the headline seems snappy and clever, then I think it embeds in the reader's mind that this is perhaps a snappy and clever story and perhaps worth reading. And if you've done that, you've done your job. If they get past the headline and down to the nut graph and they continue, hallelujah! Our readership surveys show that still some appalling percentage of our readers never get past the fold in a lot of the stories, so it's a hard job.

## So what's the secret of your success?

It's easier to tell a good headline when it's been written than it is to say how you write one. But I think the clue here at the *Journal* is that I'm in a stable of brilliant headline writers who are very clever and very gifted at doing this kind of stuff.

Brecher, who appreciates good headlines and who also has won a headline writing award, challenges us to be creative. He says, "We all recognize that there's a thin line between a really clever, funny headline and one that goes over the line." Brecher's theory is see what happens, and if it's too clever by half, he will tell you, "I think this is a little overripe and worth trashing."

You have to recognize that there'll be disagreements and people will say, "Well, I think this is one of the cases where it doesn't work and we can't do it and that's that." But in the main, we are told to go for it.

## If there were a metaphor that you felt described you as a headline writer, what would it be?

Well, I would say a hoopster. I go for the slam dunk.

I like to write heads that are noticeable and everybody notices the slam dunk, right? That's what you strive for. Not every story can take a slam-dunk headline. There are very serious matters that sometimes have to be dealt with and you can't be funny or playful about those kinds of things. There are times when you're constrained to do just the facts.

But given the chance, and especially with A-heads and some leaders, there are times when we have a license to be creative and playful, and I think we should do it.

**So it's not surprising that puns seem to be the chief currency of a lot of *Wall Street Journal* headlines.**

Absolutely true. I think a well-placed pun is a thing of wonder. The thing that we always have to guard against is overusing them and getting too carried away. You really can't use puns on stories about AIDS.

**Have you always been an inveterate punster?**

I always loved wordplay. I remember almost nothing of my English literature major career, but I do remember reading Shakespeare and being stunned at the wordplay, this clever fencing with language. I've always been an admirer of that form.

**What's your reaction to a good pun?**

To me it's a thing of great enjoyment. I try to bring a certain sense of humor to my job. *The Wall Street Journal* is a good gray lady and on one level we have to take ourselves dreadfully seriously because you've got to get it right. We're the daily diary of the American dream, as they say, and there are high standards and we're expected to live up to the high standards, and we sweat buckshot trying to get it right. On the other hand, I think you can't take yourself too seriously.

**How long does it take you to write a headline?**

Some take 22.5 seconds from start to finish, and some take four days.

We sometimes have a languid amount of time to work on these stories, especially an A-head. If it takes you two days to rewrite the story, you're thinking about the headline the whole time—at least I do. I mean, I always try to think about it.

**What advice would you offer the copy editor who is churning out several headlines a day?**

Think creatively. If it is a feature story, be playful, don't be afraid to take risks. Use what I call the "ouch test." If it's a pun and it makes you really say, "Ouch," then maybe you shouldn't use it. On the other hand, if you chuckle, then maybe you should. I think we all appreciate that there are some stories that simply don't lend themselves to puns or wordplay. Let's face it, there are some boiler plate kinds of stories where you do your reader the best service by just writing serviceable, just-the-facts headlines. I don't think every story lends itself to a featurized headline treatment. If we start hanging cute headlines on car wrecks, we're in trouble.

**Do writers ever offer their own headlines?**

Surprisingly, they don't. In the old days writers never even saw the headlines. But these days we try as often as possible to send the headline back to the reporter just to make sure that there's not some nuance that we've missed, or that we've misstated something, or have been too cute by half or something like that.

**That's decent. Most reporters have had at least one day ruined by a headline.**

That's right, and I think that's the point: to try to not have reporters' days ruined by headlines. And I think we've all had that experience, where the headline was either too harsh or it overstated the case.

**Do you break rules as a headline writer?**

There are cardinal rules that we don't break, the standard ones like not splitting infinitives, not splitting adjectives between lines. We couldn't put "Catholic" on one line and "Church" on the next line. There are rules we have to live by.

**What rules *do* you break?**

The rules that you learn in journalism school about headline writing, that you shouldn't rob glory from the story. I think those bedrock kinds of rules we probably flaunt a lot. It was a cardinal sin in journalism school when I was there that you should never write a headline that reflects pop culture because within a year or two people who read these stories will have no idea what the hell we're talking about.

**Your headline "A River Ran Over It..." violates this rule then?**

Right. That is clearly a rip-off. Unless *A River Runs Through It* survives—it's a great book and a decent movie—but unless it survives, I would suspect that some cultural anthropologist reading this years hence will have no idea of the wordplay, that's all.

And by the way, the other thing I have to say that I never do, which is, I think, breaking all laws of God and man, is that I never use a dictionary or a thesaurus when I write headlines.

**Now, I saw a dictionary on your desk.**

I look up words if I'm worried about spelling. I don't go looking for synonyms. I never do that. I absolutely never do that. It either comes or it doesn't. This is the whole point.

**It's in your head?**

It's either there or it's not there. I find that the heads I write quickly are always the best heads. If I have to struggle, beating my head on the wall, they never come out as well.

**Let's look at a serious headline, the one about the way the Church defends priests who molest. The top line—Cross Purposes—what's that called?**

The flashline. I think it's a reasonably clever play on words on both the Church's official duties and the conflict the Church feels in dealing with the parents and alleged victims of abuse.

And so it works on a couple levels, which is why we used it.

**You talked before about not robbing glory from the story. And yet the bar line of this story—"Suing Parents for Negligence"—is actually drawn from the lead.**

Yes, I did it in that case. Normally you would not wish to rob the lead. On the other hand, I thought it was such a telling detail, it's like raising a red flag. It made me want to read the story.

**It would be hard to resist reading a story with the headline, "Ruff! Ruff! Ruffage!"**

I still laugh about this headline. There is a danger of liking your heads too well. But I still think it works, after all these months, and the subheads are as close as I can ever come to pure punnery. "Pure, Greener Dog Chow," a clear play on Purina Dog Chow.

**Are the heads and subheads the last thing you do when you're editing a story?**

Right. The great thing about this story is that when it came in, it was very well reported. There were no serious holes. And the one major thing that I did was to bring up higher the element that many people find this appalling. The way the story was originally written, it was sort of—wow, here are these weird people who are turning their pets into vegetarians, and then you read way down in the story these veterinarians saying, yes, but it could kill your dog and cat. And so I thought this is a story that will work best by noting that there's a certain amount of tension over this.

**Is "Roughage" deliberately misspelled?**

Oh, yes, it's obviously a pun on ruff, ruff, which is what dogs say when they bark.

**I guess I could hear a copy editor saying, "Yeah, that's very funny, Ken, but..."**

This is our fear. There is a gatekeeper above who is known occasionally to have literal interpretations of these kinds of things. In this case, this one got by.

**Do you ever come up with a headline and decide the references are too obscure or too elitist or too common?**

Well, I think I worry more about being too common than being too obscure. We have an intelligent readership and we don't have to pander to them or patronize them.

**Your job combines story editing with headline writing. What advice would you give to a reporter who would like to write better?**

First of all, I do agree that writing can be taught, that it is an acquired skill, which isn't to say that you can teach someone to be Hemingway, but I think competent bordering on bright writing can be instilled. It takes an incredible amount of determination. If you want to be a good writer, you've got to write a lot. If you want to be a good writer, you have to read a lot, and you have to go out and find good stuff to read.

**What's your reading list for success?**

I think every journalist benefits from reading Hemingway. He's the father of us all in proving that spare prose can also be elegant. I think people who write for magazines or newspapers like *The Wall Street Journal* and who aspire to write features, realize in some ways that less really is more. I favor the taut kind of telling of tales.

**And what advice would you give a headline writing hopeful?**

Take chances; try to think cleverly. You can't say that you can't flaunt the rules of grammar. I mean, I made up a word: "Ruffage."

There is a danger of innocent, youthful headline writers trying to make everything seem sort of featurish, and obviously there are stories that are very somber and serious and that you can't be cute with. And so I think that's a valuable lesson. If you're writing a headline about the school board meeting, unless it was invaded by Martians, it probably does not lend itself to feature treatment. But if it's a story that's having fun, you should have fun, too, and join in the spirit of the thing.

# Rose Jacobius

## Finalist, Headline Writing

Rose Jacobius has written headlines for the Style section of *The Washington Post* for a bit more than a decade, first as a copy editor and for the past five years as the section's night editor. Her boss, assistant managing editor Mary Hadar, describes Jacobius's headline output as "by turns appealing pungent or funny—but always precise." They're so good, Hadar notes, they even provoke "a steady stream of letters from appreciative readers who notice these things."

Jacobius got her start in headline writing at her previous job as a staff writer for a congressional service organization. Given the weighty subjects —principally the reauthorization of the Clean Air Act and Clean Water Act—and the one-line head format, it was a challenge. ("Need an atmospheric pun?" she asks. "How about Air Apparent, on hopes of legislative action, or Knock Their Sox Off, on a plan to cut sulfur emissions.") Before that, Jacobius covered the waterfront, literally speaking, for a group of newsletters on coastal and ocean science and policy.

"Good headlines require creativity, accuracy, and an inviting tone," Hadar observes. "They must tell prospective readers what the story's about and somehow make them want to read it. Done properly, they are little art works unto themselves." Nowhere are those qualities more evident than in "The Eternity of Being 12," a Jacobius headline that magically evokes the painful interlude in a girl's life when she's no longer a kid but not yet an adult.

# The eternity of being 12

JANUARY 14, 1993

*For Chelsea Clinton's peers, an agonizing stop between childhood and adulthood.*

By Elizabeth Kastor

The girls are 12. They are talking about Chelsea Clinton. They are talking about themselves.

"I kind of feel bad for her," one says of the next president's daughter. "She has kind of babyish clothes."

"I think her parents do it so she can look all cute and innocent and adorable."

"Boys will be intimidated by the Secret Service."

"Who'd want to call your friend and tell her your secrets when the phone is tapped?"

"She won't be able to tell if people like her because she's the president's daughter or because of who she is."

"I think she's probably going to get caught up with the bad crowd because she might not have any friends and she'd want to be popular."

"She might kiss a boy and people would think she's a skank."

This is what it is like to be a girl, 12 going on 13. The old childhood laws of friendship and loyalty tremble and crack. Parents become dictators with perverse ideas about wardrobe. The hair-sprayed sophistication and black-draped melodrama of adolescence beckon. You are told to behave like an adult but are still relegated to the children's table at Thanksgiving. You are, in one girl's words, too young to drive but too old to be cute. And then there's sex—sex education, dances to which only one boy comes, and thinking it's disgusting but not being able to think of anything else.

And if it's bad enough believing to the last molecule of your body that every single girl in your science class is grading your choice of jeans, imagine knowing, as Chelsea Clinton does, that a couple million Americans actually *are* judging your clothes.

With an eighth-grader in the White House, America is in for four years of voyeuristically observed adolescence. Dating and proms and algebra. Braces and rebellion and acne.

We mark 16 as the essential turning point of youth. The doors to freedom swing open, the motors rev and the mythic bliss of teenage life falls into our eager hands along with the car keys. But as Chelsea Clinton and millions of other girls know, junior high is where the real psychological action is. Breasts emerge and girls get their periods. The glories of gossip and the inanities of parents reveal themselves. In June the boys are mere tadpoles, but when they come back to school in September they are lanky proto-men wearing after-shave and playing macho in PE.

Chelsea Clinton is halfway through eighth grade. She will turn 13 in February. Not all eighth-graders are 12 in fact, but they are in spirit—no longer children, not yet full-fledged teens. There is something magnetic about 12-year-olds, but the magnet both pulls and repels. Girl Scout executives know troop leaders either love working with 12-year-olds or go out of their minds. They are disconcerting, these kids, because they are neither one thing nor the other. At moments they are the children we gave birth to, affectionate and needy, sweet and funny. At other times they are ruthless judges, observing their parents' world with acidic disdain. But at every moment they are that most unnerving thing of all: fledgling adults, creatures in the process of becoming us. To watch them is to watch our hazily remembered past and wonder how we got to the present.

Which is not to say we understand them. Because we can't. Just ask a 12-year-old.


## THE PARENT PROBLEM

On this they agree: Parents should not attempt to be funny.

"Parents make the stupidest jokes," says Emma Saal, a 12-year-old talking with several other ballerinas from the Washington School of the Ballet. "My dad thinks he is *so* funny."

"My mom thinks she fits in with my friends," laments Lauren Proffitt.

"My dad says, 'Hey, you guys are so groovy!'" says Emma. (How could you, Mr. Saal?)

"My mother's really annoying about everything," says Jessica Sanet. (Sorry, Mrs. Sanet.)

Parents should also not attempt to be affectionate. At least not in public.

At Williamsburg Middle School in Arlington, 10 girls from the eighth grade agree that the ultimate humiliation may have occurred one day when, in full sight of everyone, a father dropped a girl off at school, honked his horn and called out that he loved her. Being kissed in the car by a mother also ranks high on the embarrassment scale, as does being asked in public if you have your lunch money.

By way of weak comfort for parents, New York psychologist and author Stanley Goldstein offers this: "It's important that adolescent girls feel that parents are annoying. At times they even attack them, because what they have to do is break the symbiotic relationship with the parents, and the more difficulty they have breaking the symbiotic tie, the more they are going to have to attack them, unfair as it may be."

In other words, girls are certain adults cannot understand them because they *need* adults to be unable to understand them.

But get a group of seventh- or eighth-grade girls together, and in between the descriptions of annoying parental behavior come flashes of empathy.

"You can't win with parents," says Hanh Diep, an eighth-grader at Williamsburg. "Never can you win."

"You can't please them," says Gina Bailey.

"They never apologize. Never," says Angela Goodwin.

And then it happens. "They can't win either," offers a tentatively smiling Olivia Shilling. "When a friend is over and they say something, I say, 'That's so embarrassing!' But the next time they don't say anything and I say, 'Why did you just stand there?'"

And with that, the conversation ends.

### 'WHICH IS THE COOL TABLE?'

Middle school is cruel. It is a self-conscious culture, shot through with rumors, with complicated dress codes and a status hierarchy shaped by the desperate desire to be that most magical thing—popular.

Millie Lawson, eighth-grade counselor at Williamsburg, stands at the door of the cafeteria some days and watches her students calculating where to sit for lunch. Which is the cool table? Do they rank high enough to walk up and pull out a chair? "They hear notes of social acceptance only a dog can hear," Lawson says.

The citizens of Williamsburg Middle School can describe its arcane customs and have suffered from them, yet they cannot escape them. They make jokes about a girl's weight and know the jokes are mean, and know they are also funny. They watch each other to see if they have met the standard, if their clothes are from the Gap, not Kmart or Ames or Montgomery Ward. "I hate when people do it to me," says Olivia Shilling. "But then I go, 'Look at those pants!'"

Adults have their bland explanations: "Adolescent girls are trying on roles for size," says Goldstein, "so they do observe others and think, 'Well, is this comfortable for me? Who am I really? Who will I be?'"

The currency in this culture is friendship, and the market is not stable. Betrayal is common. Other people's secrets are traded for the possibility of new allegiances. "You usually don't know if you have a friend or not," says Williamsburg's Angela Goodwin.

Although they do not know her, girls talk about Chelsea Clinton as if she were just one more kid in their class. Raise her name, and they get started.

She looks so young, they say, in what one calls her "pretty-girl dresses."

"And the hair," says another.

"It's just a bad perm, I think," says another.

That her curls may, in fact, be her own, and that in only a few years women may envy the wild, flowing mane is not likely to occur to your average eighth-grader. But having offered up their critiques, they pull back again, shifting in an instant from the role of unflinching critic to empathetic observer.

"She can't dress like us," says Meghan Cooney. Look around the circle of girls (well-worn jeans, leggings and sweaters, pair after pair of suede bucks) and you see that of course she is right; these are not the fashions of campaign stops and photo opportunities. Meghan and the others then go on to talk of a recent *Saturday Night Live.* "That was so mean!" several say.

It was a "Wayne's World" skit. Right after Mike Meyers waxed erotic about Al Gore's daughters, he mentioned Chelsea. He paused and the pause was pointed. "Adolescence," he said, "has not been kind."

The studio audience roared. Welcome to middle school.

## TALK TO ME

There are things they love. TV. Pets. Shopping. Music. Hanging around.

And talking. Talking to each other. Talking to anyone who will listen. Especially talking on the phone.

"They talk unnecessarily," says Tawana Hinton. A Girl Scout troop leader and mother of an adolescent daughter, Hinton has invited Arkansas Girl Scout Chelsea Clinton to join her troop. As she speaks she is smiling wryly. Adults who enjoy 12-year-olds spend a lot of time smiling wryly. "They never stop talking. No matter how you threaten them, what you do, they talk."

Sometime even the girls realize it has gone too far. Andrea Wise says her addiction to the phone grew so bad last year that when she and her friend ran out of material, they would stay on and watch TV together. No conversation. Just TV over the phone lines.

It seemed pretty stupid, so they stopped.

## THE BURDEN OF GIRLHOOD

Someday Jessica Sanet wants two daughters, a son and a beagle puppy, but Emma Saal hopes only for boys. "Because look at what girls go through," she says. "All these problems. Like their periods!"

All these problems. The studies and books and articles flutter forth at regular intervals, detailing the problems. Teachers call on boys more often than on girls, says one. Teenage girls are increasingly likely to get in trouble with the law, says another. By the time girls reach their teens, they have learned to silence their inner "voice," write professors Lyn Mikel Brown and Carol Gilligan.

In their recent book, *Meeting at the Crossroads: Women's Psychology and Girls' Development,* Brown and Gilligan argue that around 12, girls choose to be seen as "perfect" and "nice," squelching their honest feelings of anger and aggression. Their theory comes from a feminist perspective, and there are those who would take issue with their interpretation, but talk to young girls and they do describe a culture that punishes honesty and idiosyncrasy.

But then there is Malika McCray. She is thin and blond and was, according to another girl, considered the prettiest girl in seventh grade. Now, a year later, she is Williamsburg Middle School's resident iconoclast. In the course of conversation, Malika repeatedly strikes out on her own. She thinks her parents are cool, not insufferable. She derides popular jokes about "faggots and lesbos." She describes and then condemns the slang terms for white kids who hang out with blacks, Hispanics and Chinese—"wiggers, higgers and chiggers."

"She says exactly what she thinks and doesn't care," says good friend Meghan Cooney. "She's great about that."

But even Malika knows one can stray only so far from the pack. "This year, kind of being your own person is in," she says. But the definition of "your own person" is not open to any interpretation. "You still have to act right to be accepted. You have to say the right things."

## UNCOMMON DENOMINATORS

It is, of course, all too easy in our mass culture to assume that because every 12-year-old knows who Madonna is, every 12-year-old girl is essentially the same. But money and race and religion divide these kids, just as they divide their elders.

There is Amber Akram. Her parents are from Pakistan, and she expects they will choose the man she marries.

There is Hanh Diep, whose parents were left behind in Cambodia when she was taken out as a baby. She has had no word of them in years.

There is Gina Bailey. She wants to go to Harvard Law School because she likes to argue and she likes to win.

There are the members of Veronica Hartsfield's Girl Scout troop at Carver Terrace housing project: Her 12-year-olds, she says, rarely see the world beyond their apartments. They need to be freed from caring for younger siblings while their mothers work, to stay in school and avoid pregnancy and drugs, to survive.

Among the ballerinas, all but one of whom are white, the talk is of shopping and pets and bar mitzvahs at the Four Seasons Hotel, and there is appalled disbelief at one girl's comment that she knows an eighth-grader who is publicly pregnant. In a room of black girls, the talk returns again and again to racism, the girls having long ago become aware of where their lives scrape up against the larger American society.

But having talked to girls in YWCAs, schools and homeless shelters, psychologist Ann F. Caron says, "There was much more similarity than dissimilarity." Parents and their kids agree the world has changed since the adults were 12 themselves, that crime and drugs and sex have created new, more complicated equations. But given a common culture, given common expectations about what adults must be, some things never change. Mothers are doomed to be annoying. What psychologists like to call "the developmental tasks of adolescence" must be completed no matter where or when you live.

## MISSING SANTA

They speak about adolescence as if they are preparing to fall off a psychic cliff. "People expect you to start acting silly" when you become a teenager, says ballerina Lauren Jewell. Girls this age remember when they stopped playing with dolls, when the imaginary worlds of pretend adventures came to feel thin and outgrown. There is something sad in all of it to adults, who no longer plead for the future to arrive sooner.

Meghan Cooney remembers that in fourth grade it was suddenly no longer acceptable to play imaginary games. The change was painful at first, leaving the fluid, welcoming world of make-believe, "but I think I really wanted it to end. I wanted to grow up a lot." Now, however, she has found herself marooned.

"I think I'm struggling a lot between adulthood and childhood," she says, "and there's just no place for me now."

They step forward, then pull back. Tawana Hinton says the girls "want their parents to let them go, but they still have enough fear about how they'll get home. So what you do is, drive them to the subway."

You take them halfway, because that is where they live. Parents talk about children growing up too fast, but the children themselves worry that if they do not hurry, they may not get there at all.

Natalie Ford's mother tells her to slow down. "You have plenty of time," she says, but Natalie and her friend Sabreen Madyun do not believe that. "It's very dangerous in this world, and you could be taken out any time," says Sabreen. "I don't think I have plenty of time."

But they are nostalgic for the very thing they are fleeing. A group of Girl Scouts from suburban Maryland and Virginia sit around a table, absorbing cookies, fruit, cheese, potato chips and dip like small vacuum cleaners and pondering what must be given up as they move ahead. They speak wistfully of a time when they were still able to believe in Santa Claus.

"My older sister kind of brainwashed me he doesn't exist," says Nileah Bell, "but I think he does."

"I want to believe in him, but I can't," says Chandra Clover.

But although they miss Santa, they are outraged when adults fail to bestow upon them the respect their maturity deserves. They are prevented from seeing certain movies and looked on warily by saleswomen, and when they talk on the phone, parents listen in and feel free to comment.

"They treat you like an adult," says Charis Willis of the District, who is 11 but believes she knows what 12 feels like. "They say, 'Don't run! Don't run! Don't run!' You have to wear a skirt, even if it's winter. But when it comes to making a real decision, they don't let you. The main thing is, I'll never do this to my kids."

An admirable resolution. Does she think she can live up to it?

Her face takes on the fatalism of someone recognizing a rule of physics. She admits it: "Probably not."

# Lessons Learned

BY ROSE JACOBIUS

Headline writing is often 1 percent inspiration and 99 percent desperation. Nothing quite focuses the mind as do those minutes ticking past when the last hole on the page is 72 points by 58 picas.

Those few large words can be extraordinarily difficult to choose, or they can simply spring up by a kind of free association. Whether through inspiration, desperation, or sheer perspiration, however, the headline writer must take care to convey not only the idea but also the tone of the story, to help prepare the reader for the kind of story to come, and to make the headline seem truly a part of it.

The headline on Elizabeth Kastor's story about Chelsea Clinton's cohorts was serendipitous, conjured almost by the story itself. In "The Eternity of Being 12," Kastor very quickly evoked adolescence, the time between being little and being grown, a sort of purgatory on the path to adulthood. From the concept of purgatory it was only a short step to the eternity of the headline, a bit of hyperbole that emphasizes the feeling of the young girls interviewed.

The main headline contained the essence and tone of the story. The subhead, deck, bank, or readout, as it is called at *The Washington Post,* had to do the rest. It expanded on the point of the main head: Being 12 is an eternity because it is "an agonizing stop between childhood and adulthood." And it gave the news peg for the otherwise evergreen story: The new president's daughter is at the neither-here-nor-there age, so let's take a look at what it's like to be just shy of a teenager, let's talk to "Chelsea Clinton's Peers."

These necessary elements—the subject, the flavor, the facts, the peg—help to dictate the content of a headline. The limited space, and the need to grab the reader quickly, dictates that the concept be kept simple, that the words be few and familiar.

An article may be rich in detail but a headline is like haiku. Short, clear, a window on a larger world.

# Beth Witrogen McLeod

## Finalist, Headline Writing

Beth Witrogen McLeod was born in Wichita, Kansas. She graduated Phi Beta Kappa from the University of Wisconsin and has a master's degree in journalism from the University of California, Berkeley. She began her journalism career in 1968 as a summer intern at *The Wichita Beacon*. She held a variety of reporting, editing, and photography jobs in the Bay area from 1970–75 before joining the *San Francisco Examiner* where she was a reporter and editor until 1978. She spent a decade free-lancing before rejoining the *Examiner* in 1988 as chief copy editor in the Style section. She is currently senior editor of the *Examiner Magazine*. She has run her own dance and exercisewear manufacturing business, designed costumes for the movies *Willow* and *My Stepmother is an Alien,* and is the author of *Foot Notes: The Bay Area Guide to Dance.* McLeod has won several national headline contests sponsored by Hearst Newspapers.

McLeod writes headlines that captivate readers and must delight the reporters whose stories they grace. Digging into a literary bag of tricks, she creates magic out of humor, word play, alliteration, and allusion. Who could resist a story headlined, "Ken Is Out of the Box, But Is He Out of the Closet?"

# Ken is out of the box
# but is he out of the closet?

OCTOBER 20, 1993

By Cynthia Robins

The inevitable has finally happened. Ken is out.

Barbie's consort, escort, reputed boyfriend—the guy with no visible means of support (and nothing visible in his supporter)—has sprouted an earring and a lavender vest. Two visual clues (albeit sexist and stereotypical) that Earring Magic Ken is, dare I say it, gay.

For years, Ken was Barbie's mystery beau. A guy who, in the almost 30-something years they'd been together, could never commit. Barbie had the jobs, the careers. And the stuff. The houses. The cars. The boats. The soda fountains.

And Ken? He had the surfer physique and the out-of-season tan. But no job, let alone promising career. He clocked a lot of time at the beach or driving around in Barbie's pink Corvette. He had really bad hair that around 1965 got better, but it was still, er, very styled. (We straight women take a look at a gorgeous man with hair like that and just know: This cat is too groomed to be straight.) As for his wardrobe: The lavender vest is just another in a long line of fashion victimization.

"This is the gayisha one, right?" queried comedian and school board president Tom Ammiano. "The one with the earring? I heard they were going to put an earring somewhere else, but he, uh, doesn't have a place to put it. How pernicious can this be? Maybe this is Mattel's answer to safe sex."

The truth is: Barbie's ultimate accessory has now become Barbie's ultimate walker. That man of mysterious sexuality—a guy, says my friend Stephanie Salter, whose money is probably so old he's forgotten where it came from—who looks great in a tux and knows how to use the correct fork, dance the cha-cha and not hit on her. (In 35 years, has Barbie ever gone through a pregnancy?)

And now, Ken is out of the closet, or at least on the mantle pieces of hip gay men all over the country who are buying this doll and displaying it. Like John Stubbins, who has a tableau of three Ken dolls sitting in an "I Love Lucy" ashtray behind a philodendron in his living room.

"It's the first thing people see when they walk in," says Stubbins, a teacher for 15 years in the San Francisco school system sidelined for the last few years with AIDS. However, with the new Ken doll, Stubbins says, he "can't think of anything else that Ken could be with that lavender mesh shirt and lavender jacket and his earring and that c--- ring he's wearing around his neck. Seems pretty gay to me."

Of course Mattel is denying any connection between Ken and his lavender brothers. The Barbie franchise is the cash cow responsible for more than 40 percent of Mattel's yearly profits. And at times, Barbie, her friends and possessions have saved the company from itself, especially when Hot Wheels raced off the track and the video game business wavered.

For Mattel, Barbie is fairy princess (no pun intended), meal ticket and icon; so of course, they are going to stick to the party line that Earring Magic Ken is, in the practiced words of Donna Gibb, Mattel's director of media relations, "a fun, wholesome toy for young girls. The Ken doll was not intentionally designed for any audience other than our primary one, girls ages 3 to 10."

Fact is, Gibb says, Earring Magic Ken, which has become an instant camp classic, was designed by a team of women who "were amazed when all of this surfaced—that the gay community was buying this doll. It never occurred to them that anybody outside the target market would want him."

Ultimately, according to Mattel, the Earring Magic series—Barbie, Ken and three racially mixed dolls, equipped with earrings with interchangeable charms—are reflecting their market research in terms of the color palette young girls love: pinks, purples, lavenders and aquas.

"I just wish I had sat in on the marketing meetings where they decided which ear they should put the earring in," chortles David Perry, communications director of Center for the Arts. "I'm sorry, but Earring Magic Ken sounds to me like a $20,000-a-year gay catering waiter trying to look like a $40,000 Pacific Heights walker."

And isn't that the ultimate accessory?

# Lessons Learned

## BY BETH WITROGEN MCLEOD

The story comes across my desk, a fast job by a fast reporter with an eye to the exotic, a fine writer but one with a penchant for spelling errors. Her topics are often risqué, not always "family newspaper" material. But here is the reality: We are a daily newspaper, I am on deadline, I have to read and correct the story, and write the head and deck and caption in about 20 minutes. It's the main bar; it all has to be top notch. I am slot; the responsibility rests squarely on my shoulders.

The subject: Earring Magic Ken, the doll that the writer calls "Barbie's ultimate accessory, the man of mysterious sexuality." The dish: that Ken is gracing the mantles of gay men all over the country. The implication: that the reason Ken and Barbie never tied the knot is because Ken is gay. I'm laughing at the spoof, I'm rushed, it's the end of a long day, and the head order is a lulu. I must come up with a long head that has to fit vertically over several lines, plus write an unusually long deck that has to explain the head, and a caption that must be a strong element in the package, amplifying but not duplicating the head and deck.

There is no time for contemplation, so I go with my gut instinct, the first lines that pop into my head: "Ken is out of the box, but is he out of the closet?" Intuitively it seems to work on several levels: It feels clever, funny, accurate, my Holy Trinity of Headline Writing. But will it play? My boss, who must OK all cover headlines before they appear in print, is in a rush, late for a meeting. I grab her as she breezes past, point heatedly to the VCR screen and blurt, "This OK?"

She loves it. I had hesitated for a moment, thinking that my choice might not be considered politically correct, as that has become so important. But I trusted my judgment, it appeared in the paper, and won its due.

I've been at this business since 1968, and scrapped my way to becoming a headline writer after years as a reporter. "Ken" reminded me that the rules of good headline writing are the same as those for good writing: The item should be concise, it should communicate, it should be active (and contain a verb), it should draw the reader in by its snappy, punchy style.

But most of all, I realized, headline excellence requires a breadth of both intellectual and emotional background that can be drawn on to add—at a moment's notice if necessary—that extra element of surprise, or of wit that reaches the pinnacle of the highest standards. It is always the reader that a headline writer should have in mind, not one's own cleverness—or insecurity. It is a desire to give the reader a chuckle or a deep emotion, a bit of information or education, to share one's experiences in a way that we can all benefit from together.

Good headline writing comes from a love of words, a love of *playing with* words, a respect for the nuance and flow of the English language. Excellence in headlines comes from a desire to sculpt new shapes out of tiny spaces, an unwillingness to be restricted by anything but one's own imagination and commitment.

# Storytelling on deadline

## BY CHRISTOPHER SCANLAN

Twenty-two years ago, I was the police, fire, library board, and conservation commission reporter at *The Milford Citizen,* a small daily newspaper in a Connecticut suburb. This was my first newspaper job. I was 22 years old.

One weekend, I was sent to cover a drowning at a park outside town. It was a summer Sunday and the park was crowded with families who had come to escape the heat and frolic in the cool water of the lake.

There was no one in the water when I arrived, except for a fire department rowboat moving slowly across the smooth brown surface. Beneath the water, divers searched for the body of a teenage boy who had disappeared.

On the banks, families stood around, talking in hushed tones, all their games and Frisbee throwing halted by the accident. Even the children played quietly in the dirt, as if they too were mindful of the tragedy unfolding before them. Off to one side, by the cluster of police cars and emergency vehicles, the boy's family waited.

It took about an hour for the divers to find the boy on the lake floor. A diver surfaced and signaled to the men in the boat and then, suddenly, the boy's head and shoulders broke through the water.

I don't remember many details from that day, but the image of that dead boy is as clear as if I were still standing on the bank watching the rescuers carry his body onto the grassy shore. He was naked except for the long, sodden blue jeans he wore swimming. His chest was muscular and hairless and deathly white. He appeared to be sleeping. I scribbled observations in my notepad.

The boy's mother, a middle-aged woman who had waited, slack-jawed, chain-smoking, now leaned on the hood of a police car and beat a tattoo in the dust with her feet, an angry, futile rhythm.

I followed the rescue procession out of the park.

Back in the empty newsroom, I struggled for several hours to write a story for the next day's paper. This was in the days before word processors, and my desk sat beside a black Associated Press ticker. I was full of the experience, the images, the feelings, but I sat at my typewriter unable to get them onto the page.

I wrote lead after lead. I tried to describe the bitter staccato the boy's mother beat in the ground. Nothing satisfied me, and I ripped the abortive attempts out of the machine. The pile of crumpled copy paper grew in the wastebasket at my feet.

Eventually, I gave up. I surrendered to the wire service standard that clattered incessantly over that machine next to me. I don't have the clip, but I'm sure it came out something like this: "A 17-year-old Milford youth drowned yesterday at Lake..."

I've never forgotten that experience. There was a story to tell that day and I didn't know how to tell it. I didn't have the tools.

Ten years later, two of us at *The Providence Journal* shared an assignment to write a front-page daily news feature. It had to be on the news, it had to be 20 inches long, and it had to be done by 8 p.m. We soon gave our new job a name: the "heart attack beat."

At the time, it seemed like the perfect name for a punishing assignment, but when I look back on the highlights of two decades in journalism, along with the lengthy takeouts and multi-part series that consumed weeks, months, and even years of my life, I keep coming back to a handful of stories I wrote during that year.

They are stories that haunt me to this day, because I think they embody the essence of the storyteller's craft: They convey important truths about what it means to be alive, and also because I know I did what at the time I thought was impossible—I reported and wrote them in a single day.

Learning to write well with the clock ticking may be the most important challenge that today's journalists face.

But in too many newsrooms, storytelling has become the exclusive province of the feature or project writer who is given space and time denied to other writers. Good writers, those who care about the craft and want to get better at it, often chafe at the restrictions of daily deadlines.

They don't have enough time, they say, to gather the material they need—the telling quotes, the revealing detail, the senses of people, place, time, and drama—to write a story rather than an article.

Getting enough narrative information and being able to focus, organize, draft, and revise it into a story, all in the space of a working day, has to be one of the toughest high-wire acts of the news business.

But those are the kinds of stories I want to read in my paper, stories I want to read aloud to my wife and daughters and clip and save for myself, stories that have the immediacy of life.

I've come to understand that what made the difference between the frustrations of my first newspaper job and the success, if not ease, that I enjoyed writing deadline news features a decade later, were a number of tools and strategies for reporting and writing the news. Some emerged in the crucible that is the deadline experience. Others came from insightful reporters, editors, writing coaches, and teachers, either through the good fortune of personal contacts in Providence, at The Poynter Institute and the *St. Petersburg Times,* and the Washington bureau of Knight-Ridder Newspapers.

## STORIES IN THE NEWS

The police brief that Joel Rawson, my editor at *The Providence Journal,* handed me one Monday morning was only a couple of paragraphs long, but there seemed no doubt there was a story there. Over the weekend, an Amtrak train struck a teenage girl walking on the tracks. Local police credited a teenage boy with giving first aid that saved the victim's life.

Within minutes, a photographer and I were on our way. "From Jon to Lani, the Gift of Life," my 800-word account of the coming together of two very different teenagers, appeared on the front page the next day.

Newspapers are full of stories waiting to be told. Police briefs, classified ads, obituaries, the last two paragraphs of a city council brief all may hold the promise of a dramatic story. Mine the paper, as Steve Lovelady of *The Philadelphia Inquirer* has been preaching for years.

The newspaper is just one fountain of ideas. Traditionally, the story was the "news," the event or development considered significant and worthy of attention. The challenge for today's journalists is to go beyond bureaucracy, beyond meetings, and to write stories that reveal the "joys and costs of being human," as Joel Rawson described it to his reporters.

■ Examine how the "news" affects people's lives: a burglary, a bankruptcy, marriage, death, accidents. "The point is to stress the importance of getting true stories in the paper," says Jack Hart, writing coach at the Portland *Oregonian,* "human dramas that go beyond the reports we usually run."

■ Find the extraordinary in the ordinary stuff of life: graduations, reunions, burials, buying a car, putting Mom in a nursing home, or the day Dad comes to live with his children.

■ Change your point of view. Not your opinion, but rather the spot from which you see the story. Write the council story through the eyes of the Asian who asks for better police protection in his neighborhood. Tell the story of the foiled suicide attempt through the cop who talked the jumper down.

After John F. Kennedy's assassination, Jimmy Breslin interviewed Clifton Pollard, the worker who dug the dead President's grave at Arlington National Cemetery. "One of the last to serve John Fitzgerald Kennedy, who was the 35th President of this country, was a working man who earns $3.01 an hour and said it was an honor to dig the grave." From that perspective, Breslin produced a haunting column that conveyed the nation's loss more poignantly than reams of eulogies from the high and mighty.

At the bottom of the hill in front of the Tomb of the Unknown Soldier, Pollard started digging. Leaves covered the grass... When the bucket came up with its first scoop of dirt, Metzler, the cemetery superintendent, walked over and looked at it.

"That's nice soil," Metzler said.

"I'd like to save a little of it," Pollard said. "The machine made some tracks in the grass over here and I'd like to sort of fill them in and get some good grass growing there. I'd like to have everything, you know, nice."

### REPORT FOR STORY

We don't write with words, writing coach Don Murray says. We write with specific, accurate information. When Joel Rawson assigned Berkeley Hudson and me to the daily news feature beat at *The Providence Journal,* he challenged us to bring back the sights and sounds of our city and state, not just who, what, when, where, and why, but how.

How did it look?

What sounds echoed?

What scents lingered in the air?

Why did people care?

■ Get out of the office. Storytellers aren't tied to their desks. They are out in the streets. They're the reporters who show up before the news conference and hang around after it's over, the ones who interview the victim two weeks after the shooting. They know that stories don't end after the arrest or the election.

When Francis X. Clines was writing the About New York column for *The New York Times,* there were days he didn't know what he was going to write about. But, he said, if he could just go somewhere, he knew he'd be okay. "Reporters always want to witness when they write," Clines said after he won the ASNE award for deadline writing in 1989. "And when you do witness, then you know there's no way the story won't be interesting."

"You can't win the deadline writing contest unless you are where the story is," *Concord Monitor* editor Mike Pride noted when the ASNE judges gave the top deadline writing award to Colin Nickerson of *The Boston Globe* for his Gulf War dispatches in 1992.

■ Look for revealing details that put people on the page. "In a good story," says David Finkel of *The Washington Post,* "a paranoid schizophrenic doesn't just hear imaginary voices, he hears them say, 'Go kill a policeman,' and 'You can't tell Aretha Franklin how to sing a song.'"

■ Use the five senses in your reporting and a few others: sense of place, sense of people, sense of time, sense of drama. As a rookie reporter, I failed to adequately report the story of that teenager's drowning. Instead of standing there as a passive observer, I should have roamed the park, interviewing, eavesdropping. Approaching the family could have netted important details about the missing boy.

■ Write while you're reporting. Listen for quotes, find details, uncover information that you know will be in the story. Reporting my story about the girl whose leg was cut off by an Amtrak train, I interviewed her parents. I asked her father what he did for a living. Engineer, he said. Then when he said his daughter should have escaped injury, I asked him to explain. I knew I was getting an expert's opinion that I could drop right into the story.

"By all rights," her father says, "she should have been safe." But Otey Reynolds is an engineer at Electric Boat and he knows that an object moving at a high rate of speed creates a vacuum and as air rushes in to fill it, it makes a wind. "And the wind sucked her leg under the train," he said.

## FIND A FOCUS

"The most important thing in the story is finding the central idea," says sports columnist Thomas Boswell of *The Washington Post.* "It's one thing to be given a topic, but you have to find the idea or the concept within that topic. Once you find that idea or thread, all the other anecdotes, illustrations, and quotes are pearls that hang on this thread. The thread may seem very humble, the pearls may seem very flashy, but it's still the thread that makes the necklace."

■ Don't wait until you're back at your desk to figure out what your story is about. Find your focus in the field, award-winning journalist and author Richard Ben Cramer advises, so you can search for the details, scenes, quotes, that support it. The deadline storyteller must be a radar screen, forever monitoring for information that is the heart of the story.

By the time I reached the home of Lani Reynolds, the train victim, I had already obtained a police report rich with detail and had gleaned other nuggets from a variety of witnesses, including Jon Tesseo, the shy Boy Scout hailed as a hero. My notebook was filling up with quotes, facts, and revealing details, but I was still hunting for the element that would elevate this beyond the clichéd rescue story. Then Lani's mother, sitting on her living room couch, said this about the boy who came to her daughter's rescue: "He's a preppie, everything Lani disliked." And I knew I had found it. Don Murray calls the focus the "north star" that leads a writer out of the tangled woods of reporting.

■ Good writers know that a story should leave a single, dominant impression. On deadline, finding a focus quickly is even more crucial.

An effective focusing strategy came to me one desperate afternoon in *The Providence Journal* newsroom as I battled to meet my deadline and the expectations of my editor for a newsy, well-written story. They are the two questions that help me keep track of the focus of my stories as I write and read and rewrite. To this day, I still write them at the top of my video display screen, even before the dateline. They are:

What's the news?
What's the point?

Answering the first question is usually easy. The second is often more difficult, but is more crucial. Forcing yourself to state the theme may give you not only the focus; you also may hear the voice of your story.

Although by now I had my focus, rescue by an unlikely savior, I still didn't have a lead until I answered those two questions:

> Jon Tesseo is 17, the kind of boy parents look at and say, "Why can't you be like that?" Clean-cut, yearbook photographer, a Boy Scout nine merit badges from Eagle. Just the kind of kid Lani Reynolds couldn't stand.
>
> On Saturday morning, he helped save her life.

## PLAN ON THE FLY

Finding your focus will give you a destination. Now you need a map to get there. Some writers make a formal outline. Others jot down a list of the points they want to cover.

Writers are always looking for a new way to tell their story, to stretch the traditional forms, to experiment. Writing the lead often helps writers devise their plan of attack. Effective leads "shine a flashlight into the story," as John McPhee of *The New Yorker* puts it. It is the first step of a journey. Just as important, if not more, is the last step, the ending. Create your own form.

David Zucchino of *The Philadelphia Inquirer* says his deadline stories are "totally determined by the facts on hand, the amount of time I have, and the space...The form is determined by the situation."

■ Before you begin writing, make a list of the elements you know you want to include in your story. Number them in order of importance. Structure your story accordingly.

■ Look for pivotal moments that make story beginnings dramatic and irresistible:

When things change;

When things will never be the same;

When things begin to fall apart.

■ "Think 'short' from the beginning," advises Roy Peter Clark, co-author with Don Fry of *Coaching Writers: The Essential Guide for Editors and Reporters.* It's a suggestion echoed in *The Elements of Style,* Strunk & White's indispensable guide: "You raise a pup tent from one sort of vision, a cathedral from another." Staying faithful to an 800-word length will help you jettison irrelevant information and avoid reporting detours that might be interesting but that will consume valuable time.

Once the writer accumulates a wealth of material —statistics, quotations, differing opinions—confusion often sets in. What does it all mean?

Clark offers several other strategies for keeping on track:

Conceive and re-conceive the story in your head.

Rehearse your lead on the way back to the office.

Give yourself three minutes to write a five-word plan to structure the story.

## LOWER YOUR STANDARDS

The discovery of the story continues when you sit down to write it. Writers use the draft to teach themselves what they know and don't know about their subject. Saul Pett, a veteran feature writer for the Associated Press, once said, "Before it's finished, good writing always involves a sense of discipline, but good writing begins in a sense of freedom, of elbow room, of space, of a challenge to grope and find the heart of the matter."

■ Write like hell, Clark says. Wait for the adrenaline to kick in.

■ Put your notes aside before you start to write. "Notes are like Velcro," says Jane Harrigan, author of *The Editorial Eye.* "As you try to skim them, they ensnare you, and pretty soon you can't see the story for the details." Her advice: Repeat over and over, "The story is not in my notes. The story is in my head."

■ Follow the advice Gene Roberts, legendary editor of *The Philadelphia Inquirer* and now managing editor of *The New York Times,* got from his first newspaper editor, a blind man named Henry Belk: "Make me see."

■ Lower your standards. Of course, you and your editor must apply rigorous standards—of accuracy and clarity, among others—but ignoring the voice that says, "This stinks" is the first step to producing copy on deadline in time for revision. The wisest advice on the subject of writer's block comes from poet William Stafford:

> I believe that the so-called "writer's block" is a product of some kind of disproportion between your standards and your performance...One should lower his standards until there is no felt threshold to go over in writing. It's easy to write. You just shouldn't have standards that inhibit you from writing.

That's not as paradoxical as it seems.

With 35 years' experience at deadline writing, AP correspondent Saul Pett said he stopped spending so much time on leads as he used to. "We make a mistake when we're younger. We feel compelled to hit a home run in the very first sentence. So we spend a lot of time staring at the typewriter. I'll settle for a quiet single, or even a long foul, anything that gets me started."

### REWRITE FOR READERS

Good writers are rarely satisfied. They write a word, then scratch it out, or in this computer age, tap the delete key, and try again. "Non-writers think of writing as a matter of tinkering, touching up, making presentable, but writers know it is central to the act of discovering," says Don Murray, author of *Writing for Your Readers: Notes on the Writer's Craft from The Boston Globe.*

The writing process isn't a straight line. Often the writer circles back to re-report, re-focus, re-organize. Good writers are never content. They're always trying to find better details, a sharper focus, a beginning that captivates, an ending that leaves a lasting impression on the reader.

■ Role play the reader. Step back and pretend you're reading your story for the first time. Does the lead make you want to keep reading? Does it take you too long to learn what the story is about and why it's important? If not, are you intrigued enough to keep reading anyway? What questions do you have about the story? Are they answered in the order you would logically ask them?

■ Shoot for a draft and a half. Write your story once through and then go back to polish, to re-order, to refine. If your time is limited, I'd argue that it's best spent on your ending. That's the last thing readers will experience. Make it memorable. The story of Jon and Lani ended this way:

> After Lani Reynolds was taken away for surgery Saturday, Jon Tesseo called Paul Gencaralla, the owner of the men's shop, to ask for a few hours. He felt a little sick. Jon left the hospital and walked to a friend's house nearby. Before he got there, he was sick in the street.
>
> "He didn't get sick because of the gore," Gencaralla said yesterday. "An ambulance attendant had told him he didn't think the girl would make it. She'd lost a lot of blood. Jon said, 'I should have made a tourniquet.' What made him sick was the thought he didn't do enough."

Historian Will Durant once observed, "Civilization is a stream with banks. The stream is sometimes filled with blood from people killing, stealing, shouting, and doing the things historians usually record; while on the banks, unnoticed, people build homes, make love, raise children, sing songs, write poetry, and even whittle statues. The story of civilization is the story of what happened on the banks. Historians are pessimists because they ignore the banks for the river." I know now that when I covered that tragic drowning 20 years ago, my biggest mistake was focusing on the river, or in that case, the lake, where rescuers were searching for the victim. The real story was on the banks, where his family waited.

# Annual bibliography

## BY DAVID B. SHEDDEN

This selected bibliography of books and periodical articles focuses on the art and craft of writing for newspapers. Also included are items on reporting, composition, coaching, editing, and the teaching of writing. Some entries are followed by an excerpt.

### WRITING AND REPORTING BOOKS, 1993

Bowles, Dorothy A., Diane L. Borden, and William Rivers. *Creative Editing for Print Media.* Belmont, CA: Wadsworth Publishing, 1993.

Brooks, Brian S. and James L. Pinson. *Working with Words.* 2nd ed. New York: St. Martin's Press, 1993.

Cixous, Helene. *Three Steps on the Ladder of Writing.* New York: Columbia University Press, 1993.

Deford, Frank, ed. *The Best American Sports Writing.* Boston: Houghton Mifflin, 1993.

Digregoria, Charlotte. *You Can be a Columnist: Writing & Selling Your Way to Prestige.* Portland, OR: Civetta Press, 1993.

Fedler, Fred. *Reporting for the Print Media.* 5th ed. San Diego: Harcourt Brace Jovanovich, 1993.

Fox, Walter. *Writing the News: A Guide for Print Journalists.* Ames, IA: Iowa State University Press, 1993.

Fry, Don, editor. *Best Newspaper Writing 1993.* St. Petersburg, FL: The Poynter Institute, 1993.

Garrison, Bruce, with Mark Sabljak. *Sports Reporting.* 2nd ed. Ames, IA: Iowa State University Press, 1993.

Garvey, Mark. *1993 Writer's Market.* Cincinnati, OH: Writer's Digest Books, 1993.

Harrigan, Jane T. *The Editorial Eye.* New York: St. Martin's Press, 1993.

> Good editors have always recognized that it's short sighted to yank a story away from its author and completely rewrite it. Seizing control may solve the immediate problem, but in the long term it creates a new one: angry writers who keep repeating the same patterns. So good editors have always seen their jobs as a collaboration, pooling ideas with writers and together nudging a story beyond its limits.

Herman, Jeff. *Insider's Guide to Book Editors, Publishers, and Literary Agents, 1993–1994.* Rocklin, CA: Prima Publishing, 1993.

Itule, Bruce D. and Douglas A. Anderson. *News Writing & Reporting for Today's Media.* New York: McGraw Hill, 1993.

Kennedy, George, Daryl R. Moen, and Don Ranly. *Beyond the Inverted Pyramid: Effective Writing for Newspapers, Magazines, & Specialized Publications.* New York: St. Martin's Press, 1993.

> Good writers read widely. If you would write well, you must know what good writing is—the look, the sound, the feel of it. Read poetry, read fiction, read journalism. Poetry is the most overlooked and possibly most valuable source of guidance for writers who would perfect their craft. The best poets are the most efficient users of the language. Making each phrase do the work of a paragraph, creating images with a single line, they use words precisely. Read e.e. cummings for the discipline of his art, Edna St. Vincent Millay for imagery, and John Neihardt for soaring eloquence. Then emulate those masters.

Mencher, Melvin. *Basic Media Writing.* 4th ed. Dubuque, IA: William C. Brown, 1993.

Murray, Donald M. *Read to Write.* 3rd ed. Fort Worth, TX: Harcourt Brace Jovanovich, 1993.

Nelson, Victoria. *On Writer's Block: A New Approach to Creativity.* Boston: Houghton Mifflin, 1993.

> A useful exercise for writers who feel excessively vulnerable to the words of critics is to one-up the opposition by writing your own evaluation ahead of time...As if you were an objective reviewer, explain the purpose or intent of the work, and most important, its strongest and weakest features. Be as detailed as you can, and be honest in your evaluation.
>
> You now have a document against which to compare the reactions of others. If a certain editor does not like the work, you do not have to identify wholly with her criticisms; you have already defined your own positions as distinct from hers. Some of this editor's strictures you may want to accept; others, reject. Some will come as a complete surprise; others may be identical to your own. With your own review on paper (as opposed to in your head, where it is not nearly so authoritative), you are at least able to keep her viewpoint separate from yours.

Paul, Nora. *Computer Assisted Research: A Guide to Tapping Online Information,* Second edition. St. Petersburg, FL: The Poynter Institute, 1994.

Rich, Carole. *Writing & Reporting News: A Coaching Method.* Belmont, CA: Wadsworth Publishing, 1993.

Rosenblatt, Roger. *The Man in the Water: Essays and Stories.* New York: Random House, 1993.

> Rule number three, then: "Make guesses." As long as the line is made clear to the reader between what one has actually seen and what one has felt, the imagination has a place in journalism, I believe, often the commanding place. The imagination is part of reality,

too, after all. Inevitably a writer not only thinks his way into a subject; he dreams his way into it—in those dead quiet, expressionless moments when he or she unconsciously receives all the various little signals shocking the air. Somerset Maugham said, "A state of reverie does not avoid reality; it accedes to reality." I have learned to trust a dull ache in the area behind my back teeth to tell me secrets about a story—to tell me what else, besides the information of my five senses, is happening in a story. I have disregarded messages from that area to my peril.

Scott, Andrew, ed. *IRE 101: Computer-Assisted Stories from the IRE Morgue.* Columbia, MO: Investigative Reporters and Editors, 1993.

Woodruff, Jay. *A Piece of Work: Five Writers Discuss Their Revisions.* Iowa City, IA: University of Iowa Press, 1993.

What I could predict I will do when I sit down to write is not what I end up with. I want to end up with what surprises me along the way, what jumps out at me from the potential of my work and not from what I've already realized about it before I've ever started. If I'm simply writing down what I already know, it is of no earthly interest to me. And not only that, everyone else will know it anyway. Simply obvious stuff. I'm not subtle. When I sit down to write, I discover things that I have, for one reason or another, not admitted, not seen, not reflected on sufficiently.
—Tobias Wolff in *A Piece of Work*

## CLASSICS

Atchity, Kenneth. *A Writer's Time: A Guide to the Creative Process, from Vision through Revision.* New York: Norton, 1986.

Berg, A. Scott. *Max Perkins: Editor of Genius.* New York: Dutton, 1978.

Bernstein, Theodore M. *The Careful Writer: A Modern Guide to English Usage.* New York: Atheneum Press, 1965.

Biagi, Shirley. *Interviews That Work: A Practical Guide for Journalists.* 2nd ed. Belmont, CA: Wadsworth Publishing, 1992.

Blundell, William E. *The Art and Craft of Feature Writing: Based on The Wall Street Journal.* New York: New American Library, 1988.

Brady, John. *The Craft of Interviewing.* New York: Vintage Books, 1977.

Brande, Dorothea. *Becoming a Writer.* Los Angeles: J.P. Tarcher, 1981; distributed by Houghton Mifflin, Boston (reprint of 1934 edition published by Harcourt Brace).

Brown, Karen, Roy Peter Clark, and Don Fry, eds. *Best Newspaper Writing.* St. Petersburg, FL: The Poynter Institute. Published annually since 1979.

Cappon, Rene J. *The Word: An Associated Press Guide to Good News Writing.* New York: The Associated Press, 1982.

Clark, Roy Peter. *Free to Write: A Journalist Teaches Young Writers.* Portsmouth, NH: Heinemann Educational Books, 1986.

Clark, Roy Peter, and Don Fry. *Coaching Writers: The Essential Guide for Editors and Reporters.* New York: St. Martin's Press, 1992.

Dillard, Annie. *The Writing Life.* New York: Harper & Row, 1989.

Downie, Leonard, Jr. *The New Muckrakers.* New York: NAL-Dutton, 1978.

Elbow, Peter. *Writing With Power: Techniques for Mastering the Writing Process.* New York: Oxford University Press, 1981.

Follett, Wilson. *Modern American Usage: A Guide.* London: Longmans, 1986.

Franklin, Jon. *Writing for Story: Craft Secrets of Dramatic Nonfiction.* New York: Atheneum Press, 1986.

Goldstein, Norm, ed. *The Associated Press Stylebook and Libel Manual.* 27th ed. Reading, MA: Addison-Wesley, 1992.

Gross, Gerald, ed. *Editors on Editing: An Inside View of What Editors Really Do.* New York: Harper & Row, 1985.

Howarth, William L., ed. *The John McPhee Reader.* New York: Farrar, Straus, and Giroux, 1990.

Hugo, Richard. *The Triggering Town: Lectures & Essays on Poetry & Writing.* New York: Norton, 1992.

Mencher, Melvin. *News Reporting and Writing.* 5th ed. Dubuque, IA: William C. Brown, 1991.

Metzler, Ken. *Creative Interviewing: The Writer's Guide to Gathering Information by Asking Questions.* 2nd ed. Englewood Cliffs, NJ: Prentice Hall, 1989.

Mitford, Jessica. *Poison Penmanship: The Gentle Art of Muckraking.* New York: Knopf, 1979.

Murray, Donald. *Shoptalk: Learning to Write With Writers.* Portsmouth, NH: Boynton/Cook, 1990.

— *Writing for Your Readers.* Old Saybrook, CT: Globe Pequot Press, 1992.

Plimpton, George. *Writers At Work: The Paris Review Interviews.* Series. New York: Viking, 1992.

**Interviewer:** If you had to endow a writer with the most necessary pieces of equipment, other than, of course, yellow legal pads, what would these be?

**Maya Angelou:** Ears. Ears. To hear the language. But there's no one piece of equipment that is most necessary. Courage, first.

Interview with Maya Angelou in *Writers At Work*

Ross, Lillian. *Reporting.* New York: Dodd, 1981.

Scanlan, Christopher, ed. *How I Wrote the Story.* Providence Journal Company, 1986.

Sims, Norman, ed. *Literary Journalism in the Twentieth Century.* New York: Oxford University Press, 1990.

Snyder, Louis L. and Richard B. Morris, eds. *A Treasury of Great Reporting.* New York: Simon & Schuster, 1962.

Stafford, William and Donald Hall, eds. *Writing the Australian Crawl: View on the Writer's Vocation.* Ann Arbor, MI: University of Michigan Press, 1978.

Strunk, William, Jr., and E.B. White. *The Elements of Style.* 3rd ed. New York: Macmillan, 1979.

Talese, Gay. *Fame & Obscurity.* New York: Ivy Books, 1971.

Wardlow, Elwood M., ed. *Effective Writing and Editing: A Guidebook for Newspapers.* Reston, VA: American Press Institute, 1985.

White, E.B. *Essays of E.B. White.* New York: Harper & Row, 1977.

Witt, Leonard. *The Complete Book of Feature Writing.* Cincinnati, OH: Writer's Digest Books, 1991.

Wolfe, Tom. *The New Journalism.* New York: Harper & Row, 1973.

Zinsser, William. *On Writing Well.* 4th ed. New York: Harper & Row, 1990.

— *Writing to Learn.* New York: Harper & Row, 1988.

## ARTICLES

Albers, Rebecca Ross. "More Than One Way to Tell a Story." *Presstime,* October 1993, pp. 34–39.

Astor, David. "A Story About What Storytelling Can Do." *Editor & Publisher,* July 31, 1993, pp. 32–33.

Barlett, Donald L. and James B. Steele. "In Philadelphia, We Gave Readers a Long, Tough, Complicated Story, and They Loved It: Sometimes, All the 'Experts' are Wrong." *Editor & Publisher,* April 1993, p. 4.

The conventional wisdom said that people don't have time to read long stories. It said people resist reading stories that jump. It said that people don't want to be confused by a lot of numbers and cryptic terms. It said that people want packaged information, rather than narrative stories...

By all the measures of conventional wisdom, the "America: What Went Wrong?" series published by *The Philadelphia Inquirer* in October 1991 should have proved a stunning failure. No one, according to the conventional wisdom, would read it.

After all, the stories ran over 120 inches, totaling 73,000 words in all—the length of many books. The stories jumped not once but twice and were filled with numbers, scores, and scores of numbers...

But the conventional wisdom was wrong...The articles provoked the greatest reader response in the newspaper's history...The ongoing demand for reprints forced the *Inquirer* to keep going back to press for more copies, eventually publishing 400,000 reprints...George Gendron, the editor of *Inc.* magazine...noted, "...The lesson is that people, lots of people, are hungry for serious economic analysis and desperate for economic education. It's about time they get it."

Bhatia, Peter. "Bright Copy Editors Use Their Heads to Spark Interest in Stories From Almost Any Section." *ASNE Bulletin,* July 1993, p. 21.

Blackman, Michael. "You Owe the Reader a Good Ending." *The Coaches' Corner,* June 1993, p. 3.

Caldwell, Emily. "Be a Person First When Covering Stories Involving Grief." *Editor & Publisher,* Dec. 11, 1993, pp. 56, 47.

Caperton, Frank. "A Five-Step Plan to Reduce Writing Flab." *The Coaches' Corner,* March 1993, p. 3.

Case, Tony. "Impact of Editorials." *Editor & Publisher,* Nov. 6, 1993, pp. 13, 35.

Cassavoy, Ed. "Word Pictures: How to Write Great Profiles." *The Editor,* May 1993, pp. 7–10.

Chepesiuk, Ron. "Covering the Environmental Beat," *Editor & Publisher,* Dec. 18, 1993, pp. 18–19.

Clabes, Judy. "Editorial Pages: The 10 Commandments; Editorials Should be Well-Written and Say Something." *The Editor,* March 1993, pp. 17–18.

Cook, Betsy. "Those Unhappy Copy Editors: The Need to Study a Changing Role." *Editor & Publisher,* Aug. 7, 1993, pp. 48, 39.

Darling, Ian. "A Short List for Short Stories." *The Coaches' Corner,* March 1993, p. 6.

DeSilva, Bruce, Carole Rich, Bill Hart, Paula LaRocque, Virginia Black, and Jane Zemel. "The Inverted Pyramid: R.I.P.?" *The Coaches' Corner,* September 1993, pp. 1–6.

> Individual stories are served best with individual styles of writing: what we've got to do, as editors and coaches, is to encourage thoughtfulness and allow our reporters the freedom to determine the best way to tell a story: chronologically, storytelling, interpretative, whatever. We have to be prepared to accept different styles of writing on Page One, or in the business section, or the sports section, not just in lifestyle.
>
> Some stories are probably best served by the old inverted pyramid. But until we admit that that's not the only "serious" form of newswriting, we'll continue to bore, befuddle, and drive away readers.

Fanning, Kathryn. "Style: the Difference Between Poor and Good Writing." *Byline,* May 1993, p. 9.

Foreman, John. "25 Basics for Stories for the Readers." *The Coaches' Corner,* March 1993, p. 4.

Franklin, Jon. "Going the Distance." *Washington Journalism Review,* January/February 1993, pp. 21–22.

Fry, Don. "You Can Lead Readers to a Story But It's the Writing That Makes Them Drink It In." *ASNE Bulletin,* May 1993, pp. 10–12.

Fry, Don and Roy Peter Clark. "Return of the Narrative." *Quill,* May 1994, pp. 27–28.

Gersh, Debra. "Inverted Pyramid Turned Upside Down." *Editor & Publisher,* May 1, 1993, p. 22.

Gibson, Martin L. "Sometimes You Have to Throw Out Your Gems." *The Coaches' Corner,* March 1993, pp. 7–8.

Jarmul, David. "15 Ways to Get an Op-Ed Article Published." *Masthead,* Summer 1993, pp. 22–23.

LaRocque, Paula. "Are We Decimating the Language, or Destroying It?" *Quill,* January/February 1993, p. 52.

Harrigan, Jane. "The Coaches' Creed," *The Coaches' Corner,* June 1993, pp. 1–2.

Hart, Jack. "Inside Stories," *Editor & Publisher,* Dec. 11, 1993, p. 24.

Hart, Jack and Richard Zahler. "10 Steps to Better Editing: Line Editors Must Be Cheerleaders, Teachers, Critics, Planners, Confessors, Ombudsmen, and Attorneys." *Quill,* March 1993, pp. 31–33.

  What does it take to be an editor of people rather than copy? Viewing editing as a consultation, not a command: The writer's intentions for a story are just as important as the editor's. If you ask a writer to fill in the editor's blanks, you'll get a fill-in-the-blanks story; if you want reporters to be alert, interested, and thoughtful, let them know what they think matters.

Hedley, David. "Coloring the News: Markers Can Help Writers, Editors Organize Better." *Quill,* March 1993, p. 35.

Kaminski, Dave. "How to Win with Every Story." *The Editor,* April 1994, pp. 12–15.

"The Maestro Concept: A New Approach to Writing and Editing for the Newspaper of the Future." Report from the Committee on Small Newspapers, American Society of Newspaper Editors, 1993.

Miller, Lisa C. "Looking for Help? Stylebooks, Reference Works 'Evolve' with the Language." *Quill,* March 1993, pp. 36–37.

Moen, Daryl. "Give Your Readers some Chocolate." *The Coaches' Corner,* March 1993, pp. 1–3.

Rice, John. "Serve the Reader." *The Coaches' Corner,* June 1993, pp. 6–7.

Roberts, Eugene L. "Nothing Succeeds Like Substance." *American Journalism Review,* December 1993, pp. 3–4.

> Many newspapers seem to be in a race to see which can be the most shortsighted and superficial. We are relying too much—far too much—on weather maps, charts, graphs, briefs, and color.
>
> If we had looked at these devices as nothing more, or less, than desirable improvements, then our papers would have been all the richer for the additions. But in far too many newsrooms, we introduces these devices while slashing newsroom budgets and newsholes. The result, all too often, has been that instead of becoming *additions* to news coverage, the devices have become *substitutes* for news coverage. And this, in a word, is folly...We, of course, introduced many of the devices in order to reach out to the marginal readers and nonreaders. This was good. But when we started cutting back on substance, we put serious, devoted readers at risk by becoming less essential...quite simply, we are imperiling newspapers in the name of saving them.

Ryan, Buck. "Editing Takes on a New Look: Maestro Concept Meshes Newsroom's Verbal, Visual Experts to Create a Better Newspaper." *Quill,* March 1993, pp. 18–24.

Sennett, Frank. "Five Tips for Procrastinators." *Writer's Digest,* November 1993, p. 68.

Soukhanov, Anne H. "Language: Pushing the Envelope." *Presstime,* June 1993, pp. 40–41.

Stein, M.L. "In Praise of the 100-Inch Story." *Editor & Publisher,* March 20, 1993, p. 14.

Stepp, Carl Sessions. "Going Long in a No-Jump World: Papers Are More Selective about Lengthy Projects, and Good Writing is Often the Key to Getting Them In." *Washington Journalism Review,* January/February, 1993, pp. 18–20.

Sweeney, John. "The Profile, The Interview." *The Coaches' Corner,* December 1993, pp. 4–5.

"Ways with Words: A Research Report of the Literacy Committee." American Society of Newspaper Editors, 1993.

Williams, Robert J. "Let the Sun Shine In On Weather Stories." *The Coaches' Corner,* March 1993, p. 5.

Winship, Thomas. "A Better Break for Reporters, Please." *Editor & Publisher,* July 3, 1993, p. 3.

Wyatt, Robert O. and David P. Badger. "A New Typology for Journalism and Mass Communication Writing." *Journalism Educator,* Spring 1993, pp. 3–11.